C0-AVH-702

THE MULTICULTURAL CHURCH

A New Landscape in U.S. Theologies

William Cenkner,
Editor

PAULIST PRESS
New York/Mahwah, N.J.

BX
1407
.M84
M84
1995

The Publisher gratefully acknowledges use of the following material: excerpts from "Home is Where the Han Is: A Korean-American Perspective on the Los Angeles Upheavals" by Elaine Kim from Social Justice 20, 1-2 (spring and summer 1993), pp. 1-21; excerpts from *Poems of the Aztec People*, translated by Edward Kissam and Michael Schmidt, copyright © 1983, Bilingual Press, Tempe, Arizona, Arizona State University; excerpts from "The Construction of Self in U.S. Latina Autobiographies" by Lourdes Torres from *Third World Women and the Politics of Feminism*, edited by Chandra Mohanty, copyright © 1991, Bloomington and Indianapolis, IN: Indiana University Press; excerpts from "On the Pulse of Morning" by Maya Angelou, copyright © 1993 by Maya Angelou. Reprinted by permission of Random House, Inc.

Cover photography by CLEO © 1995.

Copyright © 1996 by William Cenkner, O.P., c/o Southern Dominican Province

All rights reserved. No part of this book may be reproduced or transmitted in any form or by any means, electronic or mechanical, including photocopying, recording or by any information storage and retrieval system without permission in writing from the Publisher.

Library of Congress Cataloging-in-Publication Data

The multicultural church : a new landscape in U.S. theologies / William Cenkner, editor.
    p.   cm.
Based on papers presented at a symposium held at the Catholic University of America in late April 1993.
    Includes bibliographical references (p.).
    ISBN 0-8091-3607-4 (alk. paper)
    1. Multiculturalism—Religious aspects—Catholic Church—Congresses. 2. Religious pluralism—Catholic Church—Congresses. 3. Catholic Church—United States—Membership—Congresses. 4. United States—Church history—20th century. I. Cenkner, William, 1930-
BX1407.M84M84   1995   95-31265
282'.73'08693—dc20   CIP

Published by Paulist Press
997 Macarthur Boulevard
Mahwah, NJ 07430

Printed and bound in the
United States of America

CONTENTS

INTRODUCTION

Cultural pluralism has been a constant in the American experience from the early years of this nation. It is not surprising, then, that the Catholic Church in this country embraces the same rich spectrum of cultural diversity. However, socialization in either church or nation does not always permit growth and enhancement through ethnic and racial diversity. The early tragic years of the American experiment gave witness to the cultural imperialism against the indigenous first peoples of this continent, soon followed by the black slave markets, and continued against the immigrants from the suffering and suppressed communities of Europe. Such episodes carry their own narratives of pain and oppression which continue into our own time. They are the context within which an increased movement of peoples into the United States again intensifies our cultural diversity. How will this round of inculturation differ from previous rounds, now that we can draw upon our troubled memories of an earlier history?

It is estimated that presently three thousand Catholic parishes in the United States, out of nineteen thousand, are Spanish-speaking. And although the language may be the same, multiculturalism exists within the Hispanic/Latino community itself. The more we achieve a global consciousness the more we are aware of the distinct voices within our own church and country. The African-American faces, the Asian and Hispanic faces, the faces of our first peoples, bring into clearer focus than ever the reality that a new dawn has broken within U.S. Catholic life. This can be an hour of opportunities or an hour of tragic failure. How can we live in a multicultural church in which its very diversity gives growth and enrichment to all?

The papers in this volume result from a symposium on the "Implications of the Multicultural Dimensions of the Catholic Church in the United States," at The Catholic University of America in late April, 1993. The idea originated with the Board of Visitors of the School of Religious Studies and specifically from one of its members, Virgil Elizondo, a recognized authority in Mexican-American ministry

1

and theology. It was left to a faculty committee, however, of the School of Religious Studies to articulate the scope of the symposium. The symposium reflected what an academic community does best, namely, to gather the finest theological minds to deliberate in depth on a subject of import.

The symposium initiated a face-to-face conversation among American Roman Catholic theologians who were distinct racially and ethnically. Euro-American, African-American, Hispanic/Latino and American-Asian men and women theologians gave the major papers and were the primary respondents. Fifty invited participants reflected to some degree this ethnic and racial mix. Professionals from pastoral ministry and the public arena composed nearly one half of the participants who were not from the academic community. It was soon discovered that conversations among theologians and between theologians and pastoral workers, all representing cultural pluralism with distinct and different cultural identities, must be ongoing within the church today. This volume, hopefully, will continue that conversation.

These essays make a major statement on the local church and its crucial role in working out a theology and practice of ethnic and racial diversity within a broader communion of faith. Chapter 1 speaks to self-identity in a multicultural church: M. Shawn Copeland and Marina A. Herrera, a womanist and *mujerista* theologian, respectively, speak from their own lived experience. Chapter 2, "Theology of the Local Church: State of the Question," is Joseph A. Komonchak's challenging reflection on the question of priority between the local and universal church. Gerard S. Sloyan responds initially with the example of St. Paul whose management of diversity was a major task in the early church. Chapter 3 is Orlando O. Espín's "A Multicultural Church? Theological Reflections from Below," in which he dissuades us from using the term multicultural and equally cautions against the reification of culture and experience, especially when outsiders define such terms, reducing them from the vitality they express in the life of a people. Mary Collins responds with contributions from feminist and liturgical studies. Chapter 4, "Communion within Pluralism in the Local Church: Maintaining Unity in the Process of Inculturation," by David N. Power, O.M.I., addresses the thorny issue of cultural distinctness within one faith and within post-modernism. Womanist theologian Diana L. Hayes responds with a call for more indigenous theology from American experience. Peter C. Phan in chapter 5 summarizes the work of "Contemporary Theology and Inculturation in the United States," inclusive of African-American, Hispanic/Latino, and Asian American and exemplifies the plurality of theologies in the U.S. church. Roberto S. Goizueta adds the socioeconomic factor in contextualizing religion and culture. Bishop Enrique

San Pedro, S.J., in chapter 6, "The Pastor and the Theologian," addresses, in a traditional and creative way, how the academy can better aid pastors and ministry itself. In response Edward Branch calls for a rebirth of the Catholic imagination in reformulating time, space, silence, story, and sacrament.

Other than to continue the conversation, another objective of this volume is to create a research agenda for the academy, with lines for continuing dialogue between pastoral ministers and theologians and among theologians themselves. The reader will have to tease out of the major papers this agenda which at times emerged more explicitly from the symposium discussions following these papers. Regardless, multiculturalism in the U.S. Catholic Church calls forth further research involving not only theologians but also cultural anthropologists, historians, social analysts, experts in ethnic folklore and literature; that is, writers who are skilled more anecdotally and those whose theologies exist only orally. If multicultural analysis is to succeed, the above need to be in conversation with pastoral ministers who speak for and from a culturally diverse church.

The symposium upon which this volume is based was made possible through the generous funding of a major foundation that wishes to remain anonymous, The Catholic University of America, the University Grants Endowment of this university, and the Lilly Foundation. All are sincerely acknowledged. A word of special appreciation is extended to Mary Dancy who prepared the final manuscript. This volume is dedicated to the faculty of the School of Religious Studies, The Catholic University of America, and other scholars exploring multicultural issues.

William Cenkner
School of Religious Studies
The Catholic University of America

M. Shawn Copeland

SELF-IDENTITY IN A MULTICULTURAL CHURCH IN A MULTICULTURAL CONTEXT

INTRODUCTION

The tokens of my theological responsibilities hang on the walls of my study. These prints and documents aesthetically, existentially, politically (for I take the political to invite us to discern the right and virtuous way to live) explain to the curious and remind me when I tremble of my theological vocation. There is my diploma: large and imposing; the eagle of Boston College clutching an olive branch in one talon, a palm branch in the other; in its beak a banner with the motto: αιε υ αριστε υε ιυ. Three framed prints cluster nearby. The background of the largest print has been stippled yellow, red, and black. Three curved black lines cross the canvas vertically—one at the right, two at the left. In the foreground, broods an angel—androgynous, African, black; only chest, wings, head are visible. The African angel wears a necklace of cowrie shells and a collar delicately and elaborately engraved with West African symbols. The right wing is blood-red, the left etched in hieroglyph.[1] The two smaller prints are details from Diego Rivera's mural, "The Baptism of the Indians." Men and women who created and sustained an ancient civilization are bound and forced by Spanish steel to kneel in obeisance to a new god. They are branded, then drowned in the waters of baptism; they rise, new, surprised, wounded, fearful, resigned. They have been tormented spiritually, despised culturally, tortured physically, defeated militarily (for the moment), but certainly not for love of Christ—greedy lust for gold drives the conquistadors.[2]

Other prints hang in my study, but it is to these tokens, talismans, perhaps, that I turn most often when I pause in study and writing to puzzle a question, to clarify my thinking, to change or confirm my position, to coax an idea forward. These icons remind me that I bear the considerable, and sometimes arrogant, weight of the intellectual and cultural resources which have historically funded Roman Catholic theology. My heart weeps with the Africans and the indigenous peoples whom my church and my discipline, at once, savaged and endowed. Yet, my intellectual interests and sympathies are neither crude, nor parochial. Sorcerers (Socrates' sophists) play tricks with the truth, but an authentic scholar can not willfully ignore, despise, or reject it. So, on the bookshelves in my study, Plato and Aristotle stand shoulder to shoulder with Thomas Aquinas. After them a modern muscular deluge: Machiavelli, Hobbes, Locke, Rousseau, Kant, Nietzsche, and Marx. Michel Foucault, Hans-Georg Gadamer, Antonio Gramsci, and Jürgen Habermas push against Aladsair MacIntyre, Albert Memmi, Robert Nisbet, and Cornel West. Leo Strauss commands an entire shelf, William Edward Burghardt DuBois another; Bernard Lonergan takes over four. Martin Bernal, Cheikh Anta Diop and Frank Snowden lay the ground for Eric Foner and Herbert Aptheker, Vincent Harding and Jacqueline Jones, Mary Frances Berry and John Blassingame. Maria Stewart and David Walker, Anna Julia Cooper and Henry Highland Garnet, Marcus Garvey and Malcolm X offer different strategies, yet concur in understanding and judgment with Alain Locke, Oliver Cox, C.L.R. James, Harold Cruse, and Angela Davis. Behind my desk, there is vigorous and rigorous intellectual shout: June Jordan, Andre Lorde, Bettina Aptheker, Patricia Hill Collins, Alice Walker, Toni Morrison, Lourdes Torres, Zora Neale Hurston, Dee Brown, Paula Gunn Allen, Vine Deloria, Jr., Chandra Mohanty, Gloria Anzaldúa, bell hooks, Antonio de Castro Alves, Henry Louis Gates, Jr., Michelle Wallace, Ngugi Wa Thiong'o, Trinh Minh-ha, Wole Soynika, John Mbiti, Molefi Asante, Richard Rodriguez, Clifford Geertz, Melville Herskovits, Robert Farris Thompson, Maya Deren, Eduardo Galeano, Primo Levi, Susan Griffin, and Patricia Williams.[3] These are women and men of marginal options and marginal opinions; some are members of so-called marginal races, marginal cultures, marginal ethnic groups. Their collective and personal search and practice of truth-telling strengthens my resolve.

I begin in so personal a fashion, so as not to lose the concrete, so as not to escape the difficulties, contradictions, antagonisms, and pain of historicity and our several histories. What follows is a pre-theological reflection in which I take up the topic of self-identity in three sections. In the *first section*, the paper uncovers and explores some of the meanings and implications of the terms culture, barbarism, and civilization. The aims are clarification and contextualization; the method phenomenological, heading toward thick description; the locus of investigation is the multicultural context of the United States. Given the history, exigencies, and paradoxes of the Catholic community in the

United States of America, the *second section* pursues contextualization even further. Here, I probe the meanings of culture, multicultural, global Catholic Church. Such close attention to contextualization prepares us to grasp some of the difficulties women and men of our church and of our country encounter in living and speaking their lives, their self-identities, themselves. Thus, only in the *third section* do I come to a specific discussion of self-identity. Finally, the paper concludes with a brief reflection on the intellectual, moral and existential challenges to be confronted in an American appropriation and articulation of Catholic theology.[4]

EXPERIENCES AND MEANINGS OF CULTURE, BARBARISM, AND CIVILIZATION IN THE UNITED STATES

I begin with a consideration of how the terms culture, barbarism or savagism, and civilization functioned within various contexts in Europe and in the United States. I lay out the realities expressed in these terms, while keeping a sidelong glance on their contemporary corollaries—multicultural, cultural pluralism, and diversity.

Within the intellectual, economic, political, and military parameters of Europe and North America, the notion of civilization has been synonymous with the Anglo-European approximation of the "Greek ideal" in education, fine arts, science, humanism, manners, refinement, social mores, aesthetic formation and taste. Various local or regional or national realizations and expressions of that "ideal" meant that a man or woman was considered cultured in the French sense of *savoir-vivre*. That is to say, that men and women who were considered cultured evinced the good manners, good taste, and proper comportment consonant with the Anglo-European approximation of the "Greek ideal." To this approximation of civilization as culture, infants were to be tutored and by it barbarians or savages were to be tamed. Moreover, while culture was something that could be acquired, it also was a sign of good breeding; hence, culture was a preserve of the upper classes. From this standpoint, then, nearly all other and non-Anglo-Europeans, (non-white peoples, except the Chinese and the Egyptians) were savages without civilization.

Nineteenth century anthropologists, studying so-called primitive societies, borrowed the German *kultur* and introduced the term as a contrast to civilization—a contrast, perhaps, to the heaviness and grandeur of that "Greek ideal."[5] British anthropologist Edward Tylor in his work, *Primitive Cultures*, provides us with both an early example of such study as well as a definition of culture. According to Tylor: "Culture or civilization is that complex whole which includes knowledge, belief, art, morals, laws, custom, and any other capabilities and habits acquired by man [sic] as a member of society."[6] With this definition, Tylor sought to identify the "nonbiologically transmitted [human] heritage."[7] Generations of scholars have revised and refined Tylor's definition. One standard or commonly recognized scholarly definition of culture has been authored by Alfred Kroeber and Clyde Kluckhohn:

> Culture consists of patterns, explicit and implicit, of and for behavior acquired and transmitted by symbols, constituting the distinctive achievement of human groups, including their embodiments in artifacts; the essential core of culture consists of traditional (i.e., historically derived and selected) ideas and especially their attached values; culture systems may, on the other hand, be considered as products of action, on the other as conditioning elements of further action.[8]

In the geographical, psychological, political, economic, and social context of the so-called new world, the terms culture, barbarism or savagism and civilization reconfigure somewhat differently. So-called cultured and civilized European men and women, on this portion of the North American continent, brought forth a "new nation, through a colonial, [rather than] social revolution."[9] Displaced, separated or exiled from Europe, these men and women openly acknowledged and avowed the superiority of European civilization. These "first Americans looked to their parent civilization for intellectual and cultural resources, applying these to very un-European conditions principally by means of crude imitation."[10] Thus, in America, to be cultured was to appropriate and to imitate the style and content of European civilization; in fact, to be American meant to imitate the style and content of European civilization. Yet, it is well to remember that on these terms, culture and to be cultured meant to appropriate only one regional and linguistic zone of the so-called old world, only one regional and linguistic zone of culture and civilization. British military, political, religious, and cultural-linguistic might tempered and marginalized the influence of the French, the Spanish, and the Portuguese, an influence proudly Catholic.[11]

There is, as we know full well, another and underside to the foundation of the body politic which became the United States of America and its national culture. By national culture, here, I mean what Frantz Fanon means: "the whole body of efforts made by a people in the sphere of thought to describe, justify, and praise the action through which that people has created itself and keeps itself in existence."[12]

There were children, women, and men who did not travel in order to arrive: Mohawk, Iroquois, Peoria, Creek, Seminole, Cherokee, Ute, Sioux, Navajo, Pawnee, Oneida, Zuni, Pima, Shoshoni, Narraganset, Pequot, Mohegan, Miami, Tuscarora, Delaware, Wyandot, Ottawa, Hopi. These and so many, many others who are the indigenous peoples of this land were to be removed, to be driven into American civilization and culture—or else exterminated. These children, women, and men resisted. Consider the soldiers' toast of July 4, 1779: "Civilization or Death to all American Savages."[13]

There were children, women, and men who sought passage and those who were compelled to make the voyage: young Irish girls forced by grinding poverty into indentured servitude, hungry young men imprisoned for poaching deer, debtors clamoring for a real chance, young widows and landless second sons, men and women of the European so-called lower classes escaping the brutality of lingering feudal pretensions, men and women—broken-hearted, furious, full of hope, weighed down by sorrow, flushed with daring. Thus came the immigrant, the exile, the uprooted: "Europe watched them go—in less than a century and a half, well over thirty-five million of them came from every part of the continent."[14] These men and women and children came in waves: four and a half million Irish; four million and more English, Scots, and Welsh; six million Germans; two million Scandinavians, five million Italians, eight million Poles and Jews, Hungarians, Bohemians, Slovaks, Ukrainians, Ruthenians; three million Greeks and Macedonians, Croatians and Albanians, Syrians and Armenians.[15] These were to be smoothed out, scrubbed clean of their old country ways, powdered, dressed, and assimilated into the Americanized version of Anglo-European culture—learning language, food, and modes of comportment far from their peasant class origins. These children, women, and men resisted.

Then there were the children, women, and men who neither asked nor desired to come: How many children did Africa bleed during the four-hundred years of traffic in human flesh? On some accounts, well over forty million.[16] Who were those betrayed, captured, bought, sold, traded? Igbo, Yoruba, Mandigo, Fulani, Bakango, Edo-Bini, Fon, Wolof, Bambara, Mende, Limba, Bola, Balante, Vai, Gola, Kisi, Grebo, Ewe, Fante, Ga, Popo, Bambo, Ndungo, Luba, Luango, Ovimbundu.[17] These were forbidden and denied, *de jure* and *de facto*, admission and participation in that Americanized version of Anglo-European culture. These men, women, and children were mere instruments of a master's bidding; these were talking animals, accorded only the most minimal portion of humanity. These, too, resisted.

There are children, women, and men who continue to emigrate in wave after wave: Chinese, Filipino, Portuguese, Spanish, Korean, Japanese, Haitian, Jamaican, Vietnamese, Cambodian, Hmong, Laotian, Salvadoran, Nicaraguan, Honduran, Dominican, Peruvian, Chilean, Russian, Ethiopian, Egyptian, Iraqi. These, too, are to be pressed and flattened into the gray plateau of the Americanized version of Anglo-European culture. These, too, are pushed to relinquish language, foods, dress, customs, and modes of comportment and acquire different Americanized versions of their cultures. Like all the others, these too resist.

I have been attempting to suggest some of the wonder, agony, and shame of that complex process by which so many peoples have been mingled on that portion of this continent becoming a country, a people, a nation.[18] In that meeting and mixing, teaching and preaching, creating and building, hoping and deceiving, loving and fighting, dancing and celebrating, Oscar Handlin reminds us "were gathered up people of the most diverse qualities, people whose rulers had for centuries been enemies, people who had not even known of each other's existence. Now they would share each other's future."[19] We have come to accept the scholarly consensus that there was no melting. The third and fifth and seventh generations seek and cherish, without embarrassment, those codes of conduct, ways of phrasing the body, customs of birth and death and marriage, which the first generation had hoped the second would shed, at least to some extent. For what the children and grandchildren and great-grandchildren of immigrants, exiles, and captives sought was "the culture of [their] ethnic group[s]."[20]

The culture and language of an ethnic group, what Richard Rodriguez refers to as the intimacy of the home, is to be distinguished from the public and national culture which American English (by necessity or force or choice) has given us.[21] Today, that national Anglo-European-American culture and that protean language are under even greater indictment. Our national culture draws its cultivating purposes from its origins in the romance languages and its linguistic imperialism from the British conquest. The far-ranging and insidious implications of such hegemonic normativity are captured in the designation of that national culture as classicist.[22] Men and women of classicist mentality consider culture as something static and ahistorical to be encapsulated in the universal, the ideal, the immutable. Wittingly or unwittingly, the Anglo-European version of the "Greek ideal," at once, exalts and truncates the Greek mediation of meaning. This expression of classicist culture standardizes or canonizes what is only relatively good and true through ahistorical dogmatism. And, since it despises other and different cultures, the classicist mentality betrays its own Greek foundation in wonder; it is manifestly antagonistic to other and different cultures. Moreover, in the United States (indeed, around the world today), race functions to problematize culture, ethnicity, and language. Culture has become the site of struggle.[23] And, situated as it is, in this site of conflict, the church is drawn into the fray.

CHURCH, CULTURE, AND THE POLITICS OF DIFFERENCE

The early Catholic community in the United States was complex, polyglot, and multicultural. The explorers, exiles, captives, and immigrants were anxious that religion do and mean in the new world all that it had done and meant in the old worlds. Priests and churches, women religious and schools proliferated according to cultural-linguistic needs. In a letter to the papal nuncio, Capuchin friar Charles Maurice Whelan reported that "it was necessary for a priest to know at least the Irish, English, French and Dutch languages, because our congregation is composed of these nationalities, as well also as of Portuguese and Spaniards."[24] This Catholic community was excluded from the powerful and influential processes of acculturation and socialization of the controlling and Protestant groups, even though "as early as the national census of 1850, statistics showed that the Roman Catholic Church was the largest single denomination in the United States."[25] Moreover, many Protestant groups stressed the incompatibility of Roman Catholicism with what came to be understood as American life, culture, and religion. Protestant nativist groups considered "Catholics as unassimilable immigrants, undemocratic residents whose parochial schooling and 'loyalty to the pope, a foreign power' precluded participation in republican life."[26]

I cannot discuss here the effects of anti-Catholic practices and sentiment on the collective self-understanding of Celtic-, Anglo-, European-American Catholics in the United States. We know that Catholics met rejection, ridicule, and ostracism with creative insularity. Indeed, we Catholics as an identifiable or self-identifying group have endured such exclusion well into the twentieth century, even if some of us have become "WASCs"—White Anglo-Saxon Catholics. With that epithet, John Tracy Ellis decried, I think, not merely the formal decline and loss of religious festivals and customs rooted in the dense webs of ethnicity and old world cultural mores and customs, but the winnowing and withering of robust Catholic distinctiveness, subtlety, suppleness, largess, compassion, gladness of heart, openness and openheartedness. Ellis' charge points up the enervating character of our scramble for acceptance, for inclusion, for economic and political ascendancy. And, perhaps, more importantly, it insinuates the fading of a sacramental worldview and the diminishment of what is human and passionate and celebratory in the face of pinched, acquisitive materialism and possessive individualism.

Yet, if Celtic-, Anglo-, European-American Catholics in the United States were discriminated against, Celtic-, Anglo-, European-American Catholics also discriminated—and against each other. Although cultural-linguistic separation had been a feature of Catholic life in the United States, the national atmosphere was poisoned by the slave trade, its economic systematization, and its legacy of lynching, segregation, and racism. Racism contaminated and further problematized Catholic adaptation to American culture and society.[27] For indeed, race mattered. Catholics—laity, vowed religious, as well as clerics—were slaveholders and, in most instances, maintained racially segregated parish and reservation schools and churches. Catholics found it difficult to emancipate themselves from the prevailing national attitudes about Native Americans, Africans, Latinos, and Asians. So, even today, Catholics find it difficult, institutionally and personally, to grasp that black or Native American peoples might, like Latinos, be so-called birthright Catholics. A perusal of the extant parochial registers for St. Augustine's, in what is now northern Florida, discloses two-hundred years of vibrant black Catholic sacramental life. Historian Cyprian Davis writes, "If St. Augustine's was an outpost of Spain with a large black Catholic presence, Los Angeles was an outpost of New Spain built on a black and Indian presence."[28] And, extant parochial registers for what is now California and New Mexico attest to the Catholic faith of mestizos or people of Indian and Spanish ancestry as well as mulattos, Indians, and Africans.[29] From its arrival in the new world, the Catholic Church has been the faith of peoples of different cultures.

Catholics, along with many other inhabitants of the United States, find it difficult, institutionally and personally, to grasp that enslaved Africans or Native Americans, might have had culture, were able to create culture, were cognitively equipped to improvise new forms of culture.[30] And, just as often, these same women and men cannot now grasp the reality that the descendants of those enslaved Africans have and create and improvise new expressive cultural forms. Many of these same men and women acknowledge that Mexican-Americans and Puerto Ricans and the indigenous people of the land have culture(s). Yet, they regard Mexican-Americans and Puerto Ricans and the indige-nous people of the land and their cultures as exotic, quaint, a bit out of date, but interesting. Some of these men and women collect other people's cultures. When a ritual cannot be celebrated on demand, a mask cannot be presented for inspection, a dance cannot be performed, these collectors are angry and annoyed, at not being able to consume one more piece of another people's power and spirit.

We Catholics, institutionally, collectively, and personally, have been caught up in a classicist notion of culture; the consequence of this institutional, collective, and personal location is nothing less than our impoverishment. The Second Vatican Council nudged us toward more concrete and historical considerations of culture and away from ahistorical thinking. And, increasingly, since the Second Vatican Council the notion of culture has functioned as a point of reference or a point of departure in considerations of theology of mission, evangelization, and local theologies.[31] In an effort to face up to the global character of the church, the council sought to adopt a more dynamic and concrete notion of culture. This attempt is made quite clear in *Gaudium et Spes*:

> It is a fact bearing on the very person of man [sic] that he [sic] can come to an authentic and full humanity only through culture, that is, through the cultivation of natural goods and values. Wherever human life is involved, therefore, nature and culture are quite intimately connected.
>
> The word "culture" in its general sense indicates all those factors by which man [sic] refines and unfolds his [sic] manifold spiritual and bodily qualities. It means his [sic] effort to bring the world itself under his [sic] control by his [sic] knowledge and his [sic] labor. It includes the fact that by improving customs and institutions he [sic] renders social life more human both within the family and in the civic community. Finally, it is a feature of culture that throughout the course of time man [sic] expresses, communicates, and conserves in his [sic] works great spiritual experiences and desires, so that these may be of advantage to the progress of many, even of the whole human family.
>
> Hence it follows that human culture necessarily has a historical and social aspect and that the word "culture" often takes on a sociological and ethnological sense. It is in this sense that we speak of a plurality of cultures.
>
> Various conditions of community living, as well as various patterns for organizing the goods of life, arise from diverse ways of using things, of laboring, of expressing oneself, of practicing religion, of forming customs, of establishing laws and juridical institutions, of advancing the arts and sciences, and of promoting beauty. Thus the customs handed down to it form for each human community its

proper patrimony [sic]. Thus, too, is fashioned the specific historical environment which enfolds the men [sic] of every nation and age and from which they draw the values which permit them to promote human civic culture.[32]

This definition not only maintains that human beings cannot exist without culture, but that culture, insofar as it presents and coaches men and women to real and natural goods and values, is that crucial site where full and authentic humanness flourishes. This understanding of culture affirms human creativity and historicity, the diverse ways of human living and worship. Moreover, the council acknowledges and affirms the actuality of different cultures, of a plurality of cultures and is, at least to some extent, curious and open to them.

How does this definition of culture compare with other definitions to which I have adverted earlier in this essay? The council's treatment, like that of Tylor, presents culture as something extrinsic, as something static. Kroeber and Kluckhohn also maintain this static view. However, by admitting that culture is not only "products of action," but "conditioning elements of further action."[33] Kroeber and Kluckhohn open up the possibility of understanding culture as a process, as ongoing, as dynamic, as changing, as developing. This possibility allows us to advert to human persons whose intelligence, creativity, imagination, and persistence are responsible for culture.

The notion of the politics of difference further problematizes our apprehension of culture as a dynamic process. In American English, the noun difference denotes unlikeness; it connotes opposition, disagreement, quarrel, and dispute. Synonyms for the adjective different include: diverse (suggesting conspicuous difference), divergent (stressing irreconcilability), distinct (stressing different identity and unmistakable separateness), dissimilar (focusing on the absence of similarity in appearance, properties, or nature), disparate (implying essential or thoroughgoing difference, often stressing an absence of any relationship between things), and various (emphasizing the number and diversity of kinds, types, etc.)[34] With the exception of various, the most common synonyms for difference imply negative qualities or conditions and negative relations: disagreement, dissent, discord, estrangement, dissimilarity, dissimilitude, variance, divergence, contention, dispute, disparity, inequality, unlikeness, discrimination, diversity, discrepancy.[35] The most common antonyms suggest positive qualities or conditions and positive relations: agreement, similarity, similitude, assent, consent, concurrence, accord, accordance, harmony, amity, concord, congruity, unison, and union.

If our national language reflects and expresses our national political, economic, and social class experiences, then clearly in our language, difference provokes suspicion, if not disdain. What is communicated is that difference is to be avoided. As Iris Marion Young observes, in our national consciousness, "the ideal of liberation" has been the "elimination of group difference."[36] We have preferred and fostered uniformity; we have espoused what some social theorists name the relentless "logic of identity."[37] While it is important to recall that most recent social movements emerging from oppressed men and women have challenged this ideal of uniformity, and have argued that the positive self-definition of group difference and self-determination are more authentically liberatory, this ideal continues to persist. This logic of identity denies and represses the creativity and possibility of variety, variation, diversity, and difference. Young goes on to remark that, "the irony of the logic of identity is that by seeking to reduce the differently similar to the same, it turns the merely different into the absolutely other."[38] American culture and American peoples are the products of such a logic. On the one hand, differently similar Celtic-, Anglo-, European-American men and women in the United States share the mere similarity of skin color, although they have participated in and been formed by several different cultural, social, economic, aesthetic, intellectual, historical experiences. However, in the light of skin color, often substantive differences are reduced, so that the different are rendered the same. On the other hand, those merely different (from whites and from each other) in skin color—the African, Latino, Chicano, Korean, Chinese, Japanese, and Native Americans— are absolutized as the other and ruled out of authentic human participation in our national life. And, when racial and cultural-ethnic differences are absolutized

> the response from many liberal, white[s] is, for example, to speak because they are of the dominant group. The effect is indistinguishable from not having to take any political position whatsoever in relation to the culture of the other. If one does not have to take a position, then difference has been preserved as absolute and so has the dominant social order.[39]

Thus, literary critic and author Hazel Carby interrogates "the relentless logic of identity," on the one hand, and the inadequacy of the commonsense notion of difference, on the other. Carby importunes us to challenge the structures of power and domination that are at work in the "racialization of the social order."[40]

In our curiosity, openness, and eagerness to embrace and affirm the new (to us) cultures of people whom our church, our theology, and our ministry, first, have brutalized, then, ignored, what questions might we ask: What issues and questions do we avoid? What problems and answers do we suppress? Do we avoid discussions of race altogether? Do we pretend to be colorblind? Do we raise issues of race with Cubans or Chicanos or Latinos or Koreans or Filipinos? Do we consider that these people may be victims of white racism and white racist supremacy? Or do we save racial questions and considerations for those of African descent? Do those of us who are of Celtic-, Anglo-, European-American heritage ever think about our own race? Do we even recognize that having this option is a point of privilege? What does it mean for us to read books about and by men and women of other races, of other cultures, but never relate humanely to those same people? Do we evade discussions of cultural difference? Do we take difference as an insurmountable border on the cultural frontier? Is this avoidance of difference a new and other form of racism?[41] What does it mean to appropriate the cultural possessions of another and controlled group, while ignoring the living, flesh and blood, members of that group? How do we learn from men and women of other cultures without dispossessing them of their heritage? Have we grown tired of the turn to experience in doing theology because of whose experience it is? Do we really want the new perspectives which may emerge when we invite African-American and Latina and Korean women to participate in doing theology? And if their perspectives do not appear radical enough for us, what is our response? Are we prepared to wait for new women and men in ministry to discern their work and the Spirit's work in them? Are we prepared to wait as long as it takes? Or, do we want to decide that change and control its outcomes?

EXPERIENCES AND MEANINGS OF SELF-IDENTITY

The very term self-identity is characteristic of modernity; hence, an account of self-identity has to provide an account of modernity as well.

The term modernity calls up images and ideas of innovation and novelty, of interruption and discontinuity. Modernity is, as both Anthony Giddens and Daniel Bell suggest, "a post-traditional order."[42] For our purposes here, I take modernity to refer to a set of assumptions which undergird culture, commerce, and religion. Those assumptions include the rejection in social relations of that oppressive heaviness, formality, and rigidity so intrinsic to and typical of feudal societies; disdain for (Victorian) bourgeois order, coherence, and commerce; awareness and self-conscious preoccupation with the problems of art; first suspicion, then disregard, for religion and religious norms; and the assumption that the moral and social center of society is not the group, the tribe, or even the city-state, but the autonomous individual.[43]

What is self-identity? Again, Giddens:

> Self-Identity is not a distinctive trait, or even a collection of traits, possessed by the individual. It is the self as reflexively understood by the person in terms of her or his biography. Identity here still presumes continuity across time and space: but self-identity is such continuity as interpreted reflexively by the agent.[44]

Identity, self-identity, is not found simply or merely in behavior, although behavior is an important clue both to ourselves and others. Nor is self-identity taken primarily from the reactions of others, although feedback regarding our self-presentation is crucial; of course, so are love, regard, and emotional and physical intimacy. Stable self-identity is formed in the critical, narrative, and practical struggle to reflexively maintain personal integrity or authenticity. Stable self-identity addresses ongoing responses to basic questions of human life: the meaning of existence and being, finitude and human life, the experience of others, the experience as other, the continuity of self-identity.

In the context of racialized multiculturality, let me reformulate and briefly explore the experience as other and the continuity of self-identity.

A predominant experience in the attempt at self-identity in the United States for most children, women, and men who are red, black, brown, or yellow is experience as "other." The problematic for the other is constituted by trust in the face of historic bad faith. The man, woman, or child who is other thinks: "My own skin renders my own country, my own state, my own city, my own neighborhood a potentially hostile place for me. In the face of an overweening history of bad faith and betrayal by whites, can I trust my self, my being, my life to a white man or woman? Can I trust my self, my being, my life to any other person? Can I risk placing my self in someone else's hands?"

Tina Plaza examines this problematic in reporting on a threatening incident experienced by a Mexican-American man in El Paso, Texas.

> [In November 1991] Ben Murillo...suddenly found himself looking down the barrel of a Border Patrol agent's revolver while driving two of his football players to a game at rival Jefferson High School.... "I pulled into a Dairy Queen parking lot, thinking that maybe I had a taillight out," says Murillo. "But one of my students said, 'Coach, they think

you're a wetback.' Then I turned around and saw the muzzle
of the officer's revolver pointed at my face."

Murillo was extremely frightened, [and] told the officers
that he was a varsity football coach at [the local high
school]. "'I have two varsity players with me and I'd
appreciate it if you'd shoulder your gun,' I told the officer.
And he said, 'I'd appreciate it if you'd shut up.'" The officer,
Murillo says, was holding the gun in two hands, with his
arms fully extended, an account confirmed by several
witnesses.[45]

Not surprisingly, Plaza's report of Ben Murillo's experience evokes
those terrible and terrifying scenes from the video—Rodney King,
prone on the ground, being beaten by police wielding batons. King and
Murillo share the mere similarity of dark skin, skin darker than that of
the police officers who are bent on subduing and arresting them.

The problematic for the darker skinned other is the problem of
trust in the face of historic bad faith. In far too many social, economic,
political, intellectual settings, the darker skinned other is stigmatized,
demonized, absolutized as a different ontological other. The man,
woman, or child who is red, black, brown, or yellow wonders: "I speak
another language. Can I make myself understood? Will the other man,
woman, or child who is white try to understand me? Will this one care
to listen? Am I being prejudged?" And fictive as they may be, racialized
societies remain life and death situations for those who are marginalized and controlled, despite their assumptive economic or social
location.

Consider Elaine Kim's experience as other. In an article, "Home
Is Where the Han Is: A Korean American Perspective on the Los
Angeles Upheavals,"[46] Berkeley professor Elaine Kim discussed the
social construction of race and culture. Kim's essay, written for
Newsweek magazine, charged the news media with manipulating
tensions between Korean-Americans and African-Americans "to divert
attention from the roots of racial violence."[47]

I asserted that these lie not in the Korean immigrant-owned
corner store situated in a community ravaged by poverty
and police violence, but reach far back in the corridors
of corporate and government offices in Los Angeles,
Sacramento, and Washington, D.C. I suggested that Koreans
and African Americans were kept ignorant about each other
by educational and media institutions that erase or distort
their experiences and perspectives. I tried to explain how

racism had kept my parents from ever really becoming Americans, but that having been born here, I considered myself American and wanted to believe in the possibility of an American dream.[48]

However, *Newsweek* readers' who identified themselves as descendants of eastern European immigrants were outraged at her essay. Kim's effort to trust in this possibility was met with anger, resentment, and a discourse of violence. In her essay, Kim called for greater under-standing across the cultural divide. Readers labeled Kim's views as "paranoid, absurd, hypocritical, racist, and childish"; and Kim herself was deemed "spoiled, ungrateful, whining, un-American."[49] Kim reports that she also received letters of encouragement and support, letters of solidarity from "Norwegian or Irish Americans interested in combating racism," as well as from Korean Americans, African Americans, Chinese and Japanese Americans, and Native Americans."[50] However, the hate mail she received discloses the underside of the declared and undeclared value of difference.

Kim's assertion of self-identity is met with the demand for conformity, for the repression of all that is uniquely different. And several of the letters berate Kim for her self-identification as a Korean-American, rather than as an American.

> Ms. Kim appears to have a personal axe to grind with this country that has given her so much freedom and oppor-tunity....I should suggest that she move to Korea, where her children will learn all they ever wanted about that country's history.[51]

> You refer to yourself as a Korean-American and yet you have lived all your life in the United States...you write about racism in this country and yet you are the biggest racist by your own written words. If you cannot accept the fact that you are an American, maybe you should be living your life in Korea.[52]

> I am a white American. I am proud to be an American. You cannot be black, white, Korean, Chinese, Mexican, German, French, or English or any other and still be an American. Of course the culture taught in schools is strictly American. That's where we are and if you choose to learn another [culture] you have the freedom to settle there. You cannot be a Korean-American, which assumes you are not ready to be an *American*. Do you get my gist?[53]

Who cares about Korea, Ms. Kim? And what enduring
contributions has the Black culture, both here in the U.S.
and on the continent contributed to the world, and man-
kind? I'm from a culture, Ms. Kim, who put a man on the
moon 23 years ago, who established medical schools to train
doctors to perform open heart surgery, and...who created a
language of music so that musicians, from Beethoven to the
Beatles, could easily touch the world with their brilliance
forever and ever and ever. Perhaps the dominant culture,
whites obviously, "swept aside Chicanos...Latinos...African-
Americans...Koreans" because they haven't contributed anything that made—be mindful of the cliché—a world of
difference.[54]

Bad faith permeates the response of "white Americans" to Kim's free
expression of ideas. Critical, loyal dissent is to be rejected in favor of
mindless agreement or shameful silence; in matters of race and
multiculturalism, these are preferred to truth. Kim's experience as
other points up that even in the domain of ideas, self-expression,
assault is to be expected.

In racialized societies, women and men may form their self-
identities and they may claim or forge them. Thus, continuity of self-
identity itself receives a new location. Lourdes Torres in her commentary on the work of Cherríe Moraga, Aurora Levins Morales and
Rosario Morales, and Gloria Anzaldúa helps us understand this on two
planes. Following Michelle Cliff, Torres affirms the paradoxical
claiming and embracing the very identity a person may have been
taught to despise. To do this, the man or woman or child in question
"must work through all the cultural and gender socialization and
misinformation which has left them in a maze of contradictions."[55] The
task is to develop a new discourse which incorporates the often contradictory aspects of gender, ethnicity, class, sexuality. Torres identifies
the radicalness of their project in the authors' refusal to settle for any
one position. Identity politics as self-identity neither bemoans personal
and collective suffering or personal circumstances, nor ranks
oppressions. Rather, identity politics as self-identity leads to creativity
and resourceful resistant power.

In the case of continuity of self-identity, racially stigmatized
children, men, and women may or may not claim their given racial,
cultural-ethnic heritage. They may attempt to pass as cultured or they
may claim their past and the past of their great-great-great grandparents
or they may forge a new, distinct identity out of disparate and modern
elements. When racially stigmatized children, men, and women claim

and struggle for self-identity, in the process they are emboldened and pushed to discovery and, in particular, to self-discovery. In this process, they explore just who they are and who they might become, explore just where they have come from and where they might be going.

Here is the first stanza of "Ending Home" by Rosario Morales and her daughter Aurora:

> I am what I am.
> A child of the Americas.
> A light-skinned mestiza of the Caribbean.
> A child of many diaspora, born into this continent at a crossroads.
> I am Puerto Rican. I am U.S. American.
> I am New York Manhattan and the Bronx.
> A mountain-born, country bred, home-grown jibara child,
> up from the shtetl, a California Puerto Rican Jew.
> A product of New York ghettos I have never known.
> I am an immigrant
> and the daughter and granddaughter of immigrants.
> We didn't know our forebears' names with certainty.
> They weren't written anywhere.
> First names only, or hija, negra, ne honey, sugar, dear.[56]

In this poem, Rosario Morales and Aurora Morales explore the creation of identity in an internationalist, multicultural context. Joining their identities, dissolving some of the differences between them, the two authors create something new, something more than the sum of the parts of their identities. Both the displacement the women chronicle and the poem are "way[s] of surviving."[57] The poem emerges in questioning a variety of relationships, a variety of possible identities, and ways to sustain an identity in the face of enormous hostility and despair.

CONCLUSION

Our present multicultural predicament raises three challenges to those of us in the Catholic Church in the United States doing theology. The first of these challenges is an intellectual one. In these last days of the twentieth century, we need to take responsibility for a theological mediation of the Christian faith which accurately, adequately, and authentically grasps and apprehends our differentiated experiences in this country. Our church and our people need a serious, theoretically rigorous, historically grounded theology capable of meeting the level of human suffering, disregard, disdain, and human abuse in this country. We need a theology that analyzes our national culture and is willing to struggle with our conflictual and contradictory experiences, social locations, and intellectual positions.

We need a foundational theology which takes the cultural, the multicultural, the pluricultural seriously. We need a theological anthropology that faces up to the neglect of youth in our cities, to unemployment, to the spread and use of drugs, to crime, and to gross poverty, and real heartbreaking suffering. We need a practical political theology grounded in the concrete daily lives and pains and joys and prayers of those little ones whom God loves so graciously. Moreover, we need a theology of hope that seeks transformation concretely here and now, that not only analyzes instances of oppression, but systems of oppression, exploitation, and control as well. We need a philosophical theology that supports and sustains, not only resistance and rebellion, but authentic creative transformation on a human scale in society and history as well.

The second challenge flows from the first: it is a moral challenge. Put simply, the surviving native peoples, blacks, Latinos, Koreans, Jews need a Celtic-, Anglo-, European-American theologian to do for the United States what Johann Baptist Metz did for Germany. We need some intelligent, self-sacrificing, generous, human and moral man or woman to analyze critically and thoughtfully for his and her community, the implications, dynamics, structures, customs, beliefs, and practices of white racist supremacy as these arise from within racially constructed, ethnically erased white communities and as they engage children, women, and men of different racial, linguistic, ethnic-cultural heritages. We theologians must assume responsibility for our complicity in sustaining past oppressive social orders through our silence. If we believe that we are the mystical body of Christ, then it is we who are united across time and space in the blood and grace and love of Christ.

The third challenge flows from the first and second, and it is an existential challenge. Celtic-, Anglo-, European-American theologians must identify their respective social locations. This neglect leaves the best of our male theologians open to the charge of positing a kind of universal viewpoint and cripples the work of the best of our female theologians because racial self-critique and analysis do not figure in their discussions.

I began with the tokens of my theological vocation; I close with them. Rivera's prints were purchased on a Sunday afternoon walk through my neighborhood which is (Orthodox and Reform) Jewish and African-, Celtic-, Anglo-, European-American. I was working on the final revisions of an essay; blocked, I took to fresh air. The Hadassah

Consignment Shop was open. Although the prints were old, the quality of their colors remained rich and vivid. On market value, the price was cheap, less than ten dollars. On the ledger of history, they are an invaluable, yet sorry prize. Still, Rivera's aesthetic courage prompts me as a theologian to seek out the decentered and the displaced, to make space in order that they might use me to speak their sad and beautiful truths. This is part of my theological calling. These prints hang above the brooding angel, African, black, darkly dark, the one wing is dipped in history's bloody suffering, the other bears culture.

Compactly, then, this is how I self-identify in our multicultural church. If I am to be an authentic human person, an authentic theologian, I have not much choice. I am called to be an insurgent intellectual.[58] Indeed, if I do not choose, others will choose for me, and they are too eager to do so: pasting this or that stereotype on me with little notice and less regard for my intellectual training and interests, my preferences, my choices, my oversights, my social location, my appropriation of complex multiculturality, my blunders, my development, my growth. The material for my struggle is the Word. And as an old Aztec poem has been translated to read in part: *Perhaps with words / you will be pierced, broken / to understand.*[59] Perhaps, we all shall—by the grace of the Word made flesh.

Marina Herrera

RESPONSE TO
M. SHAWN COPELAND

I am pleased to continue the line of thought opened by Shawn of what will hopefully be only the beginning of many conversations on the subject that is being addressed. I am related to Shawn in circuitous but nevertheless important ways that have left us with similar imprints in our self-identity, both in spiritual and cultural ways. She has approached the complex issue of self-identity and multiculturalism from a unique and rich perspective, quite different from mine but with clear convergences in a common life shared in Adrian, Michigan, in theological school, in our experiences of discrimination on the basis of gender, race or ethnic origin, and in our deep concern for justice and community. Remarkable convergences when you consider the distance and difference between her starting point in Detroit and mine in the small town of Banø on the southern coast of the Dominican Republic. Her hometown is the automotive heartland of the world; mine is known only to Dominicans because of its milk fudge (*dulce de leche*), and its beautiful women, and to Cubans for being the birthplace of Máximo Gómez, the fighting general of their liberating forces at the turn of the century. Perhaps, the only similarity in both towns was the presence of committed religious who dedicated themselves to educating the young and left in our youthful psyches the imprints of the power of the Word to free and to inspire.

My self-identity was forged in a remarkably multicultural environment in the day-to-day interactions of living in family and town. My parents had merged Italian, Spanish, Basque, Portuguese, and Taøno blood and by some indications, even Russian and Armenian. Our parish was run by Canadian Scarborough missionaries, our school by Carmelite Spanish sisters, and our main restaurant by Chinese. My extended family had room in its warm embrace for twin black women whose grandparents had been stranded on a passage to the eastern islands of the Caribbean in search of the freedom denied them here before emancipation. The worst sins (or virtues depending on your political affiliation) of my town were not racial but ideological, attacking the tyranny of the dictator Trujillo who held a strong grip on the island in the years of my childhood and adolescence. There was no sense in my childhood that different skin color meant inferiority. Most families exhibited the gamut of skin colors. An accented Spanish was a sure entry into a circle of admiration and appreciation on the part of the locals who immediately perceived foreigners speaking Spanish as friends trying their best to communicate.

My home offered a contrast to my early experience in the United States where I was presumed intellectually, academically, and culturally inferior because my upbringing until my late teens took place in Santo Domingo. My application for admission to Fordham University in graduate theology was denied on the grounds that my English might not be good enough. The decision was quickly reversed when I informed the department chair that I would be interested in translating one of his books into Spanish and that I had good publishing connections in Latin America. He was even more surprised when he showed me one of his French translations and I was able to read it for him without hesitation. I was exempt from taking the French language exam required by the department, and the admissions committee was called to an extraordinary meeting two hours later to interview me and approve my admission. One educated in the Dominican Republic meant that the study of both English and French was compulsory. No one would be considered prepared for living in the modern world without at least three languages. Those two were indispensable to our survival as a trading partner with Haiti and the United States.

Such multicultural experiences were enhanced and expanded by my interest in understanding the religious dimension of life as manifested in different spiritual traditions. My interest included a taste of Asian religious thought from Professor Thomas Berry, the geologian, made supple and body-conscious by Yoga; a communal experience in a Methodist study experience for a summer in Chicago; and work at the United Nations as a representative of the Dominican Republic during my last two years in New York. I felt a unique affinity for tackling some of the issues of discrimination and injustice experienced by members of other cultures.

I saw my interest in theology, education, culture, and intercultural communication converging when I was invited to initiate a position in the Department of Education of the United States Catholic Conference in 1977. This new position was entitled "Specialist in Religious Education for Minorities." After one week in my new job I went to Msgr. Thomas Leonard, Secretary of Education at the time, and asked him to clarify for me which minorities were to be my concern. The question had been triggered by the many calls I received as soon as the news release had been dispatched by Catholic News Service. Congratulatory messages were mixed with inquiries from the Office for the Handicapped as we then called it, people from Dignity, Native Americans, and the Office of Black Catholics. "Considering that the only minorities in the church are the bishops," I said very seriously to Msgr. Leonard, "and certain that the title does not include them I feel we should find a different title in order not to cause confusion." He approved my request and I went off to redefine my title and the scope of my office. After checking how other episcopal conferences classified similar offices, I found in Canada the closest to what I was looking for. This was "Office of Multicultural Catechesis." Whereupon my job description as Specialist in Multicultural Catechesis was imprinted on my office door. The efforts in secular multicultural education were in their infancy and no one had yet connected the description to religious education.

I went to the Catholic Conference as the U.S. National Catechetical Directory, *Sharing the Light of Faith*, was being prepared for its final vote which took place three months after I arrived. I could do little to alter what was already well set in stone. But there were a couple of lines within the Catechetical Directory that presented an opening which proved most fruitful. In Catechesis for Persons with Special Needs (chapter VIII, C), the directory spoke about the need to adapt catechesis to a pluralist society and called for the adaptation of catechesis to take into account the social and cultural differences of its members. It said, "the Church recognizes within the unity of faith, diversity, need for equality, charity and mutual respect among all the groups within the Church and society." I must add, however, that the picture that accompanied article 194 of the directory was that of a kind elderly sister trying to speak with a child who seems to suffer from some form of cerebral palsy. It is no wonder that shortly after it was published, and following the earnest desire of the bishops that it be implemented, a diocese published a book of resources of audio-visual materials and one of the segments included was materials for the culturally handicapped. The degree of my shock over this bizarre interpretation of the Catechetical Directory was compounded by the indifference of my colleagues to the issues involved when I expressed my dismay to them. Obviously, there was serious need for the raising of consciousness as to what it is to be culturally different.

Furthermore, the directory called for the adequate preparation of catechists, giving attention not only to language but also to modes of thought, cultural particularities, customs and symbols. It pointed out that catechetical materials should respond to those special needs, and that more is needed than a simple translation or a change of pictures. Catechetical material should reinforce the identity and the dignity of ∿ the members of each group. And it added this statement: "Even in homogeneous areas and parishes, **catechesis should be multi-cultural**, in the sense that all should be taught to know and respect other cultural, racial and ethnic groups. The members of minority groups should be invited and encouraged to participate in the religious and social functions of the church."

The Catechetical Directory made other important points that have served as the springboard of my efforts in these years. First, the word multicultural was written with a hyphen. When I see it written that way, it is a flag for me that the users consider it a new term, expressing a new reality that is not quite easily understood by those reading the document. In my experience, working since 1975 with issues of intercultural relations and as a member of SIETAR (The Society for Intercultural Relations, Training and Research), multicultural is written as one word expressing that such is the way of life in our world, our country and our Catholic Church. The word in hyphenated form also conveys that the users are tentative about the legitimacy, validity, and gifts of the many cultures with claims to a rightful place in the community without necessarily "melting" their unique cultural characteristics with those of the controlling culture.

Second, the way in which the Catechetical Directory phrased the issue of special needs conveyed a very static concept of culture on the part of those who wrote it and those called to implement its teaching. Adaptations to the different needs of the culturally different are considered essential, while it does not suggest who is responsible for those adaptations nor the role that the recipients can and should play in the creation of those adaptations. The questions are asked as if the host culture knows what the other cultural groups need and want.

Third, the directory seems to convey a widely held belief among religious education professionals: the ways of the church in the United States are superior to the ways of the church in those parts of the world where the culturally different originate. There is no suggestion that the church in the United States needs to heed what *Ad Gentes* observed in its ground breaking statement: "The young churches borrow from the customs, traditions, wisdom, teaching, arts and sciences of their people everything which could be used to praise the glory of the Creator, manifest the grace of the saviour or contribute to the right ordering of Christian life" (art. 22). While the Roman Catholic Church has a five hundred year history of uninterrupted presence in my country of birth and in most of Latin America and almost the same for the Philippines, the question of the catholicity of the newcomers is always posed in terms of the church in the United States (that recently celebrated the bicentennial of the first diocese), assuming a position of seniority in regard to those other churches.

What the Catechetical Directory included is the first stage in a process of developing a comprehensive understanding and praxis of what a multicultural church is. This process necessitates the acquisition of cultural literacy that includes anthropological understandings that go beyond those developed by scientists from the controlling cultures while observing peoples from so-called underdeveloped cultures. It also necessitates the creation of ecclesiological structures for intercultural dialogue based on the premise that at the heart of the faith we share is the belief that grace determines one's place in the community of believers that we call church.

The first step in developing a process to achieve cultural literacy is to understand culture from a dynamic perspective.

In order to arrive at that perspective we need to go beyond Clifford Geertz' definition of culture, and those inherited from most anthropology classes. They have left us with the impression that culture can be transplanted, transmitted and dissected; that it is an objective reality; that it can be understood with the analytical tools created in epistemological systems derived from meanings usually nonexistent in the cultures being analyzed. Culture ought to be seen as the process of giving meaning to all our relations (people, friendly and unfriendly, God, nature, things). My starting point for this definition is Luzbetak's[1] notion of culture as a total shared design for living. In that sense it is easy to understand the power that family, school, church, and society have on our self-identity. This definition points to the need for those from the established and controlling culture to make significant adjustments in their role of ministering to those in transition from other cultures. The newcomers are the only ones who truly know and experience the redefinitions that they are making or need to make in order to function successfully within the new culture. Their burden can be made heavier by an attitude of condescension, paternalism/ maternalism, or self-pity. Their burden can be lessened by the sensitivity of those who understand the positive and negative power of the controlling culture to reshape self-identity. They need to welcome newcomers not as potential members of an old Catholic Church of the United States, but as indispensable members of a new Catholic Church of the United States, one not yet born but in which the gifts of faith from all the cultures are brought to the altar and allowed to interact, challenge, and enhance each other. For the most part church practitioners have been assigning us meanings that most often do not correspond with the ones we had received from our first self-defining environment. That is why, for example, I see myself as a missionary to the United States, a culture that even from the Dominican Republic in 1960, was obviously anti-Catholic given its notorious racist stance. Church leaders in the United States need to hear the meanings the culturally different attach to the church and then proceed to make adaptations and adjustments in a way in which the church's self-identity is expanded to include the expectations and aspirations of the new groups and those not so new but who also feel like outsiders.

The second step in the process is to become particularly adept in knowing the crucial importance of naming oneself, one's relations and others in the process of acquiring a healthy self-identity.

When we feel power over persons or things we feel we can name them, depending on the place we assign to them in our overall design for living. Essential in the development of ecclesial structures and catechetical approaches that are conducive to the development of the multicultural church is the way in which we name not only the persons from those cultures, but also their rituals and symbols. It is customary, for example, to refer to the religious practices that come from outside the United States as folk religion, popular religiosity, in order to distinguish such practices from mainstream religiosity. That which is called popular religion by theologians from the dominant culture (and even by some from the outside cultures well versed in the epistemo-logical systems of the insiders) is the attempt of missionaries in the past to enculturate the faith in the surroundings to which they brought the official religion. What I experienced growing up in Banø, which I am often reminded is only folk religion, were practices affirmed and blessed by the official church of my country, practices sown by Spanish, and in the second half of this century, by Canadian missionaries. We need to find ways to improve our pastoral language in order not to offend the religious sensibilities of people from different cultures. In settings where Catholicism was not challenged by Protestant influences, its members did not need to approach the faith as an academic exercise for the purpose of defending it, but rather as a total way of life that was celebrated and affirmed by the entire social and civic establishment. While we Latin Americans with a Catholic education could relate the names of the great saints and missionaries of the past, North American Catholics were prepared to recite the answers to the *Baltimore Catechism*. Neither of these learned and culturally defined responses to the faith we share constitute qualifications for counting ourselves among the blessed on the day of judgment.

Third, we need to develop intercultural approaches for deciding pastoral norms in those areas that affect the ecclesial life of those who come from different cultures with long established Catholic traditions.

This issue is often muddled by those who look at the ecclesial questions raised by a multicultural society from the perspective of dogmatic questions that seek to redefine the relation of the local church to the church of Rome. Prior to that is the issue that sets the cultural style and mode of a local church as the sole arbiter for deciding the style and mode of ecclesial participation for people with a very different experience of church. We are not talking about the issues related to bringing the faith to those who had never heard it, but to people whose continuous membership in the church is older than the local church that now makes the decisions for them. Deciding on pastoral norms for a multicultural society is perhaps the most difficult ecclesial task the church must face in the next decade.

Norms are always derived from the criteria of the controlling culture. So it is, for example, that the medical establishment asks "Why do women live longer than men?" in trying to understand longevity, and proceed for the most part to study men and not women. If the question were posed, "Why don't men live as long as women?" and use women as the norm for long life, we might be closer to breakthroughs in increasing the human life span. When taken to the ecclesial realm, we may cease to ask Hispanics why they do not go to church, but ask church officials instead, "Why isn't the church more welcoming to Hispanics?" or ask Hispanics, "How welcomed do you feel in the church?" Such a change in the way of posing questions would necessitate a radical shift in the perspective of what constitutes the norm and in the way we measure those aspects of ecclesial life that are driving Hispanics away from the faith tradition that has been a significant aspect of their self-identity. Or it may lead to findings that reveal why the Catholic Church is the spiritual home of only 2 million African-Americans at a time when the same church is showing explosive growth in Africa.

Intercultural understanding demands that we no longer measure people from the perspective of those who, because they ask the questions, feel they are the measure against which all things are validated or understood. It is time that those from other cultures be welcomed not only to pose questions from different perspectives to those answers that had always been taken for granted, but also to participate in the formulation of the new answers required in the finding of pastoral solutions. Thus a more welcoming and representative church is born.

This search for pastoral practices that do not invalidate the Catholic experience of other cultures would prepare future priests to give more satisfying answers to new questions. A family of Mexican immigrants was ready to baptize their youngest child; however, on the wrong date. When the family was denied baptism by a Chicago priest who wanted this Mexican family to learn first how the church operates in this country, the father asked, "I have had five other children baptized, is baptism different here?" The explanation and the tone in which an answer was given left the family convinced only of one thing: Yes, baptism is different here and the main difference is that you have to pay more for it!

We need to abandon many of our definitions of race and culture in order to accommodate the new human reality that is being born and that makes many of our definitions totally invalid. This lack of cultural sophistication is best seen in a recent column by Ann Landers who responded to a white woman asking for advice to help her Korean-Hispanic adopted daughter fill out the forms where race is requested or required. Ann Landers' response was, "Have her choose Asian or Hispanic until she decides which is her identity." Ann Landers' simplistic solution is a clear indicator of the naiveté regarding the complexity of self-identity. Such complexity arises when the norms for judging one's racial make-up have been invalidated by the greatest racial mixing the world has ever known, not to speak of the cultural hybrids that we all are.

The last United States census identified the number of those belonging to other races as having had a growth of 45% or some 9 million people. No one doing demographic studies seems to attach any significance to this group of people. To me it signals a radical change in the awareness that persons of mixed race are having and their refusal to accept the box provided by the census bureau to present a valid picture of who they are as persons. They are aware that ours is a nation of hybrids for which the labels of the past are no longer valid. Not only is the United States the de facto cradle of a new human genetic pool, but also the possible birthing place for the world church of which Karl Rahner spoke.

The church, since it was born in the upper room with the Pentecost experience, has been concerned about its need to communicate the message of Jesus to people from outside the culture of his original band of followers. It was true as the church moved through northern Africa, southern, central and northern Europe, Asia, and starting five hundred years ago, the Americas. That task remains but it is different from another one faced by the church in the United States: how to preserve the faith of those who acquired it in one setting and having transplanted themselves to a new society learn how to maintain it, grow in it, and continue to be involved in their faith community.

In the United States, the church has been Eurocentric in its leadership and congregations, though its flavor and style has been varied and at times contentious as reflected in the struggles of diverse ethnic prelates from the beginning of its history. There were always Native Americans and African-Americans to preach to and convert; and in our time many other groups as well. What is radically different now is that ethnic and racial groups from outside are speaking with their own voice, in cadences, rhythms, accents and images that were not given to them by the culture that has dominated the destiny of this land. There are now ethnic and racial theologians, intellectuals, and writers who speak in the language of the controlling culture and demand that they be considered from a perspective other than the one prescribed by those who only saw them in a relationship of control and power. Ideally, every theological and pastoral conference should include persons from different cultures to help frame the questions and look for solutions in unsuspected areas to the pastoral issues we face. Another possibility, sometimes more productive in academic gatherings, is to have persons from the controlling culture whose pastoral life and work outside their own culture has enabled them to ask questions and offer new avenues of thought from the perspective of the outsiders.

Insiders who have asked questions from outside their cultural matrix are Peter at the first Council of Jerusalem, and Fray Antonio de Montesinos to the representatives of the Spanish Crown attending mass on the third Sunday of Advent in Santo Domingo in 1511.

Peter's, "Why do you now want to put God to the test by laying a load on the backs of the believers which neither our ancestors nor we ourselves were able to carry?" (Acts 15:10) broke the ideological impasse created by those who wanted to restrict the circle of the saved to the Jews. Montesinos: "Tell me, who gave you the right to declare such a hateful war against these people?....Why do you oppress them to the point...that from the excessive work you force upon them...you kill them in order to mine and acquire gold each day?....Are these people not men? Don't they have rational souls? Are you not obliged to love them as you love yourselves?..."[2]

It is difficult for those who create a language, determine its categories and its norms and have authority to impose them, to understand the perspective of those from outside who use a different language, different categories and lack any worldly authority or power. It is difficult for them, too, to accept dissenting voices from within their own ranks who dare to suggest a new pattern of relationships. We are all quite familiar with the struggle of Peter in the early church; we have not been equally exposed to the reaction of the Crown to the questions asked by Montesinos:

> I also saw the sermon which was delivered by a Dominican
> friar called Antonio Montesinos, and even though he always

preached in scandalous ways, what he said has left me in astonishment because what he said does not have any good theological foundation, nor canons nor laws according to what the scholars, theologians and canon lawyers say who have seen the grant that our very Holy Father Alexander VI made to us...so it is reasonable that you will impose on the one who preached it...some punishment because his error was very great.[3]

Allowing persons from outside cultures and those from within their own controlling cultural matrix who have "inter-pathy"[4] to pose questions and seek solutions to the dilemmas presented to the church by the multicultural society is the best approach to move the church beyond the present intolerance and misunderstandings of many of its ministers. The survival of the church in the next century is linked to its ability to allow newcomers to be involved in its transformation.

The questions of a multicultural society need to be framed from the perspective of the pastoral issues confronted by pastors, catechists and other pastoral ministers in the day-to-day unfolding of their ministries with and for people whose faith tradition is constantly devalued and misunderstood. In that context, participants should come with different perspectives and representative of the broad range of possibilities in the solutions or insights to the questions asked. How can an Hispanic woman theologian respond to the question of self-identity as framed by an African-American woman theologian, both of whom do not seem to have had their self-identities crushed or even dented by the negative self-definitions we have been decrying? We women, African and Latinas, lucky enough to have had our self-identity shaped by those who were already doubters of their own inherited cultural biases, are ready and willing to continue conversing with each other as to what it means to be African and Hispanic in the church in the United States. We also ask new questions of bishops, theologians, and cultural anthropologists and even offer suggestions to solve the pastoral dilemmas that the church confronts today. The multicultural society and church can come about in a process in which the members of all cultures find a way to come together to seek, express and give meaning to our new relations as church, city, nation, and world.

In order for that to happen we need dynamics of interaction that reject confrontation and pursue communication in every form, downplay competition, facilitate collaboration, take responsibility for the conflagration of our cities, and seek by every possible means to celebrate our common divine origin and heavenly destiny.

But to get there the words from an old Spanish poem give me

inspiration: "Caminante, no hay camino se hace camino al andar."[5] This is true of the church in the United States. There is no already-made road for us to follow; we must build it with the participation of all those willing to open up the way to new directions. May each one of us in the power of the Holy Spirit be willing to join hands with all the different Catholic groups in this great land in building the new reality; a church where all feel at home in fulfillment of Jesus' vision and mandate to his disciples.

Joseph A. Komonchak

THE THEOLOGY
OF THE LOCAL CHURCH:
STATE OF THE QUESTION

This conference addresses one of the major themes in the theology of the local church as this has developed in the decades since the close of the Second Vatican Council. This remarkable development has had three principal points of focus: (1) identifying the constitutive principles of the church and where and how they generate the church; (2) clarifying the meaning of catholicity as diversity integrated into unity; and (3) exploring the responsibility for the genesis and activities of the local churches.[1] It is the second of these that lies at the heart of our discussions here. The conference title, "Implications of the Multicultural Dimension of the Catholic Church in the United States," draws together the two themes that pose the central problem. Namely, multicultural refers to diversity, but this is a diversity that exists within the one Catholic church in the United States, a church that is not one unless the diversity is integrated into unity.

It might even be argued that our theme of diversity-in-unity provides the key for a concrete theology of the church that can deal adequately with the other two principal themes. Ecclesiologists deal with the constitutive principles of the church—what makes it a distinctive human community in the world; but often what results from this necessary effort is only a formal or heuristic ecclesiology of universal application, one that needs to be filled in by reflection on where and how it is that this one church comes to be and to act as an historical subject. This requires a consideration of the meaning of catholicity as a dimension intrinsic to the reality of the local church and to the communion of local churches that is the one universal church. Finally, only a reflection on the local churches as the concrete subjects of the realization of the one church provides a properly theological basis for the recovery of a sense of their responsibility as historical agents.

I will discuss two themes that emerged from the ecclesiology of
Vatican II, the generative and constitutive principles of the church as
realized in the many churches and the theological significance of
cultural particularity in the genesis of the church in the churches.

THE SECOND VATICAN COUNCIL

When the Second Vatican Council began its work, Catholic ecclesiology was dominated by a universalistic ecclesiology. The word
"church" was normally used in the singular and referred to the single
worldwide religious community and organization directed by the pope.
The inability of the First Vatican Council to complete its projected work
on the church, which would have included a discussion of the place
and roles of bishops in the church, had as one of its consequences an
immense emphasis on the jurisdictional and symbolic role of the pope.
Tendencies toward uniformity and Roman centralization, which had of
course been present and effective for centuries, reached something of
an apogee in the reign of Pope Pius XII. A passage in his encyclical,
Mystici Corporis, is illustrative. After discussing how the mystical body is
governed both invisibly and extraordinarily by Christ and visibly and
ordinarily by the pope, Pius XII devoted a paragraph, that reads almost
like an afterthought:

> What we have thus far said of the universal church must be
> understood also of the individual communities of Christians,
> both Latin and Oriental, from which the one Catholic
> Church is made up [ex quibus una constat ac *componitur
> Catholic Ecclesia*]. For they too are ruled by Jesus Christ
> through the power and voice of their respective bishops.
> Hence, bishops must not only be considered as the nobler
> members of the universal Church since they are united by a
> very special bond to the divine Head of the whole Body and
> are rightly called "the principal parts of the members of the
> Lord"; but besides, as far as his own diocese is concerned,
> each one, as a true shepherd feeds the flock entrusted to him
> and rules it in the name of Christ. But in exercising this
> office, they are not fully autonomous, but are subordinate to
> the lawful authority of the Roman Pontiff, although they
> enjoy the ordinary power of jurisdiction that they receive
> directly from the same Supreme Pontiff.[2]

You will note that the word "church" is here reserved for the universal
church; the dioceses over which bishops preside are not called churches

but individual communities of Christians. And while bishops are, of course, described as shepherds of their own flocks, their jurisdictional authority over them is said to derive, not from ordination or by reference to their local churches, but from immediate delegation by the pope. It was not entirely surprising, then, that some theologians and canonists during the reign of Pius XII spoke of the church as if it were a single vast diocese with a single universal bishop at its head.

The influence of this universalistic ecclesiology is even evident in one of the first efforts to reform it, Karl Rahner's unfortunate theory of the episcopal college which sees it as a sort of board of directors for the governance of the whole church. If on this view, a collective directorate would make the universal governance more collegial, the basic vision of the church is still that of the whole universal body for which decisions would be made, not, if I may press the image a bit, by a single chief executive officer alone but by him in some kind of collegial association with his board of directors. The traces of this vision of the church remain today, even in some proposals for increasing the role of the college of bishops, for example, in the Synod of Bishops.

Given this widespread and often almost unconsciously influential vision of the church, it is not surprising to find traces of it in the ecclesiology of the Second Vatican Council. What is surprising is that within less than five years, the council was to provide a basis for a revalidation of the local church and to begin the movement toward a reconceptualization of the one Catholic Church as the communion of local churches. It did this through two chief emphases in its theology of the church: by its renewed attention to the distinctive spiritual principles of the church as realized in local communities of faith and by its redefinition of catholicity as diversity-in-unity.

THE CONSTITUTIVE PRINCIPLES OF THE CHURCH

In several passages the council described what I may call the distinctive generative principles of the church: what it is that makes the church the church and distinguishes it from all other human communities. In summary, these are the call of God, the word of Christ, the grace of the Spirit, the sacramental communion of faith, hope, and love, and the apostolic ministry. These elements constitute and animate the distinctive life of the church. This represents the repudiation of an ecclesiology that focuses chiefly on the institutional dimensions of the church: the identification and distribution of authority. It is because of these conciliar emphases that in the years since ecclesiology has focused instead on concepts such as those of the people of God, communion, and mystery.

But the council did something else. It drew attention to the fact that these divine principles do not generate the church on some abstract level, but only in local communities of faith. Two passages in *Lumen Gentium* are here quite crucial. In the first the council addressed a question similar to the one posed by Pius XII in the passage from *Mystici Corporis* cited above. But the council's language is significantly different:

> As the Roman Pontiff, as the successor of Peter, is the principle and visible foundation of the unity both of bishops and of the multitude, so individual bishops are the principle and center of unity in their particular churches, which are formed in the image of the universal church and in and out of which the one and only Catholic church exists (*LG* 23).

Note, first, that dioceses are here now described as churches.[3] The crucial reference remains, of course, to the universal unity, for which the pope has distinct essential responsibilities, but the distinct and essential responsibility of bishops for the unity of their own churches is stressed more forcefully than in *Mystici Corporis*. And above all, a reciprocity in the very reality of the one Catholic Church and of the individual churches is firmly established. On the one hand, the particular churches image the universal church; on the other hand, the one Catholic Church exists only in and out of the particular churches. These two affirmations, which can appear to be in some tension with one another, are not further clarified in this passage or anywhere else in the conciliar texts. That task of clarification is left to theologians, but before addressing it, we should look first at another important text of *Lumen Gentium*.

It appears in the paragraph in which the council takes up the bishop's sacramental tasks in his church. It begins with a reference to the eucharist, "from which the church ever derives its life and growth." And this leads into the following set of statements:

> This Church of Christ is truly present in all legitimately organized local assemblies of believers, which in union with their pastors are themselves also called churches in the New Testament. For these assemblies are in their own localities the new People called by God, in the power of the Holy Spirit and in full conviction (cf. 1 Th 1:5). In them believers are gathered together by the preaching of the Gospel of Christ and the mystery of the Lord's Supper is celebrated.... In each altar-community, under the bishop's sacred ministry, a manifest symbol is displayed of that charity and "unity of the mystical Body without which no one can be saved." In

> these communities, although they are often small and poor or
> scattered, Christ is present through whose power the one holy
> Catholic and apostolic Church is brought together (*LG* 26).

Here the council's attention has moved to infradiocesan eucharistic
assemblies such as parishes or other authorized communities. The
focus is on the eucharistic assembly, and this passage represents the
council's appropriation of the adage that "the church makes the
eucharist and the eucharist makes the church." The biblical grounds for
calling these assemblies churches are recalled and then are explained
by the presence in them of the constitutive principles of the apostolic
ministry, the gospel of Christ, the power of the Spirit, and the
eucharist. These small communities are not called churches by some
sort of convention, but because in them Christ is at work, gathering his
one and Catholic Church.

These two passages of *Lumen Gentium* give the essential reasons
for the revalidation of the local church. The one and Catholic Church,
the communion of faith, hope and love, is the community brought into
existence by the call of God, the word of Christ, and the grace of the
Spirit and through the apostolic ministry. These principles generate and
characterize the one church as the universal communion of believers,
and I take this to describe what is meant by "the image of the universal
church": if a particular community does not assemble around these
distinctive principles, it cannot be called a church. But here is the
essential point: this one mystery of communion in turn is only realized
locally, when believers gather under the gospel, in the Spirit, and for the
eucharist, and when their assemblies are in communion with one
another under the authority of a bishop. The one mystery of the church
is only realized in the many local particular churches.

These two conciliar affirmations forbid one from indulging either
of two ways of thinking of the relationship between the one universal
church and the many local churches. The first would see the universal
church as the result, in some second moment, of a federation of local
churches, perhaps something like the World Council of Churches.
Individual assemblies of believers would first exist in some sort of
independence and only subsequently decide to confederate into a single
universal church. The other view would see the local churches as
derivations of a pre-existent universal church. The latter would exist
somehow and somewhere first and then, perhaps principally for
administrative reasons, would divide.

Nearly everyone who writes about these issues agrees that these
two positions are unacceptable.[4] But this has not prevented the question of the relationship between the one church and the many churches

from being posed in terms of a priority of one to the other. It has to be admitted that the conciliar text (*LG* 23) does pose a question that can, mistakenly I think, be stated in terms of priority. If the individual churches are in the image of the universal church, must not the latter have priority? But if the one church exists only in and out of the individual churches, must not the latter have priority? Both positions have been defended in the literature, as when, on the one hand, it is said that only the universal church is comprehensive, including the church in heaven, that the local church depends on the universal church, that the universal church has preeminence and absolute ontological priority (Mondin); that as the church-from-above, the mystery of salvation, it exists in all the local churches (Boff); that Christ founded only the universal church and not the particular churches (Bertrams, C. Colombo, Bandera, d'Ors); that the universal church is the exemplary, efficient, and final cause of the local church (Bertrams); that only the universal church can be the universal sacrament of salvation (Bertrams, Bandera) and is assured by Christ's prayer of being indefectible and infallible (C. Colombo, Bandera), and holy (C. Colombo); that the universal church precedes the local church temporally (Ratzinger).

Explicit assertions of a priority of the local church are rarer. Bruno Forte defends its *primato* because the church that is born in the eucharist is by priority (*prioritariamente*) the local church and in the sense that "there is no truly ecclesial act which is not by origin (*originariamente*) an act of the local church." Severino Dianich argues that the necessarily particular event of the communication and reception of the faith is the "first principle" of the church from which all other elements are derived as developments of its universal virtualities.

The considerable recent Roman concern about one-sided claims for the local church may also be directed against various movements in favor of the basic Christian communities and the communities which claim to be constructing "the church from below." This would seem to be the case, for example, in Cardinal Ratzinger's vigorous reply to the claim that a local community may be said to have a "right" to the euchar-ist. The recent working-paper on episcopal conferences expressed the fear that a one-sided emphasis on the local churches was threatening "the ontological and also historical priority of the universal church over the particular church." "The Petrine Primacy itself, understood as 'plenitudo potestatis,'" it argued, "has no meaning and theological coher-ence except within the primacy of the one and universal church over the particular and local churches."[5] The same concern and similar language appear in the recent letter of the Congregation for the Doctrine of the Faith, "Some Aspects of the Church Understood as Communion."[6]

There are many fine things in this document, particularly in the early sections on the trinitarian and eucharistic grounds of ecclesial communion. But the second section, on the universal church and the particular churches, raises some questions and has received some serious criticisms from both Catholics and other Christians.[7] The Congregation is concerned about some (unidentified) people whose idea of the communion of churches is one-sided, weakening "the concept of the unity of the church at the visible and institutional level. Thus it is asserted that each particular church is a subject complete in itself, and that the universal church is the result of a reciprocal recognition on the part of the particular churches." In response the Congregation warns that, "as history shows, when a particular church has sought to become self-sufficient and has weakened its real communion with the universal church and with its living and visible center, its internal unity suffers too, and it finds itself in danger of losing its own freedom in the face of the various forces of enslavement and exploitation" (#8).

The historical reminder is useful, since in fact nearly every schism has originated from excessive emphasis on national, racial or ethnic particularity. But the Congregation then goes on to argue a more problematic case when, in order to insist that the universal church is not "the result of the communion of the churches," it asserts that "it is a reality ontologically and historically prior to every individual particular church." Here is how it makes its case:

> Indeed, ontologically, according to the Fathers the church-mystery, the church that is one and unique, precedes creation and gives birth to the particular churches as her daughters. She expresses herself in them; she is the mother and not the offspring of the particular churches. Furthermore, temporally, the church is manifested on the day of Pentecost in the community of the 120 gathered around Mary and the Twelve Apostles, the representatives of the one unique church and the future founders of the local churches, who have a mission directed to the world. From the first the church speaks all languages.

> From the church, which in its origins and in its first manifestation is universal, have arisen the different local churches as particular expressions of the one unique church of Jesus Christ. Arising within and out of the universal church, they have their ecclesial character in her and from her. Hence the formula of the Second Vatican Council: "*The church in and formed out of the churches*" (*ecclesia in et ex*

ecclesiis)." Clearly, the relationship between the universal church and the particular churches is a mystery and cannot be compared to that which exists between the whole and the parts in a purely human group or society (#9).

Not content with the "image of the universal church" language of the council, the Congregation borrows from a recent speech of Pope John Paul II in order to balance the "*in et ex quibus*" phrase of *Lumen Gentium* with a new phrase: "*ecclesiae in et ex ecclesia.*" It may be helpful to quote the paragraph in which, addressing the reciprocal relation between universal church and local churches, the pope offers this formula:

> This reciprocity, while it expresses and preserves the respective dignities, adequately illustrates the shape of the church, one and universal, which finds in the particular churches at once its proper image and its place of expression, since the particular churches are formed "in the image of the universal church and it is in them and out of them that the one and single universal church is constituted." The particular churches in their turn are "*ex et in Ecclesia universali*": it is from it and in it that they have their ecclesial character. The particular church is "church" precisely because it is a particular presence of the universal church. Thus, on the one hand, the universal church finds its concrete existence in every particular church in which it is present and active and, on the other hand, the particular church does not exhaust the totality of the mystery of the church, since some of its constitutive elements are not deducible from a pure analysis of the particular church itself. These elements are the office of the successor of Peter and the episcopal college.[8]

It is not clear to me that the new phrase proposed by the pope and by the Congregation is necessary since everything it appears to intend is already present in the conciliar affirmation about the "image of the universal church." On the other hand, I would not be in principle opposed to the intention of the new phrase: to say that the one church exists in the many particular churches and that the many particular churches exist in the one church in fact is not a bad representation of the conciliar ecclesiology.

But it is precisely this mutual interiority or reciprocity that makes it a puzzle to me how one can even ask the question of priority on either an ontological or an historical level. If local church and universal church exist within one another, how is it possible to set them over-and-against one another as if they were distinct and the problem were how to relate them. Ontologically, (1) there cannot be a church except in time and place, gathering specific men and women in communion of faith, hope and love; and (2) a local community is not a church unless it is also universal or catholic in its constitutive principles: catholic both because the whole of the mystery of the church is realized in it and because the mystery that makes it a communion in Christ is the same mystery that makes every other community a communion in Christ. Historically, the paradigmatic case of Pentecost makes it clear that the church was born both local and universal. The assembly gathered in Jerusalem and yet it included representatives of all the nations, all of whom heard the one message in their various native languages. It was in this Jerusalem assembly that the universal church was already realized, and it was as a development and realization of this original catholicity that other particular and local churches were founded.[9]

The Congregation seems particularly concerned with the assertion attributed to some unidentified people that the universal church is "the result of a reciprocal recognition on the part of the particular churches." But the theologians who speak of reciprocal reception and recognition do not imagine it as if there were some second moment, after the constitution of local churches, when they look around, see that they all agree about certain things, and then decide to form a federation. All the theologians who have spoken about reciprocal recognition would repudiate the idea that the universal church results from a second moment after the constitution of the particular churches. What is meant, at least as I would put it, is that the mystery of communion that makes the church to be the church, whether locally or universally, consists in the common incorporation of its members, together, into Christ, a communion in Christ which takes conscious form in the common faith, hope and love that, first locally, make Christians the one society of the church in a particular place. That is what makes it true that in the individual congregation we are no longer Jew or Greek, slave or free, man or woman, but we are all one in Christ; this is already the realization of the catholicity of the church, and it is an intrinsic and constitutive dimension of being the church even locally. The concrete reality of the local church is the reciprocal reception of one another as brothers and sisters in Christ.

Similarly, the universal church *is* the communion of the local churches; it does not result from, it *is* their reciprocal reception of one another as all the beneficiaries of Christ's word and grace. What is realized locally is what is realized universally. What is called the universal church is this common and universal consciousness among all Christians and among all particular churches. Apart from this embodiment in this common consciousness, the universal church is, as Pope

Paul VI said, an abstraction; what Henri de Lubac called a mere "*être de raison,*" what scholastics call an "*universale ante rem.*" This common consciousness includes all the elements that make up the church: the one call of God, the one word of Christ, the one grace of the Spirit, the apostolic ministry of pope and bishops, etc.

THE CONCRETE CATHOLICITY OF THE CHURCH

There are reasons for thinking that the concern that some theologians are one-sidedly stressing the local church derives from the developments, both practical and theoretical, that have followed from the second major emphasis in the council's revalidation of the local church: its theological legitimation of local particularity and diversity. This is apparent in many passages: in the discussion of the distinct patrimonies of patriarchal and ritual churches (*LG* and *OE*), in the Decree on Ecumenism, and especially in the Decree on the Church's Missionary Activity. Let us concentrate, however, on a single text which well expresses the basic orientation that is necessary in order to make the ecclesiology I have just outlined concrete and which has received also a very perceptive commentary from the present pope.

The passage occurs in *Lumen Gentium's* discussion of the church's catholicity:

> This character of universality that adorns the People of God is a gift of the Lord himself by which the Catholic Church effectively and unceasingly strives to recapitulate all of humanity with all of its gifts under Christ the Head and in the unity of his Spirit. In virtue of this catholicity the individual parts bring their own gifts to the other parts and to the whole church so that the whole and the individual parts grow from the mutual communion of all and from their common effort to reach a fullness in unity (*LG* 13).

Catholicity is here more than geographical universality, which would, after all, be verified if the same stamp were to imprint the same figure everywhere. The assumption is that humanity is concretely diversified and enriched by a variety of gifts of God reflected in their historical and cultural particularities. Catholicity is achieved when all these gifts are recapitulated, brought together under Christ's headship and in the unity of his Spirit. All of the parts and the whole church enrich one another through their mutual communion, and the result is a "fullness in unity," a phrase that might be taken as the council's definition of catholicity.

The presupposition of this effort, of course, is that the local churches themselves undertake the task of bringing the particular local gifts God has given them into its unity in Christ, the task that we are now accustomed to speak of as inculturation. It is these gifts, confirmed, purified, or elevated by the gospel, that the local churches bring to one another, enriching one another, and achieving the fullness in unity of the one now concretely Catholic Church. It will be noted that on this view the universal catholicity of the one church, in an only apparent paradox, requires the effort at local particularity. Locality is not the opposite of catholicity, but its realization.

All this is brought out powerfully in a remarkable commentary on this passage of *Lumen Gentium* offered by Pope John Paul II.[10] The council's discussion of "particular churches with their own traditions" leads one to see the universal church "as a communion of (particular) churches and, indirectly, as a communion of nations, languages, and cultures." The pope noted contemporary emphasis on the special Christian experiences which the particular churches are having in the sociocultural context in which each is called to live:

> Such special experiences concern, it is stressed, the Word of God, which must be read and understood in the light of the givens that emerge from their own existential journeys; liturgical prayer, which must draw from the cultures in which they are inserted, the signs, gestures, and words which serve adoration, worship, and celebration; theological reflection, which must appeal to the categories of thought typical of each culture; ecclesial communion itself, which sinks its roots in the Eucharist, but which depends for its concrete unfolding on historical and temporal conditions that derive from insertion in the milieu of a particular country or of a particular part of the world.

Note that in the pope's mind the distinctive experiences to which he refers are not described simply as marking the cultures in which the churches are located; they are said to be distinctive Christian experiences, distinct realizations of the church precisely in its unique mystery. Note, too, that the points of mutual influence in the encounter between a church and its culture do not concern minor or peripheral areas: it is its reading of the word of God, its worship, its existential life, and its theological reflection that are affected by a church's insertion into a particular historical and cultural context. Individual churches derive their distinctive identities from these necessarily particular encounters between the gospel and cultures.

It is customary, of course, after such an affirmation of particularity to stress the need for unity, and the pope himself issues such a warning. But what is most remarkable about this commentary is the immediate reference point to which he directs attention. Where one might have expected him to refer directly to the need for unity with the universal church, he refers instead to the other particular churches:

> But to be fruitful, these perspectives presuppose respect for an unavoidable condition: such experiences must not be lived in isolation or independently of, not to say in contradiction to, the lives of the Churches in other parts of the world. To constitute authentic experiences of the Church, they must in themselves be synthesized with the experiences which other Christians, in touch with different cultural contexts, feel called to live in order to be faithful to the demands that flow from the single and identical mystery of Christ.

The pope's subsequent invocation of the phrase "mutual inclusion," has the same reference:

> In fact among the individual particular churches there is an ontological relationship of mutual inclusion: every particular church, as a realization of the one church of Christ, is in some way present in all the particular churches "in which and out of which the one and unique catholic church has its existence." This ontological relation must be translated on the dynamic level of concrete life, if the Christian community does not wish to be in contradiction with itself: the basic ecclesial choices of believers in one community must be able to be harmonized with those of the faithful in the other communities, in order to allow that communion of minds and hearts for which Christ prayed at the Last Supper.

In other words, the comparison is not between special Christian experiences and some imagined unitary universal Christian experience, but between the special experiences of one church and those of the others. It is indeed the one church of Christ that is present in all of the individual churches, but there is no one church whose experience serves as a criterion for the individual churches. The unifying criterion is not found on the level of experience, which is always concrete and therefore varied; the unifying criterion is the fact that all of the individual churches arise from their attempts to be faithful, locally, to "the demands that flow from the single and universal mystery of Christ."

Finally, the pope presents the special role of the Apostolic See as the service of this catholic unity: "to see to it that the 'gifts' to which the conciliar text alludes flow towards the center of the church and that these same gifts, enriched by the mutual encounter, flow out to the various members of the Mystical Body of Christ, bringing them new impulses of fervor and of life." An exercise of this Petrine role, which also illustrates the at times disorienting effect of this shift in ecclesiological perspective, can be found in the pope's remarks elsewhere, in a speech to Australian aborigines:

> The Gospel of our Lord Jesus Christ speaks all languages. It esteems and embraces all cultures. It supports them in everything human and, when necessary, it purifies them. Always and everywhere the Gospel uplifts and enriches cultures with the revealed message of a loving and merciful God. That Gospel now invites you to become, through and through, aboriginal Christians. It meets your deepest desires. You do not have to be people divided into two parts, as though an aborigine had to borrow the faith and life of Christianity, like a hat or pair of shoes, from someone else who owns them. Jesus calls you to accept his words and his values into your own culture. To develop in this way will make you ever truly aboriginal.[11]

What in the world, we might be tempted to ask, would an aboriginal Christianity look like? The pope does not attempt to give an answer, but he does warn against using some other type of Christianity as a criterion; he does not want aborigines simply to borrow someone else's Christianity the way they might borrow someone else's hat or shoes. Aboriginal Christianity will result from new distinct Christian experiences, whose only criterion is the gospel itself.

These papal reflections suggest that the real terms in which our discussion should be framed is not the relation between the universal church and the local churches, but the relations of mutual inclusion that exist among the latter. It may even be possible to say that the communion of the many local churches is, in fact, the mutual inclusion that exists among all the local churches, and that the role of the bishop of Rome is not best conceived as one of mediating between a local church and the universal church, imagined as something above all the local churches, but between one local church and the other local churches, in order to assure that the "special Christan experiences" that derive from their socio-cultural particularities do not contradict one another but that, harmonized with and enriched by one another, they may constitute a genuine communion. In other words, the communion that constitutes the universal church is precisely the mutual inclusion of all the local churches.

The mutual inclusion that defines the communion among the churches, then, is richer than often appears in the literature. Most authors discuss this inclusion solely in terms of the divine principles of the church, word, sacrament and ministry, leaving out of consideration their reception in the believing community. But if this reception—which constitutes and defines the concrete realization of the local churches—is ignored, there is nothing to relate; one has only the universal divine principles of the genesis of the church. It is only when these generative principles are received and appropriated as the vital Christian principles of distinctive communal engagements with history and culture that there is anything for one to observe, understand, relate, compare, judge, evaluate and harmonize. The very question of infraecclesial harmony only arises because the reception of the single and universal mystery of Christ never generates the one church except as the many local churches.

A local church arises out of the encounter of divine and human freedom that generates its distinctive Christian experience. It is the integration of these concrete experiences into a catholic synthesis that constitutes the real challenge of catholicity at all levels of the church's existence, local, regional, national, or universal. The various churches bring to one another not only their natural cultural gifts, but their special Christian experiences generated by the encounter between gospel and cultures. The achievement of catholicity requires the symphonic harmony of all these special, local ecclesial experiences.[12]

I have tried here to explain some of the developments in the theology of the local church that have most to offer to multiculturalism in the United States. The one that is most pertinent, of course, is the renewed appreciation of catholicity as diversity-in-unity, of what the council called fullness-in-unity. In this vision, catholicity and local particularity are not polar opposites, as they are too frequently taken to be. Local particularity, what we are calling multiculturalism, is instead a necessary element of concrete catholicity.

But this catholicity is also more than diversity and particularity; it is an integration of this cultural diversity into a fullness, into a wholeness, around Jesus Christ and in the Spirit. That integration has to take place at every level of church existence: in small communities, in parishes, in dioceses, in regional and national groups of churches, in the one Catholic communion.[13] At every level catholicity means fullness-in-unity. For that reason, catholicity is not an attribute external to local communities of faith, found only when they assemble in a universal community. It must characterize every assembly of Christians, of which it must be true that here there is no Jew and Greek, no male and female, no slave and freeman, but all are one in Christ. A community in which such integration of all is not accomplished falls short of being a realization of the one and Catholic Church. Catholicity, in that sense, is a constant challenge for every assembly of believers, beginning with our own.

Gerard S. Sloyan

RESPONSE TO
JOSEPH A. KOMONCHAK

Alan Segal writes in his exploration of the change effected in Saul's life and the changes he effected in the lives of many, *Paul the Convert. The Apostolate and Apostasy of Saul the Pharisee*: "The issue for Paul is the management of diversity, so that it does not become divisive. Unity is possible if the diversity that can lead to disunity in the community is overcome...."[1] Segal's context in that place is the mixed communities of Jewish and pagan stock—the latter largely God-fearers when not full Jewish proselytes—to whom he brought the gospel or whom, evangelized by others, he addressed by letter. We know from Paul's correspondence that as regards Jews, whom he described as "under the law," or gentiles, those "outside the law," or "the weak," yet another class of Jews ill at ease with disregard of dietary law, he became, respectively, a law-observant, a non-observant, and an abstainer from foods he felt free to eat. He gave as his reason that he might by every means possible "win some of them" (1 Cor 9:20–22). "Unity is possible"—I repeat Segal's dictum—"if the diversity that can lead to disunity is overcome."

The ecclesiological question Professor Komonchak has raised is, how much cultural diversity is compatible with unity? The discussion in 1 Corinthians 9, from which I have quoted, is not about diversity between Jews and non-Jews as distinct religious traditions, but about customs, folkways and claims of superiority within the communities of those who believed in Christ. St. Paul framed rabbinic arguments in order to convince ethnic pagans, who could scarcely have understood them, of the truth of the gospel; among gentile believers he became far more Hellenist than he ever was in his diaspora youth, to the distress of observant Christian Jews who learned of his practice, including "James and Cephas and John...the acknowledged pillars" (Gal 2:9), as he called them with respectful irony. Did Paul's strategy succeed? The record is fragmentary, making it hard to say.

We know this much, that the Hellenist strain so won out over the Hebraic in the two or three generations after his lifetime that his disciples, the authors of Colossians and Ephesians, deserve to be called the first inculturated "apostles of the gentiles" because they addressed some problems of Graeco-Roman paganism Paul did not address. Paul's principle of cultural adaptation, we know, resulted in some serious ethnic Jewish losses. His churches, despite the strains that he himself reports, seem to have survived on his terms during his lifetime and the generation after him. The answer to their unity surely lies in the unequivocal faith he professed, from which he permitted no deviance. In that unity of faith lay his authority.

Professor Komonchak has identified the principles for a multi-cultural unity in diversity in the Catholic communion as modern western and Roman ecclesiology sees it. He has not reviewed the painful history of Christian tribalism (understood popularly, not technically) over the centuries, other than by referring briefly to "national, racial, and ethnic particularities." What he has done is remind us, with the help of some recent conciliar documents, that "the one mystery of the church is only realized in the many local particular churches." There is no first and second moment in which the universal church results from a federation of local churches or brings them into being as constituent members of a preexistent universal church. This is true despite the ambiguity of the statement in *Lumen Gentium* that individual churches are "in the image of the universal church," a statement which has caused recent ecclesiolog-ical writers to adopt the one position or the other.

Lumen Gentium declares that, in virtue of the church's catholicity, its "fullness of unity," the individual parts of humanity bring their gifts to other parts and to the whole church. This expresses well the main concern of this conference. Is it so? Such has always been the church's theology in principle, but every conceivable expression of ethnic and cultural pride has beclouded it. What demon lurks in the human heart to make what is centripetal, by the Spirit's design, centrifugal? The present bishop of Rome could not be improved on as he spelled out, in his 1985 address to the Roman Curia,[2] what this fullness, this catholicity consists in. It is the experiences of various Christians in their cultural contexts synthesized with those of others; it is the mutual inclusion of each church within all the others as an ecclesial reality, a harmonization of the basic ecclesial choices of believers in the churches that make up the one church. All this is necessary if a community of minds and hearts is to prevail. The special experiences of a common faith that some have had, the pope said, must be made available to others. The logic of this, as Professor Komonchak points out, is that "there is no one church whose experience serves as a criterion for the individual churches."

What may have been culturally fitting for Antioch, Rome, Constantinople, or Canterbury in days of missionary expansion is no longer compelling for a global church or churches. The question is, did the members of the curia hear the Roman patriarch whom they serve? And was the pope listening to himself? We must wait and see if the concrete and varied experiences of the individual churches, none of which is a cultural criterion for all the others, are rooted in their attempts to be faithful, locally, "to the demands that flow from the single and universal mystery of Christ" (to quote Pope John Paul II). These churches will present a varied array of liturgical practices, popular pieties, and theological outlooks that stem from their linguistic and cultural differences. Such variety will be divisive only if a common faith in Christ is lost sight of. It remains to be seen whether these rich differences—and they are that—will be viewed with equanimity by the mother of churches, as Rome describes itself.

How is this mosaic of cultures showing forth the one face of Christ to be achieved? First of all, it already exists, although hesitantly, in some sectors of the globe. The pope in his travels is exposed to such expressions of faith in every land and corner of a multicultural land, and he approves them. "Jesus calls you to accept his words and his values into your own culture," he said vigorously to Australian aborigines.[3] But there are new Australians in that land from Europe and Asia. Their bishops, who are in no sense missionary bishops, should feel free to let flourish expressions of Chinese or Italian or Ukrainian piety without hindrance. That is the very matter at issue. They should do the same with the British-Irish Australian culture that is the matrix of the other cultures.

If a bishop has full apostolic authority in his diocese, even though Catholic faith acknowledges the same authority in every diocese to the bishop of Rome, local bishops should be able to oversee freely the expressions of faith of the people or peoples they are charged with. I say freely, meaning without nervous oversight of a body half a world or an ocean away. If a bishop has been deemed capable of protecting and promoting the apostolic faith in his diocese, and all of them have, he should be able to discern any departure from the ancient faith in the way it is being preached or taught or celebrated. Having outsiders tell him is an affront to his episcopal authority.

Some bishops over the centuries have themselves been salutary innovators. Some have always welcomed preachers and teachers from outside. But, in the main, the varied expressions of Catholic faith have come from the people themselves. They may have practiced alien forms for a century or two but gradually they have made them their own, whether by language or text or gesture or other modification. Now bishops know how earnestly the chief shepherd has exhorted them to be "through and through, aboriginal [read Hispanic-American, African-American, upper Mississippi or lower Mississippi European] Christians." "The Gospel [thus interpreted] meets your deepest desires. You do not have to be a people divided into two parts...."[4]

What, then, of the danger of fragmentation, that is, some portion of a people worldwide no longer recognizable as Catholic, even though evangelized out of the ancient Roman See?

Resistance to conformity to Christ could bring about such fragmentation. Bishops falling out of communion with other bishops or with the bishop of Rome could do it. People so ethnically or linguistically centered that they will not accept the authority of their bishops could do it. But fragmentation will not come with diversity in unity unless some persons or peoples do willful and stupid things.

I close with a practical observation. There are Catholic parishes in Los Angeles that have seven Sunday masses; one English, one Mexican-Spanish, one for Central and South American Spanish speakers, one Vietnamese, one Chinese, one Korean, one Guamanian. For Portland, Oregon, add in Ethiopian. One parish, you ask, or seven worshiping communities using the same church? One parish if the pastor has good judgment and if they all do something Catholic together at some times. One parish because professing one faith and celebrating the mystery of faith in a rite that is recognizably the Roman Rite, but oh, so differently interpreted.

To come closer to home: one first communion celebration or two or three? Some masses in an African-American mode and others in the white American style with which older parishioners may be more comfortable? If these culturally diverse Catholic people can do nothing together or cannot participate in each other's celebrations of eucharistic faith, they have lost the Catholic spirit. If they find themselves enriched, even by the unfamiliarity, the strangeness that meets their eyes and ears, they have learned something of what it means to be Catholic.

Orlando O. Espín

A MULTICULTURAL CHURCH? THEOLOGICAL REFLECTIONS FROM BELOW

On Sunday mornings Christians throughout the world profess their faith through the words of the Nicene-Constantinopolitan creed. They say, "We believe in the church, one, holy, catholic and apostolic."

It should seem clear that the essential catholicity of the church must strongly imply cultural diversity. Without the variety of human groups, languages and cultures that jointly are the one people of God, the church cannot think of itself as Catholic, unless this mark of the community is demoted to a mere geographic note. Faith and baptism open the doors to the ecclesial communion, and not passports, colors of skins, or places of birth. This should seem clear since it was settled, after all, at the apostolic council of Jerusalem (Acts 15).

However, when nearly two thousand years later we are still discussing the same basic subject, questioning about the place of cultural diversity within the church, weighing its doctrinal import, and still finding (all too frequently) attitudes and decisions that directly contradict the professed catholicity of the church, one may seriously wonder if the issues of catholicity are, indeed, that clear. One may wonder if cultural diversity has been accepted as the norm and as an essential and distinctive mark, and not just as a tolerated inconvenience in the church. One may question if other mechanisms and attitudes, which may ideologically robe themselves in the language of religion, might be operative within the church.

CULTURAL DIVERSITY IN THE AMERICAN CHURCH

I start from the assumption that cultural diversity in the church is not, at heart, a theological or doctrinal problem. It seems to me that although there are (on this subject) many associated theological topics that certainly merit reflection, cultural diversity cannot be discussed as a problem for the church without yielding to the nonsensical and dangerous premise that the very existence of cultural diversity causes theological or doctrinal problems to the church. To believe this is equivalent to holding that roundness (which is an essential dimension of a circle) causes problems for the circle as circle.

At heart we might be dealing with questions of conversion, of repentance, of practicing what we preach, or even of recognizing cultural idolatry on the part of dominant elites in the church. We might also have to confront serious pastoral and organizational difficulties. But I frankly wonder how cultural diversity can still be (after the council of Jerusalem) really such a major doctrinal or theological issue in itself, unless the supposed doctrinal difficulties were in fact covering over other more embarrassing questions and options.

But then, I am speaking as one of nearly half of all North American Catholics, whose theological contributions are usually considered peripheral to the otherwise serious dialogue held among the members of the other half. For U.S. Hispanic Catholics there is no theological difficulty (and certainly not a doctrinal one) with cultural diversity within the church. We take roundness as a normal dimension of any circle.

For us, and probably for all non Euro-American Catholics, the questions of cultural diversity in the church are pastoral, organizational, even political questions, but not theological or doctrinal. But as I said, we are not usually heard in the theological dialogue within the dominant half.

These issues become theologically controversial for us, however, when we (the other half of the church) are constantly challenged to explain and justify, indeed legitimize, our right to exist and remain culturally distinct within the North American Catholic communion. We have to use the tools of academic theology in order to show over and over again that the fundamental decisions of the apostolic council of Jerusalem are still applicable today. Therefore, the issues of cultural diversity become doctrinally and theologically important for us because of the dominance of one half of the church over the pastoral and academic agenda of the whole church (a dominance that forces our theological or doctrinal defense); but not because the issues of cultural diversity in Catholicism are, in themselves, problematic or in doubt.

Each half of the U.S. American church arrives at the theological table to discuss cultural diversity, therefore, from different perspectives and with different needs. I suspect that the dominant, Euro-American part is baffled by its increasing and unexpected confrontation with the demographic reality of American Catholicism. Indeed, there might be

some surprise at the ever-louder challenges to Euro-American ecclesiologies and ecclesiological assumptions. In the battlefront of pastoral
care most ministers, ordained or not, might be discovering that they
were trained for a church that does not and will not exist. Their
ministerial training was probably based on premises that do not reflect
the full and culturally complex reality of contemporary Catholicism in
the United States.

I think it is clear, therefore, that I come to this theological table
very much aware that I am a member of a very specific half of the
church in our country. For me cultural diversity is not a theological or
doctrinal problem, because for me the catholicity of the church is not a
theological or doctrinal difficulty. Nevertheless, I realize that this is not
the case for many in the other half. And I do not mean this in an
accusatory way but, rather, with hope.

After all, if we face the issues of cultural diversity in American
Catholicism, and do so frankly and fraternally, it might mean that we
can put our emphases, pastoral and theological, on the complex task of
proclaiming the reign of God in today's world (which is the mission of
the church) and not worry as much about the intraecclesial discussion
of whether "gentiles" should first become "Jews" in order to be
considered truly Christian.

I was asked to indicate issues that from below (which term I assume
to mean the perspective of the dominated half in the American church),
need further theological research and reflection. Given this task, I will
point with some discipline to those issues and why I think we should
research them more thoroughly. The method chosen, therefore, does
not thoroughly investigate and discuss any one subject, but covers an
array of topics. The one thread running throughout the entire discussion, as will become very apparent is the premise that culture (as
defined in the social sciences) is of extraordinary importance for
theological reflection, having a profound impact on key doctrinal issues.

I could have chosen a type of presentation that would have made
me sound theologically Euro-American with a slight Hispanic accent.
Instead, I decided to represent to you, as authentically as I could, what I
sincerely believe to be a theological perspective from below, attempting
to be and sound Hispanic, with perhaps a slight Euro-American accent.
In our American church we have learned not to speak directly, at least
not when we are the so-called minorities. It is now my choice, however,
to be direct.

There are two fundamental clusters of issues, in my opinion, that
have to be dealt with in American ecclesiology. The two clusters have a
direct impact on the question of cultural diversity, and they both
include areas and topics that need further research. In the first cluster

the ecclesiological dimensions or connections might not be clear (even though the questions dealt with there are foundational). I hope that some of the theological consequences and ramifications will become obvious in my discussion of the second cluster of issues.

CULTURE AND THE IMPLICATIONS OF DEFINING CULTURE

The act of defining culture. To speak of cultural diversity, or of any of its dimensions, assumes an understanding of culture. It often seems that we are all speaking about the same reality, employing the same definition of culture, and yet, in fact, quite different and often conflictive and mutually exclusive understandings of culture may be operative in any given discussion. This is especially true when the interlocutors in the discussion do not share the same social class or cultural background.

Any description of culture raises a number of questions, some of utmost importance. Scholars can and should argue about the most adequate description of what is culture, but it seems clear that they are only attempting to discover common denominators among diverse, shared styles of humanness or of praxis in quite distinct and living human communities.

In my view, culture is, more fundamentally, the historically shared means and ways through which a people unveil themselves as human. And the most basic means and ways for this unveiling are the social construction of reality and the discovery of meaning within and through that socially-constructed reality.[1]

The act of defining culture, however, is most problematic. It would be utterly naive to assume that the act of defining what is culture is not, in itself, a cultural act. Furthermore, and more importantly, the act of defining culture either in reference to cultures other than one's own or in reference to the shared culture of one's society grants the definer an extraordinary power over meaning, reality and truth. Therefore, more crucial and substantive than the scholarly discussions about the more adequate definition of culture is an investigation of the meaning, function and possibility of the act of defining culture and of those who exercise it.[2]

Let me borrow the distinction between the Greek concepts of *praxis* and *poiesis*.[3] Here *praxis* refers to doing and being, while *poiesis* refers to making and producing. Developing Roberto Goizueta's suggestive analysis,[4] *praxis* and *poiesis* can arguably be used to understand the act of defining culture.

If *praxis* is human life, being and acting humanly, with no purpose other than itself, then it might be said that *praxis*, by its very nature, is culture since there can be no human life that is not cultural. But by the same token, what is human in human life is precisely that which is cultural. Or, as I said above, culture is the means and ways through which a people unveil themselves as *praxis*, as human.

On the other hand, if *poiesis* is human work, then it might be argued that *poiesis* is also the result of culture to the degree that it is only human work, and what is human and work is ultimately culturally defined. Both *praxis* and *poiesis*, because of being cultural, are also communal at their root, given that culture is always communally created and sustained. This in no way erases the role of individuality, but it does place it within its real-life, communal and cultural contexts.

When and by whom can culture be defined? I would argue that a culture can be adequately defined only when the definer stands outside of it and, therefore, does not participate in the given construction of meaning and reality of the culture being defined. Otherwise, if someone attempted to define a culture from within, that act of defining could be no more than an intracultural act blind to the dimensions and portions of reality that are hidden by the very culture being defined. Only from outside its given culturally constructed reality can a culture be defined. But then, is this an adequate definition of that culture?

Furthermore, the act of defining a culture can only occur if the culture defined is first reified, made into an object of study and observation. But the moment a culture is objectified it has lost, precisely, its quality of living humanness in the life of its creators and bearers. It has stopped being *praxis* (human life in itself), and it has been turned into *poiesis* by the act of the definer. Life is transformed into product. In other words, the definer has taken possession of the human life of the creators and bearers of a given culture and made that life into an object of study, and reified its human perceptions of meaning and reality so that they may be understood from outside the living humanness that created them.

The act of defining a culture demotes its meaning and reality from human to object. But perhaps more crucial, the act of defining gives the definer power over those whose culture is defined.[5] They, too, are demoted from human beings to objects. The definer assumes the role of determining what is or is not acceptable and reasonable, of establishing what is or is not culturally coherent and authentic in the culture defined. The humanness of other people's lives is thereby confiscated and their shared *praxis* judged by the objective criteria set by the definer.[6]

More crucial in this process is the often unspoken fact that the one defining other peoples' cultures might be misunderstanding and utterly missing these cultures' core of lived meaning and reality. The very act of defining has transformed living *praxis* into objectifying *poiesis*, thereby missing what is defined as meaningful and reality-constructing culture. Therefore, what is ultimately studied and defined is not a living culture but the definer's reified and, in turn, culturally-determined perceptions of other people's means and ways of being human.

One may wonder, however, to what degree the one defining another culture would accept as valid and adequate (more so, accurate, objective or neutral) the definitions of his/her culture that might be forthcoming from the people whose culture he/she attempted to define in the first place. In other words, how would the definer react if the table were turned around? Perhaps, in the first place, it had never occurred to the definer that he/she could be defined by someone culturally different. I do not think that I exaggerate if I describe the possible reaction as one resembling outrage or dismissal if the definitions of the definer's culture did not fit his/her experienced and socially constructed reality and meaning. That is, if the table were turned around and the definer had become the defined, the latter would include, as essential criterion of truth, the other's definition of meaning and reality from the experience of the defined's shared *praxis*. Unfortunately, this criterion of truth does not seem to have entered into consideration earlier, when the definer had the sole power to define. Implied in all of this, of course, is the social reality of power and of control over the criteria for interpreting cultures.

Interpretation as an exercise of social power. If I may be forgiven the sin of simplification, I could argue that in both socialist[7] and capitalist thought that which moves history and shapes societies are the forces of the economy and the struggles they unleash. These two schools might interpret and explain the forces of the economy and the unleashed struggles in quite different ways. But they both grant economy a paramount role in forming and directing human history. Christianity, of course, disagrees with both, but it has had difficulty surviving in the modern world without somehow adapting itself to one or the other.[8] For all our claimed ecclesiastical independence from all social systems and ideologies, however, it seems that the church has never existed without borrowing quite heavily from the surrounding social systems and ideologies.[9]

Both socialism and capitalism treat culture, and what it implies and involves, either as a tool to directly or indirectly improve the forces at work in the market, or as an epiphenomenon that tangentially influences the real issues of human history. Both of them, therefore, deprive culture of its humanness and of its role as the human in human life (that is, in *praxis*), and turn it into work, *poiesis*. The assumptions and methods of scholarship designed in the long shadow of both classical socialism and capitalism have assumed as fundamentally correct this reification and instrumentalization of culture vis-à-vis the needs of the forces of economy. Why?

I would argue that once it is assumed as correct that culture is, at best, tangential to the forces of the economy, and that the forces of the economy are self-evidently at the core of human life and history, then it has to be assumed that human *praxis* (*qua* human) is economic.[10] That which is human life in itself, with no purpose other than itself, cannot be ultimately human in either classical socialism or capitalism because lack of purpose negates the foundations of that which is economic. Human life itself, from that perspective, can only be human if instrumentalized, if aimed at a purpose.[11] The profit motive and the American work ethic are deeply intertwined with this view.

Given this context, which still holds in most of the North Atlantic world, some very serious epistemological and ethical questions must be asked: What can truth be, and how is it established? What is real in that perspective, plausibly given that reality is constructed socially? What is ethical and good in a world built on the forces of the economy? What is rigorous, solid scholarship?[12]

If the North Atlantic world in which we live is founded on the preeminence of the forces of the economy and on the economic instrumentalization of humanness, I see little reason to be surprised at its ethical and cultural crises. As interpreted from below, the North Atlantic societies seem to have lowered their image of what is human to that which is purposeful and ultimately useful. Human life as human, its means and ways of humanness, and thus culture and *praxis*, appear as ideological appendixes to reality (viewed as foundationally economic), or as attempts at soothing an increasingly dehumanized collective conscience. Unfortunately, but expectedly, these processes of dehumanization have become hidden and are denied in the ideological perception of culture operative in most of the North Atlantic world. Interpreted from below, this perspective on the dominant world will not be considered acceptable, however, because in this case the definers, the subaltern, do not have the social power necessary to have their definitions heard in society.[13]

In my view, the socially dominant will continue believing that they do not need to pay attention to the definitions of their dominant culture offered by the subaltern of society. Since within North Atlantic cultures it is assumed as reality that they are more advanced, developed and objective than any other culture after advancement, development, and objectivity have been defined by the meanings culturally accepted as true within the North Atlantic societies themselves. It then becomes impossible for them to think that more primitive or less sophisticated societies could be able to define North Atlantic cultures in meaningful or important ways.

Furthermore, and continuing to speak from below, the act of defining another culture cannot be interpreted as a neutral or ethically innocent act, especially when the culture defined is the human in the life of communities that hold little or no power in society.[14] That act of interpretation would become, as seen from below, an act that reifies their life and thereby dehumanizes it. It deprives the dominated of the category human in the eyes of the dominant, turning them into objects of study. It assumes in the dominant the power to establish or define what is really human in the subaltern of society. The *praxis* of those below, which unveils their socially constructed and shared means and ways of being human, becomes real to those above only when it is received as the product of those who reflect from above. The cultural interpretations of the dominated are often seen as peripheral or as data for the reflection of the supposedly more serious scholars from the dominant segments of society.[15]

In brief, there is little neutrality or innocence in cultural interpretation. Only if a defining group has power can the hermeneutic perspectives and epistemological assumptions of that group be taken as the criteria for accuracy in the interpretation of the defined cultures. Powerless groups, although they might have their definitions of other cultures, do not have access to the contexts where the dominant in society establish the criteria for truth and reality.

To define is to exercise power, not in a raw political sense, but in the subtle and more important sense of guiding a society's construction of reality and meaning. And as can be expected, the defining group will seldom if ever lead its society to a perspective of reality and meaning that would imply the group's demise as social guide. Hence, as long as the society's configuration remains, and as long as the dominant hermeneutic perspectives and epistemological assumptions continue to be operational, the subaltern segments of that society, that is, those below, will not stand an equal chance of influencing or even successfully reaching the overall society with their expressions of themselves as living cultures, as human beings, and therefore as equals in humanness and not as problems to be studied.[16]

The adequate symbolization of culture. Cultures can and do express themselves. Expression, in this sense, is not definition. The latter assumes that the definer stands outside that which is defined. Expression, on the other hand, demands that the expressor first be part or directly have experience of that which is expressed.

In reference to cultures, this is not, therefore, an exercise of power, and it is not to be understood as *poiesis*. It is, on the contrary, the communication and historical embodiment of socially-constructed reality and meaning. It is symbolization of the human in human life. In this sense, it is *praxis*.

Cultural expression is, at bottom, the symbolization of socially-constructed reality and the meaning(s) it bears in the experience of a people. Which symbolization of culture is more adequate for a given culture? It is that which truthfully expresses the socially-constructed reality and meaning(s) of the people.[17] This necessarily means that adequate symbolization can only come from within, as expression, and not from without, as definition. Adequate symbolization is that which is expressed through the culturally authentic and therefore intrinsic symbolic system of a people.[18]

To bring another symbolic system and impose it on a people, demanding that through it they express their socially-constructed reality and meaning, the human in their lives, is to prevent the very expression that is supposedly sought.

Furthermore, the imposition of an external symbolic system on a human group assumes that this group is socially vulnerable. Indeed, vulnerable enough that it might be made to take on the imposed system for the purpose of symbolizing its culture. This would, in turn, provoke the alienation of the people from their own reality and meaning, since by adopting an imposed symbolic system they would have lost their only adequate means of expression. And the social and personal consequences of cultural alienation would be immense. The imposition of an external symbolic system on a socially weaker people is tantamount to the conquest of their socially constructed reality and meaning.

Multiculturality or cultural diversity. One question that needs to be dealt with is the possibility of multiculturality. Can it exist in human life and not merely as a theoretical construct? I would argue that it cannot exist in human life.

The cultural diversity of humankind is evident and that is not doubted here. We have groups of people who are human, hence cultural in a wide variety of ways. Their *praxes* are quite distinct. And this distinctiveness allows for their identification as this or that community. But one thing is cultural diversity and another is multiculturality.

The latter term assumes that a group can have more than one culture as its human *praxis*. In other words, multiculturality means that a given group can be human and unveil itself as human in more than one way. It also means that there can be more than one socially constructed reality for that group. On both counts, the possibility of multiculturality is absurd.

It seems rather impossible that multiculturality could ever be found as part of reality, since reality is socially constructed. Even when a human group appears capable of functioning in more than one cultural context, what is in fact operative is a type of culture resulting from *mestizaje*[19] which is, in turn, born of prolonged contact (usually the consequence of conquest, invasion, or sustained immigration). The culturally *mestizo* do not have two or more cultures, which is the premise of multiculturality. In fact, the *mestizos* have only one culture, that of *mestizaje*, and it is this one culture that allows them to maintain and function within their socially constructed reality and symbolic systems.

Multiculturality is not cultural diversity. The latter is evident and natural. The former, however, is a theoretical image that wishes to describe the ability of one human group to create, sustain, function, comprehend reality, and much more in more than one way. Since this theoretical multicultural group does not and cannot exist, one wonders about the purpose behind the use of multiculturality, and behind the insistence that it be implemented or somehow fashioned in society. Perhaps one should ask: Who is most interested in multiculturality instead of cultural diversity? Who would benefit the most from the supposed implementation of multiculturality? In fact, who is in charge of defining multiculturality and judging when it has been sufficiently achieved?

I would argue that the insistence on multiculturality hides the fear of and the inability to deal with cultural diversity. Multicultural discourse and attempted action seem to imply the quest for equality and inclusiveness. In fact, however, it assumes that there is an already established reality to which others are now welcome. But the newcomers are not invited to participate as equals in the reinvention or establishment of an altogether new reality which is also theirs. No. The discourse of multiculturality makes room for them in an existing cultural context which happens to be the context of the dominant in society. Multiculturality is, therefore, a mechanism to co-opt the dominated into accepting as most real the social constructs and meaning of the dominant.

Cultural diversity, however, involves no such domination. The acceptance of diversity assumes as valid and important the right of the other to remain and live as other. It respects diversity because it assumes it to be a necessary dimension of humanness, like roundness is to a circle. It assumes such because the socially-constructed reality of those accepting cultural diversity understands it as perfectly real and normal. When this assumption cannot be made, the difficulty lies not within cultural diversity itself but within the socially-constructed reality of the group that experiences the difficulty. I think that historically, social dominance, and the aspiration to dominance, impede the assumption of cultural diversity as valid and evident.

In this first cluster of issues, I have indicated processes and elements that are involved in the act of defining culture. I have suggested the need to understand social power as operative in the process of interpretation, and the impossibility of authentic cultural expression if adequate symbolization of culture is prevented. I have also explained why multiculturality is not possible.

The topics discussed in the first cluster of issues are foundational to any North American ecclesiological reflection. Not in the sense that scripture might be foundational, obviously; rather, foundational as human life might be. All of these issues certainly merit, and indeed require, further research on the part of theologians in the United States.

What does this first cluster of issues have to do with the impact of cultural diversity on the American Catholic church?

THE ISSUES OF CULTURE IN AMERICAN ECCLESIOLOGY

It seems that culture and cultural diversity have not been prominent categories in Euro-American ecclesiological analysis. Perhaps they have been considered too sociological, or too anthropological, or too relative to be taken seriously as theological categories or analytic tools. Euro-American ecclesiology has usually dialogued with other theological disciplines, a great deal with canon law, and externally with philosophy and history. Seldom has Euro-American ecclesiology sat down at the table of the social sciences, and even less often taken their contributions as theologically significant beyond the descriptive or problematic. In this Euro-American ecclesiology has been very different from Latin American ecclesiologies of every ideological shade. But culture is, indeed, an inevitable element in all theological reflection, whether we are aware of it or not. This indicates the need to seriously dialogue with sociologists, anthropologists, and the like. The social sciences point to dimensions and results of theologizing that we are too embarrassed to recognize and are perhaps too quick to deny. Whether we feel comfortable with them or not, the insights and contributions of the social sciences cannot be dismissed in the task of theologizing.[20] At the heart of most of these sciences there is, from their different methodological and terminological perspectives, the study of culture.

In my preceding discussion, I hope to have at least conveyed the extraordinary and determining importance of culture for human living, and how a reflection on culture can turn out to be quite oppressive if it is not conscious of other underlying issues and processes. It seems that the best methodological option is to make explicit and reflect upon that which is already there.

There are certain themes in ecclesiology that, seen from below and from cultural studies, require further theological research. These themes might be profitably discussed using the foundations we have laid in the first cluster of issues. I will limit myself to those that seem most pertinent to this discussion.

Ecclesiological models and the culturalness of Jesus. By ecclesiological models I mean the types of church life and policy that have been and are proposed and attempted in real life. These types are based on what is understood to be the mission of the church. Ultimately all ecclesiological models will appeal to Jesus and to the authority of the apostolic generation, either as the latter remembered the mission and teachings of Jesus or as it exemplified several specific models.[21]

One fundamental component of all ecclesiological models, however, is seldom brought forth by theological reflection. It is culture. It seems evident from history that all ecclesiological models are possible only within the cultural frameworks that allow them to be thought of as plausible and, therefore, meaningful in socially-constructed reality. Throughout the history of Christian theology, ecclesiological models have been so bound to the cultures of the periods that it seems hard to explain why the cultural grounds of the ecclesiological models are seldom explicitated. Even the creedal description of the church as "one, holy, catholic and apostolic," which implies an ecclesiological model, assumes cultural definitions of oneness, holiness, catholicity and apostolicity that might not be universal. Anyone involved in the interpretation of the conciliar definitions of Christian antiquity knows that.

Furthermore, our modern ecclesiologies' appeal to Jesus and the apostolic generation are so culturally constructed that they reflect the symbolizations, blind spots and biases inherent in our own cultures.[22] Two evident questions are: Why do these ecclesiologies not notice their culturalness, and why do they purport to have universal validity as ecclesiological models?

We have all heard Chalcedon's statement that Jesus the Christ is one person in two natures, human and divine. What might not be readily recalled is that, in its definition, Chalcedon emphatically also says that "the distinctiveness of each nature is not nullified by the (hypostatic union). Instead, the properties of each nature are conserved...." The council also explained, earlier in the same definition, that Jesus the Christ is "of the same reality (homoousion) as ourselves in all respects as far as his humanness is concerned, sin only excepted."[23]

Now, if what we saw in our earlier discussion is true, namely, that what is human in human life is fundamentally that which is cultural, then the definitive embrace between the human and the divine, that in history became Jesus, can be understood as the embrace of the divine with the cultural. This embrace is not with some generic cultural dimension which does not exist, but with one specific and concrete culture. And this definitive embrace, extraordinarily concrete as it was, we Christians believe to have had universal salvific consequences.

In other words, if we take and interpret Chalcedon seriously, the cultural Galilean Jewishness of Jesus, which in ancient Palestine was quite specific, stands as indispensable to the definitive embrace we call the hypostatic union. Furthermore, this cultural specificity does not cancel the universal salvific validity of Jesus but, on the contrary, makes it possible. I sometimes wonder if the idea of human nature might not be better understood today as (or at least substantially modified by) culture.[24]

I would not be surprised if anti-Semitism among Christians might have been more than tangentially responsible for the traditional downplay of the cultural Jesus and for the disregard of the role of culture as a component in dogmatic definitions. Put differently, it is quite possible that western Christian culture, with its unfortunate anti-Semitic bent, might have in turn caused its own blindness to the issues and role of culture in doctrine and theology. If Jesus is deculturalized, he is dehumanized and, in an aberrant and hollow sort of way, might thereby be thought of as universal.

Let me address the two questions I raised previously: Why do modern ecclesiologies not explicitate their cultural specificity, and why do they claim to be universally valid? If reference to Jesus and his mission is part of how an ecclesiology is grounded, then cultural analysis must be an integral part of that grounding. I do not mean that this analysis be merely or mainly for the sake of a better archaeological description, as if cultural interpretation were indispensable only as a hermeneutic tool in relation to Jesus, his mission and his time. What I am suggesting is that given the fundamental relation between humanness and culture, and thus for dogmatic as well as anthropological reasons, the analysis or interpretation of culture must become part of all ecclesiological grounding. Furthermore, the presuppositions and methodologies for this cultural interpretation or analysis must be explicitated.

If it is evident today that Jesus and the apostolic generation cannot be adequately interpreted without a study of their cultures, then it stands to reason that subsequent Christian generations cannot claim privileges of universal validity without submitting their ecclesiologies to cultural interpretation. But, as we saw in the first cluster of issues, an adequate interpretation of culture can only occur from without that culture. Hence, the creators of the ecclesiologies can be evaluated in their universal claims only by those who do not share their pretensions.

As we saw earlier, the more social power a group has accrued, the greater the latter's inclination to promote its socially-constructed reality and meaning(s) as universally valid. And a group's theologies are part of its cultural package.

I suspect that contemporary ecclesiologies from above do not explicitate their cultural specificity because, theologically, their reference to Jesus has not taken seriously enough his Galilean Jewishness as well as some of the dogmatic and methodological consequences of the hypostatic union. At best, these ecclesiologies seem to have admitted the necessity of cultural interpretation for the sake of archaeological accuracy, but have not seen cultural analysis beyond an ancillary role.[25] These ecclesiologies, therefore, believe that they can put forth models of church and discussions of the latter's mission that are not rooted in real-life humanness, which is always cultural.

The claims to universal validity put forth by many modern ecclesiologies (progressive and conservative alike), therefore, start from a perspective of universality that sees it as inimical to the culturally specific or to the anthropologically aware in methodology. Since it is apparent that this supposed enmity can only exist if the universal savior had not been an ancient Galilean Jew, I suspect that anti-Semitism and a heavy dosage of imperial pretensions have greatly contributed to such enmity.

From below it seems evident that blindness to cultural specificity and to the foundational reasons behind the cultural analysis and critique of models, as well as the unfounded claims to the universal validity, come from sociologically naive premises and insufficient theological grounding. It also seems that only the ecclesiologies of the socially secure and powerful can pretend that this naivete is possible at all.[26]

Ecclesiological models, the reign of God, and the mission of the church. Any ecclesiological model will ultimately have to appeal to the mission of Jesus and of the apostolic generation in order to ground itself in normative Christian tradition. This immediately brings up several topics of utmost importance, but by far the most crucial one is the dawn of the reign of God. Any ecclesiology or ecclesiological model must bring the impending arrival of the reign of God to the fore, because this was the message of Jesus and, therefore, the essence of the mission of the church. This is culturally important.

It is established in biblical studies that Jesus of Nazareth preached the impending dawn of the reign of God in human history. This message stands at the center of everything else he might have said or done. Here is certainly not the place for a thorough discussion of the meaning of the reign of God or the God of the reign. However, it is impossible to consider ecclesiology without bringing the theme of the reign of God to center stage. If the proclamation and symbolization of its impending dawn was Jesus' core message and mission, then the reign must figure prominently in the church's own message and mission. The proclamation and symbolization of the arriving reign of God must also be a priority for the church.

What would this world be if God reigned? What would our daily reality be if the will of the compassionate God were done "on earth as it is in heaven"? To announce that the reign of God is an impending reality has urgency and makes sense only to the degree that the listeners understand what the consequences of the dawning of the reign would have for them. This implies that if daily reality, that is, socially-constructed reality, is not perceived as being profoundly affected by the arriving reign, then the message and the messenger of the reign can be dismissed, without much ado, as either irrelevant or not credible.[27]

How do the listeners of the message of the reign understand it for what it is intended to be? How do they perceive that the arriving reign of God profoundly and irrevocably affects their daily socially-constructed reality? And assuming that they understand and accept, how do they symbolize and live this understanding and acceptance?

It is a premise that the reign of God, in first-century Jewish Galilee was not understood as referring to individuals or even to a collection of individuals. It was, on the contrary, a communal hope. But it is also a premise that communal hopes can only be imaged culturally. In other words, the message of the reign of God was understood because it was culturally imaged, culturally symbolized. This is evident.

As a matter of fact, there would have been no message about the reign of God or about the God of the reign if it had not first been considered plausible in the socially-constructed reality of first-century Jewish Palestine. Plausibility within the parameters of the real, which parameters are always socially established, is the foundational condition for understanding the reign of God.

How the original listeners conceived the message and symbolized what it meant could only have occurred through the epistemologic tools offered them by Jewish culture. Jesus understood and preached the reign of God and the God of the reign in specifically Galilean, Jewish cultural images. For his message to be plausible and meaningful, he had no other possibility. His mission, utterly dependent on the proclamation of the impending dawn of the reign, assumed as valid vehicles the means and ways of Jewish culture.

I suggest what is already evident, namely, that human cultures are valid and important vehicles for understanding and symbolizing the impending arrival of the reign of God. I would go a step further to suggest that the reign of God cannot be plausibly understood as arriving except in the fashion and to the degree that human cultures permit (specifically, the cultures "doing" the understanding). Moreover, the reign of God cannot arrive if its impending dawn is not allowed as plausible by a people's reality, because reality is socially-constructed. There is no reign of God if a people cannot ask and answer, through ways and symbols culturally meaningful to them, what would our world, our reality, be if God reigned.

Ecclesiological models can be acceptable only to the degree that they proclaim and symbolize the arrival of the reign of God among the people where the church is. Proclamation and symbolization can only occur through culturally meaningful ways and symbols. Where do people find these? In their *praxis* the means and ways of unveiling the human are shared in human life.

Only a *praxis* that meaningfully unveils a new symbolization of the human in human life can meaningfully image the dawn of the reign of God. *Poiesis*, in this case, would reify the reign and would further lead to an aberrant objectification of the mission and life of the church. Hence, a valid ecclesiological model must engage in the promotion of the reign as human *praxis* and not in the establishment of church as *poiesis*.

Every ecclesiological model reflects the culture of those who create and find it meaningful. This implies that ecclesiological models are not, necessarily and of themselves, endowed with universal validity. They are valid only to the degree that they are cultural means of unveiling the new *praxis* provoked by the arriving reign of God.

Therefore, the transfer of any given ecclesiological model outside of its original cultural context may occur only in two ways: first, if the cultural context of the people receiving the transferred ecclesiological model share the same fundamental *praxis* with the creators of the model; or, second, if the people promoting the transfer of their ecclesiological model impose it on the recipients because of the latter's social vulnerability. In this second case, evidently, any claim to the universality of the transferred ecclesiological model would amount to little more than a theological legitimation of conquest. As a consequence, a transferred ecclesiological model will become the recipients' own model only to the degree that their culture is forced to change in the image of the promoters of the model, as well as to the degree that the recipients can enter into a process of ecclesiological *mestizaje*.[28] Without a theological *mestizaje*, not always pleasant or desired, any attempt at transferring an ecclesiological model will be destined to fail because it will be deemed foreign and invasive by the people who are suffering its imposition. If a model of what it means to be church does not become *praxis*, that is, means and ways of unveiling the human in their life, for the ones receiving the transfer, then the survival of the model will be due to the success of its imposition. It will lead to ecclesial participation as chore, as work, and not as life-revealing: *poiesis* and not *praxis*.

Were this situation to happen, the ecclesiological model would become a serious obstacle to the authentic proclamation and symbolization of the reign of God and of the God of the reign.[29] The promoters of the model, by impeding (probably through religious legitimation) the development of a more culturally significant manner of being church, might be depriving different communities of the message of the reign. It could be argued that, in this case, an ecclesiological model would become an idol and its promotion idolatry.

In this context, therefore, it seems that a multicultural model of church cannot be contemplated as possible, or even as good or desirable. An ecclesiological model that attempts to establish some kind of multicultural community is doomed to fail by the very nature of what culture is. The only alternative is the conscious acceptance, defense and promotion of what already exists: a church that is a communion of culturally diverse communities, each with its own symbolization of what it means to be Christian, and each with its own means and ways of unveiling the human in their humanness. These communities are not multicultural, rather, each is culture-specific. It is the entire church, as a communion based on faith and sacraments, that is Catholic and culturally diverse.

A multicultural ecclesiological model implies the cultural invasion, under pretenses of catholicity, of the most socially vulnerable communities within the church by the most socially powerful ones. It would be the latter who define and impose what is meant by culture, multiculturality, and how they are implemented in church life.

CONCLUSION

The North American Catholic Church is culturally diverse. Theologians should continue to reflect on the implications of current and future attempts at multiculturality within the church in the United States. Otherwise, in the name of catholicity, we might become providers of legitimating discourse for cultural invasion and for the perpetuation of the above and below conditions. The unfortunate fact that, among Christians, we can speak of each other as being either above or below is an accusation against the legitimacy of our ecclesiological models.

I do not assume that the communities that are part of our Catholic communion in the United States are impermeable to one another, nor do I advocate that they should be. I believe, however, that too much is implied by and at stake in ecclesial options for multiculturality, while very little has been thought through, especially as the multicultural discourse and subsequent decisions might affect those that, together, form the non-dominant half within the North American Catholic Church.

In the real ecclesiastical world (in dioceses, parishes and other institutions) our people are systematically ignored whenever they challenge the premises of the well-intentioned multicultural model. They are treated as either spoilers or somehow opposed to good theology (the latter, of course, defined as good by the same people who might be advancing a multicultural model). In the real ecclesiastical world, the theological and pastoral concerns of the dominated half have not been heard, or have been dismissed, all too frequently in the name of a multicultural model that is supposed to be promoting the exact opposite results.

It seems to me that the best future open to the North American Catholic Church is eventual cultural and religious *mestizaje*. In the meantime, as we walk toward that new ecclesial model, we have to recognize the immediate need for respect and promotion of cultural diversity as it exists in real life, not as a problem that needs solution but as a gift from God that awaits grateful welcoming, even in professional theology.

American theology, I think, is called to a reflection that contributes in the manner of theology to a more humanizing *praxis* for all, and not to a discourse that can legitimize the cultural and social superiority of some Catholics over others. The church of God is not, and cannot be, a parody of George Orwell's *Animal Farm*.

Mary Collins

RESPONSE TO ORLANDO ESPÍN

In responding to his assignment to speak about issues that seem to need research in the viewpoint of someone doing theology from below, Orlando Espín begins by lamenting the very implications of the language. While it might have been possible to interpret the language of above and below to refer to the respective viewpoints of church office holders and church members on issues that need further research (or, alternately, of academics in their ivory tower above the fray, and pastoral workers in the field below) Espín takes the view that above and below refer to those Catholics who have achieved some measure of status through assimilation into the U.S. society and those who remain socially marginal. Whichever approach to the topic might have been taken, Espín acknowledges that above and below are existential ecclesial locations. And although he is ordained as a priest of the church, he nevertheless identifies with the view from below. Professor Espín also expresses a firm hope, namely, the possibility of a redemptive *mestizaje*, a community of faith in which above and below are no longer relevant descriptors. But he insists that we pay attention now to our actual ecclesial reality. Our ecclesial situation is contentious because of what we see from our respective viewpoints. Espín identifies his voice as coming from the non-dominant half of the American Catholic Church. He gives voice to a critique, arising from "our people," both of the Catholic Church in the United States and of the work of ecclesiological reflection. In the context of his paper and his own work as a theologian, the voice is that of Spanish-speaking Catholics. He does not so clearly identify "you people."

Yet it is evident in context that at least one feature "you people" have in common is that we are English-speakers. In the Catholic Church in the United States, as in the public life of the country, English-speakers are dominant, even though not all English-speakers participate equally— African-Americans are the obvious case in point—in that dominant culture. As second feature of "you people" is that those so identified have a greater hold on institutional power than the people we dominate.

72

The dominant English-speaking milieu is where institutional power is located.

CULTURAL PLURALISM AND
ECCLESIOLOGICAL PRESUPPOSITIONS

Having acknowledged Professor Espín's pespective, let me move to the focal issue in the first part of his paper: how those who are dominant in doing the work of theology and especially the work of developing a theology of the local church deal with—or fail to deal with—the fact of non-European cultures in the Catholic Church in the United States. He distinguishes two potential orientations in contemporary ecclesiological reflection: the way of the multiculturalists and the way of the cultural pluralists. He himself affirms the orientation of cultural pluralism, although he thinks that theologians who identify with the dominating half of the Catholic Church in the United States are committed to multiculturalism.

Here I found myself working to tease out what is only implicit in Espín's discussion. He sugggests that a Catholic posture that affirms cultural pluralism says, "let the Catholic faith find its embodiment through the expressive forms of each and every cultural community." Every culture is a worthy bearer of the gospel revelation of salvation in Jesus Christ and can give an authentic shape to faithful discipleship.

By contrast with such a commitment to cultural pluralism as the foundation for a contemporary Catholic ecclesiology, Professor Espín, viewing things from below, sees multiculturalism as a much less promising stance. Multiculturalism presumes that the ecclesiological constructs and institutional forms generated by the dominant culture are normative. These stand in judgment over against the communal achievements and aspirations of other cultures, finding them other, finding them alien or deviant or deficient or inferior, as interesting perhaps, but not to be taken with full seriousness.

But viewed from below, from the viewpoint of Spanish-speaking brothers and sisters in Christ, sons and daughters of Latin America, it is the Anglocentric American church, the child of the Eurocentric church, which is other. The Anglocentric church is short-sighted, living with delusions of grandeur. One of the delusions of the Anglocentric church is that others (Hispanics/Latinos, Asians, Native Americans, African-Americans, etc.) want to be in—or should want to be in—our present well-ordered Catholic Church.

A second delusion of the Anglocentric church in the United States, as the child of the Eurocentric church rising from Hellenistic culture, is that it can set the terms for the participation of all in the church. The proposition of the ecclesiological multiculturalist is: accept this center, which is objective and normative. In turn, we can make room for you to bring in some of your possessions. To this, Espín says no. Why? A multiculturalist ecclesiology leaves a dominant center intact; it is not yet open to the mystery of a redemptive *mestizaje*. He argues rather for cultural pluralism, because this orientation affirms the value of multiple organizing centers of the one faith in the God of Jesus Christ. It affirms that there are many ways of being church.

THE HIDDEN FOUNDATION: CLERICAL CULTURE

In addition to positing two typical ecclesiological postures, cultural pluralism and multiculturalism, and an as-yet-inaccessible ecclesial *mestizaje*, Espín speaks to several foundational issues basic to all the research and reflection theologians do in the construction of local ecclesiologies. First, he warns us of problems associated with any act of theological definition, since definition involves a cultural exercise of power and an assertion of normativity. Next, he calls for all practitioners of the theological art (for I think it is art, depending as it does on acts of imagination) to move beyond illusions that our work is culture-free and objective, and to move toward fuller awareness of the need for intelligent subjectivity in the work of theological reflection and writing. Third, he points to problems associated with the use of models in theological reflection, especially models of the church. His caution is that all such models, too, are cultural products.

I am more sanguine than Espín that many contemporary ecclesiologists are using the tools of critical history and social sciences in their theological reflection on the local church. On the other hand I wish Espín himself had ventured being more explicit on this point of ecclesiological models as cultural products. Was he hoping that we would all recognize, at the heart of his critique, allusion to the hidden problem posed for all ecclesiological renewal in the dogmatic constitution on the church, Vatican II's *Lumen Gentium*, and in the 1983 Code of Canon Law which structures the church in the spirit of the constitution? Whether or not this was his hope, I find it essential to name the problem here.

I have written elsewhere about the unexamined persistence of a classical clerical culture, a culture grounded in imperial Roman public order that in turn undergirds Roman Catholic ecclesiology.[1] It is a culture that refuses to allow the presence of women at its center and refuses to receive all the gifts of women. This classical clerical culture—a high culture from its own viewpoint—is distinguishable from the various cultures of western Europe in which Christianity took root and in which popular Catholicism persistently flourished. European Anglo-Saxon and Celtic cultures are no more identical with the Roman clerical culture that overlayed them than are Visigothic/Spanish, Native American and African cultures. Acts of theological definition emanating from the imperial Roman clerical religious imagination long ago suppressed the development of local ecclesiologies in western Europe. Such definitions continue this suppression to this day, not only in the African or Latin American church, but also in the Catholic Church in the United States. The ecclesiatical order set out as normative in *Lumen Gentium* cannot support the full ecclesiological pluralism that Espín is promoting.

WOMEN'S THEOLOGICAL PERSPECTIVES

At this point I want to note the first of two remarkable omissions in our theological reflection in this conversation. Reference to the work of feminist theology as a form of liberation theology has been given no more than a token nod, even though Hispanic/Latino women writers have been articulating a distinctive *mujerista* theology for some time.[2] Fuller inclusion of Catholic women's theological critique of multi-culturalism and cultural pluralism would have brought into focus both gender and class issues, as these shape culture and church alike. While it is not possible for a single discussion to do everything, still gender analysis cannot be passed over as a secondary issue in theological reflection on the local church. Without attention to gender issues, an ecclesiology affirming cultural pluralism will yield no greater possibilities for women than the viewpoint of multiculturalism being critiqued here.

Further, had the *mujerista*—womanist—feminist conversation influenced the shape of this and other presentations, the problem of class as an ecclesiological issue would have been as central to the presentations as it has been to the group discussions. Catholic women who have been involved in feminist theological reflection for the past quarter century have struggled honestly with and taught one another to recognize and affirm the importance of social location in the theological enterprise. Race, class, and gender analysis are all part of feminist theological method.

Whatever real differences are to be found in the theological writings of *mujerista*, womanist, and feminist theologians because of their different social locations, all Catholic women of whatever class share the experience of otherness projected upon them by traditional theological acts of definition about the nature of the church and roles and relationships in it. The hierarchal structuring of relationships organic to *Lumen Gentium*—which distinguishes communities "legitimately organized" (LG 26) from those whose organizational style is unauthorized—assures that there will always be locations below and above in the church of Jesus Christ: the ordained above the baptized, men above women, those who hold church office above those who embody the good news of salvation in the marketplace.

In this matter of exposing the concealed culture supporting all ecclesiological discourse, let me make one final point from a feminist perspective on Professor Espín's indictment of contemporary ecclesiology. The Euro-Catholic imagination has long been structured by explanatory models (what Sallie McFague calls "metaphors with staying power"[3]) of the saving grace of Christ that have come to be understood as normative models for the church. In the course of time, implications of these models (what the medieval scholastics might have named arguments from fittingness) came to accorded ontological density. The interpretation of Jesus' death as a sacrifice, for example, has carried in its wake a theology of cultic priesthood and a construction of a sacral order that elevates celibacy to a higher state of human being.[4] The interpretation of Jesus' relationship to the church as that of bridegroom to bride in a patriarchal culture has carried in its wake a theology of headship and submission extrapolated to the domestic, diocesan, and the universal church.[5]

Professor Espín's paper asks U.S. Euro-Catholics to trust that peoples like himself, rooted in non-European cultures, experience and name saving grace in ways that will give rise to other metaphors and explanatory models for being church on mission in this historical and cultural moment. This is good news, at least to those of us Euro-Catholics who, like him, weary of trying to come to self-identity as disciples within the dominant ecclesiological paradigm. But some Euro-Catholic women are also engaged in the contemporary search for new metaphors and explanatory models for ecclesiological reflection, and are moving in their search to the very heart of the doctrine of the Trinity.[6] I am sympathetic with Espín's hope that the Catholic faith as it has been received and lived by marginalized peoples has the power to re-evanglize those who dominate. But I am also wary of theological projects that do not attend overtly to gender issues in culture. We need inspiration to refresh our imaginations, to take us beyond our dualisms of above and below, to help us to recognize and to commit ourselves to the praxis of the dawning reign of God, to reorder ourselves as the church of Jesus Christ. But in a Copernican universe, above and below are locations relative to our peculiar perspectives, reminding us that we must finally be open to conversion from whatever direction grace might come.

LITURGICAL PRAXIS AND THE RENEWAL OF ECCLESIOLOGY

The second omission from our discourse is any exploration of the Catholic people's rituals—those officially identified as liturgical and those celebrated as popular—as data for the work of theological reflection on the mystery of the church. Because the data of ritual performance is difficult to turn into text for analysis, theologians generally overlook ritual performance as a source of theological meaning. This discussion would seem to confirm that it is a problem endemic to systematic theologians as systematic theologians. Because Professor Espín has treated this matter elsewhere in his work, however, its absence here is the more notable.[7]

When the Christian people assemble for worship, liturgical and popular, they embody their understanding of saving relationships revealed to the church through the Spirit of the risen Christ. The normative shape of the church's liturgy has been given to us by those acts of theological definition Espín has discussed; official liturgy is hierarchically ordered. But it is certainly appropriate to inquire: How else are Christian peoples giving visible shape to themselves as the church of Jesus Christ? What other organizing and symbolic centers are already in evidence when Catholic people gather in particular places in response to particular human concerns? How do these other shapes of the church impinge on the shape celebrated in the official liturgy?

There is not time here for discussion of this issue of the assembled church as the embodiment of the saving grace of Christ. Let me note simply that some Christian feminist groups have begun to develop a process of ritualizing grounded in ecclesial praxis. Their process involves critical and constructive retrieval, exploration, and celebration of the meaning of their faith in Jesus Christ.

At its best, such Christian feminist celebration is not based on some naive romanticism that the fullness of truth and wisdom is already present in the marginalized, just waiting to find expression when the established are moved aside. Movement toward truth requires transcendence of whatever limits are tied to the genuine achievements of both past and present. So good feminist liturgical praxis requires the participation of "organic intellectuals."[8] Such participants can contextualize within the tradition and set out for group reflection what is emerging and what is being rejected in its rituals. In this process of celebrating and reflecting, the authenticity of both the old and the new expressions of Christian ecclesial community can be probed.

Such critical liturgical praxis does not have to be restricted to feminist groups; it can be pursued in any gathering of the Christian people. It will be essential in the construction of local theologies on the

way to the redemptive *mestizaje* that Espín holds out as a hope.[9] Because
I have been observing and reflecting on what happens in women's
ritual construction, I find credible the basic argument of Espín's paper.
The central organizing symbols for the new ecclesiology will emerge
from within the local church, in what it does as well as how it thinks.[10]

A CONCLUDING CAUTION

Let me underscore a solid measure of agreement with much of
Espín's viewpoint and then express a reservation. I agree that the
writing of theology, like "the writing of culture," is an exercise of power
that must be subject to critique. So my overall response to his discussion
has been oriented to affirmation of this position rather than to critique
particular positions taken within the course of the argument. I have
affirmed his research agenda, rather than offering an alternative view
from below, even while I noted that a feminist theology of liberation, as
well as womanist and *mujerista* theologies, are unacknowledged allies in
the project he is proposing. Yet I have a reservation.

Professor Espín's affirmation of pluralism in ecclesial praxis as a
matter of theological principle is a legitimate demand for the contemporary renewal of the theology of the local church. Yet he does not
mention here two correlative obligations: communication from church
to church; and exercise of a ministry of hospitality of one community to
another. These obligations must be honored. All locally contextualized
appropriations of the message of salvation are inevitably partial.
Without mutual dialogue and hospitality, without regular shared praxis,
we put our ecclesial communities beyond critique. We may gain the
capacity for self-definition but evade invitations to self-transcendence,
to repentance and conversion. Feminists, womanists, and *mujeristas* have
generally coached one another painfully to that level of understanding.
The failure to learn humility disciplined by the critique of the larger
community is what got the dominant clerically constructed church into
the present situation of dominance in the first place.

David N. Power, O.M.I.

COMMUNION WITHIN PLURALISM IN THE LOCAL CHURCH: MAINTAINING UNITY IN THE PROCESS OF INCULTURATION

The title of this paper might suggest a prior concern for keeping unity, as though the plurality were given and the process of inculturation under way. In fact, in addressing the issue it is imperative to assure adequate respect for cultural diversity, and for particular cultures, before it is possible to talk about unity or communion.

As a word, *inculturation* is so broadly used that it has come to mean nothing other than that faith has been, and must continue to be, given expression in a variety of cultural forms. What that implies can be grasped only by reflection upon that correlation in the past and on the challenges of the present. As for the future, the best term to use is probably "organic progression".[1] When a people comes to believe in the gospel as brought to it couched in the cultural forms of the messenger, it then begins to find expression of its faith in forms that emerge from the culture's own religiosity and modes of understanding. Thus, whatever other meaning might be given to the word, multiculturalism is here understood as communion across cultures, or communion between communities living their faith out of a diversity of cultures, without attempting to reduce all to some common fusion of cultural faith expressions.

The issue being considered is not cultural pluralism in churches across the world, but communion within a local church that is facing up to its own inner cultural pluralism. Reflection must refer to this reality. This requires a consideration of the past as well as of the present. The Christian faith came to this continent in a variety of European cultural expressions but the church has not hitherto been very open to its expression in other cultures. In the past, for a living people embarked on a particular historical venture the apt cultural expression of the faith

79

helped to mediate multiple identities: that derived from the place of
origin, that of being Catholic, and that of being a U.S. American. It also
had to mediate the transitions, geographical and cultural, involved in
merging identities. These two tasks continue to be important today, in
varying degree for different cultural groups. They have to be accomplished, however, while allowing for the integrity of diverse cultural
realities.

A working hypothesis in this paper is that unity is achieved and
maintained through a communion in otherness, developed, to borrow
a phrase from Emmanuel Levinas, out of an ethic of the other. The use
of this approach to multiculturalism was suggested already by Johann-
Baptist Metz, and he traced the principle of the acknowledgment of the
other back into Jewish and Christian roots.[2] But how is polycentrism to
be retrieved from a past which often vigorously suppressed otherness,
despite these roots? Before we can talk of keeping unity, therefore, we
have to ask what rightful pluralism has to be fostered in the light of a
past which never came wholly to terms with this phenomenon. In brief,
in the U.S. American church that embraces many cultural groups how
do we begin to find the ways to acknowledge the otherness of the other,
and to consider the present in the frank light of the suppression of
otherness in the past. Cultural pluralism is thus the issue of taking
respect for the other, the demands that follow from respect for the
other, and reconciliation with the other, as the basis for communion
and unity in Jesus Christ. Only from this can a communion within
cultural diversity ensue.

As prelude to my paper, I would like to borrow from the dedication of the book to which Metz refers in the above-cited article, *La
Conquête de l'Amérique. La question de l'autre*, by Tzvetan Todorov: "I
dedicate this book to the memory of a Mayan woman, devoured by
dogs." The dedication shows Todorov's concern to keep alive the
stories that must not be forgotten, and which if remembered provide
the means to grasp why diversity has been refused and some clues as to
how it may yet be acknowledged, without the other appearing to be a
threat.[3]

With the question of the other as key to the nature of unity within
multiculturalism, five distinct steps are taken in the course of this paper
that may help us to think through the issues involved, in the hope that
such understanding may enliven action. First, brief consideration is
given to the cultural moment in which the western world and the
church as a whole are presently caught. Second, two pertinent kinds of
story are evoked from the past, the one set being stories of suppression,
the other being stories of the church itself. Third, based on stories of
the immigrant church, the role of ethnicity in religious expression is

recalled. Fourth, an analysis of otherness is undertaken, based on the book of Todorov. Fifth, the physiognomy of a multicultural church communion is tentatively opened to consideration.[4]

NAMING THE MOMENT

THE CALL WITHIN THE CATHOLIC CHURCH

The leadership of the church in the United States has in recent years hearkened to the call of newly stirring voices and has guided us all in the consideration of a newly acknowledged ethnicity and plurality. There have been pastoral letters and pastoral programs for various cultural bodies, such as Hispanics/Latinos, African-Americans, Native Americans, or Asians. In the first place, this pastoral strategy shows a new interest in those who have been here for a long time but who have been relegated to a subordinate role. In the second place, it reveals a familiar but odd human mixture of fear and eagerness in face of the new, as we witness fresh and more diversified migrations to the continent.

The plurality of cultures is clearly not reducible to the issue of race and skin color. From within black communities, for example, we hear of a diversity that is as great as the diversity among Irish, Polish and Greek white people. In the pastoral letter of black bishops, "What We Have Seen and Heard," we read:

> To be Catholic is to be universal. To be universal is not to be uniform. It does mean that the gifts of individuals and of particular groups become the common heritage shared by all.[5]

Later in the letter, the bishops comment:

> ...the African-American cultural heritage is vast and rich. The cultural idiom of American Black people has never been uniform but has varied according to region and ethos. African, Haitian, Latin and West Indian cultural expressions continue to this day to nurture the Black American cultural expression.[6]

What the bishops are asking in this and other documents is how to mediate between the diverse identity of being black, being Haitian or African or West Indian, being American, and being Catholic. They are affirming the efforts of black Catholics, whether of long-standing in the country or new to the country, to find their own voices and define their own identities. In the process they wish to aid them to make whatever cultural and social transitions the moment requires. In some respects this recalls how church communities and pastors in the past sought to help new immigrants to make comparable transitions, with both gains and losses in the strategies adopted and the experiences lived. While in the history of the immigrant church, however, a certain Roman identity was kept across cultures, black and Hispanic communities today show a greater movement toward defining their own identities, free from Eurocentric modes of thought, power and expression. Within the larger picture, and in the efforts to achieve communion among all Catholic communities, what could a new cultural awareness on the part of all mean for African-Americans or Native Americans, if the continental church can accept solidarity with the American past in which their reality was denied, whatever part Catholicism played in this denial? What does it mean for the churches that have long provided the dominant models of being church?

Besides groups of European origin, African and Hispanic Americans of long standing, among Catholics today there is a wave of new immigrants from such places as Vietnam, Laos, Haiti, Guatemala, or Nicaragua, making up their own particular Catholic communities. Reflection on the past, as it affected both the oppressed and immigrants of European origin, can open up new ways for receiving these communities with due respect for their cultural diversity, and with due regard for their rights, and with due attitudes of hospitality to their own distinctive ways of being.

THE MOMENT IN WESTERN CULTURE AND SOCIETY

The particular moment in cultural history at which this question of multiculturalism is raised for the church affects the approach that is taken to it. It is, in fact, difficult to reflect on culture at a time when the security of cultural maps and paradigms is much open to question.

Jean-François Lyotard, in an essay entitled "Universal history and cultural differences," notes a series of events which symbolically mark the dissolution of the cultures, ideologies, and institutions, of modernity. He names Auschwitz 1945, Berlin 1953, Prague 1959, Budapest 1956, and May 1968. Reading these symbols, he sees in them signs of the failure of rationality as life's and society's guiding force, of the fallacy of dialectical materialism as an analogy for history, of a refutation of the doctrine of parliamentary liberalism, and of the crisis of economic liberalism.[7]

In one brief paragraph, Lyotard conjures up the failures of the major ideologies of the period which we refer to as modernity, when nations and peoples thought to take their destiny into their own hands on the basis of humanity's inner capacity to create a new world:

rationality, historical materialism, democratic liberalism, and economic liberalism have all proved inefficacious in building a society that promotes the human good for all, a community of nations that lends to global peace, and a harmony between humankind and the earth on which it dwells. After the famous "turn to the subject" on which so much was built, we are in a world of the "loss of the subject," human persons and communities prone to forces which they do not understand, mystified by the consequences of their own actions, and without even a language or ritual system that can give people a clear sense of identity and meaning.

While the symbols listed by Lyotard affect the west in general, we might well recall symbols that touch particularly on the cultural strain of life in the United States. Here, too, there are potent symbols of date or place to evoke the nation's own moments of cruel desperation and checkmate: Chicago and Watts 1968, Saigon 1975, Watergate 1972, Los Angeles 1992, to name some that come readily to mind.

These symbols may seem a sad and pessimistic list, but it is needed to keep ourselves alert to what our communion in faith has to mediate. Not only must it mediate faith and hope in Jesus Christ, but it must mediate social and cultural transitions that both guard and enhance life. Not only must it mediate social and cultural transition, but it must do so in a time when the parent society and the parent democratic idealism are coping with a wide-ranging disillusionment and are struggling to find values on which a country can build a human community that realizes the ideal stated in the motto *e pluribus unum*.

Far, however, from simply lamenting this dissolution of hegemony, however painful it may be for many, it ought to be taken as a moment of opportunity. The hegemony broken, new voices can be heard and new shape given, out of fresh resources, to life on the continent and to life within the churches.

THE MOMENT IN THE AMERICAN CATHOLIC CHURCH

For this to be so for the Catholic Church on the continent, people of all communities need to come to grips with what has happened in the last few decades. During the Second Vatican Council, the Catholic Church seemed to discover modern ideals. Coming out of an age wherein it found it necessary to strongly protect the faith and its own liberties, it had discovered a way to live as a baptismal community, rather than as social pyramid. It also began to explore avenues toward communing with other churches, with other religions, and with the national and international bodies that sought to build a community of nations grounded in the principles of freedom and justice. However, it soon began to experience its own inner and deeply ingrained weaknesses and to realize the frustrations involved in negotiating the extraordinary transition to which it had opened itself by its synodal decrees and its new synodal idealism.

Though one is not justified in discounting the gains of thirty years, by and large one has to acknowledge that the transition has shown up an inner tension and manifold weakness in the communal life of the church here in this country. We continue to struggle over a ritual system and an ethical teaching which in many ways fail to integrate the experiences and needs of believers, or to mediate coherence between citizenship and a life of faith, or to offer a way of responding to the civic tensions and struggles that have been mentioned, so that the church may indeed be a sign of the fullness of human unity.[8]

The weaknesses that have emerged cannot be understood simply as weaknesses of the moment, or administrative weaknesses, or weaknesses of a current loss of faith or Christian ethic. They cannot be overcome by recovering the past, as though it could instantly reveal to us a firmer foundation. Most of the weaknesses are inherited weaknesses. They are built into the history of the church, so that the strength and the life to be nurtured by looking to faith and tradition can come to us only if we are ready to face these structural, institutional, doctrinal and ethnic weaknesses that are so interwoven into the mediation of the life of the Spirit that it cannot be understood or enhanced except in their recognition.

That is the only way of understanding how the faith community is responding to the social and cultural situation of which the church finds itself a part, while it faces the possibilities and the tensions of multiculturalism. Even a cursory glance, after all, shows us how conflictual some of the responses are, how terribly different to each other they are. In broad terms, one may speak of the shaping of church community as a counter-cultural force, looking for a language and strategy that serves not only its inner needs but its role in society as a whole. Yet even as one says this, there is the awareness that churches or church members are working in two different directions. Some find ground in the ideals of neoconservative reversionism,[9] while others look to a community-based evangelical witness. Some espouse conversation with the ideals born of modernity but are countered by those who express abjuration of these ideals. In even more concrete manifestations of faith-based tensions, there is in many places the emergence of a non-clerical and non-patriarchal church, especially in forms of leadership and of liturgy, while at the same time there is a strong neoconservative opposition to this emergence, expressed in many areas, inclusive of ecclesial life and ritual, political participation, and ethical discourse.

The failure of rationality and of the ideals of the Enlightenment remind us that we have to probe both cultural traditions and human nature to find life resources, not accounted for and not drawn upon in modernity's project. In an analogous manner, the church's inadequacy in drawing on the life of the Spirit, as evidenced by its inherent weaknesses, is a warning sign that there are resources that have not been tapped in ecclesial traditions and in the charisms of members. Looking to the power of narrative and drawing particularly on marginal or forgotten stories is an important way of retrieving meaning and energy from the past into current enterprises. It is dangerous, of course, because in revealing the power of a tradition in new places it also discloses the failure of those institutions and forces which have been canonized or deemed to be the primary forms of mediation.

REMEMBERING FROM THE PAST

Remembering from the past is a community act that takes shape as a necessary critical force for the channelling of present effort. It unfolds, in the words of Johann-Baptist Metz, a dangerous memory, revealing both failures where not expected and life-forces where not suspected.

As we look to our American past, we have to take note of the ways in which faith communities were party to cultural failures, and at the ways in which cultural influences shaped the development of church life.

In retrieving dangerous memories, there are first the stories of conquest and oppression, all the stories that reveal how both cultures and institutions were built on the denial of the other.

In a recent book on the place of religion in the construction of U.S. society and American culture, Jon Butler uses the notion of the "spiritual holocaust" of African heritage to show how white society and white churches approached blacks and the institutions of slavery, with long-standing effect on the place of African Americans in church and society.[10] By spiritual holocaust, he means that the African religious and cultural system as system was destroyed at the hands of slavers.[11]

The later history of black religion on this continent demonstrates its resilience and vitality, so that in fact its cultural power was never completely suppressed.[12] It enabled people to express the hope of freedom in the midst of slavery, and allowed them, out of their culture resources, to forge particular ways of translating the Christian idiom. The look back to the beginnings cannot be avoided if the whole story is to be retrieved and its dangerous power unleashed. Without resort to reversionism, for black people of African heritage a place in society and in church has to be forged through the retrieval of this religious and cultural heritage, as well as through a retrieval of the stories of oppression and of the vitality of life among slaves.

The religion and culture of Native Americans fared no better. As Jay Dolan comments in his book, *The American Catholic Experience*:

> The mission system involved not only a total revolution in Indian culture, but a new way of thinking about the supernatural, a new way of viewing the earth and its fertility, and a new understanding of personal and social relations. The irony is that the Spanish believed that this program of conversion and acculturation would be completed in a short space of time....It never worked that way, however.[13]

One could profitably read his account of the inadequacy of missionary methods, including the failure to take learning Native American languages seriously, since the priests harbored the supposition that true doctrine had to be communicated in Spanish or some other European language.[14]

Such stories have, of course, to be read within the context of the conquest of the Americas and the violence done to indigenous peoples, as this is brought to attention in the work of Todorov already cited and of which more will be said shortly. It is against that background that we see the involvement of the church in the American republic in the destruction of Native American culture.

CONSTRAINTS WITHIN THE LIFE OF THE CHURCH

Apart from Christianity's contribution to the holocaust of Native Americans on the new continents, and to the African-American spiritual holocaust, there were episodes in the inner life of the church which made it difficult for it to guide its members in taking their place in the public arena or to address these or other issues as believing Christians.

It is not peculiar to life on this continent, but it has to be admitted that the church here did not find an easy solution to the participation of the laity in the governance of the church. The example of John Carroll's problems and of his changed stance on a number of issues, after he assumed episcopal leadership, is known. Early in his life, Carroll advocated a liturgy in the vernacular and favored the laity's part in parish organization, just as he was concerned about having a church that could easily dialogue with republican interests. As recounted by historians, after he was made bishop these interests met up with practical difficulties and in the end yielded to a greater preoccupation with the centralization of authority, whether at home in the bishop or world-wide in Rome.[15]

Within the larger context, the emergence of a local church, with its own traditions, institutions and ritual, was of course hampered by the Roman refusal of language, culture, rite, traditions, memories, in Rome's vexatious U.S. encounters with non-European cultures, as well as by the Roman reaction against the influence of modernity as it appeared in the history of the church in the United States.

Such are the stories never to be forgotten. There are the stories of the oppression of black peoples and of Native American, in which Christianity played its role. To these there would need to be added the stories of the oppression of people of mixed Native American and Spanish blood, or indeed of Asian immigrants. The effort here has been primarily to go back to the beginnings, rather than to survey the entire history of the continent. Added to these stories, in more direct relation to the inner life of the church, there is that of the church's failure, even among European immigrants, to become a church of the baptized in the full sense of the word.

ETHNICITY AND RELIGION

It is already obvious that cultural heritage was operative in the life of black churches and in recent years it has been extensively investigated in the life of Spanish-speaking churches.[16] In order to illustrate this point greater attention is given here to the story of European immigrant churches.

Several histories have been written in the last few decades which show the part that ethnicity played in the religious expression of these peoples. Their particular cultural heritage was vital to the religious factors which served to mediate the transition of peoples from one continent to the other, from one national affiliation to another, and to mediate a place for them in face of the demands of being American or of finding a way of participating in the life of this new world, without being submerged by other forces.

Ethnicity is defined by Andrew Greeley and David Tracy, as "religious, racial, national, linguistic, and geographic diversity".[17] Along with others, they both argue that ethnic experience is a legitimate source of theological reflection. In Tracy's phrase, any classical expression of a particular ethnic religious heritage possesses a public, not a private character. This is so because transcendent realities must be spoken of in ways that draw from the language, heritage, and traditions of particular cultures.

One has therefore to ponder the life of the community, as it is built on patterns and experiences that are proper to its members' particular heritage. The history of Catholic immigrants cannot be told simply as a history of diocesan and parochial institutions or rituals, such as mass practices, schools, hospitals or parish organization. Within the *locus theologicus* of history, one has to include the ways in which parents passed on the faith, the vocabulary used by people to speak of God, Christ, Mary, human life, and that enigmatic area of faith expression that goes under the generic heading of popular devotion. Recently, Philip Gleason has lauded Jay Dolan and James Hennessy for writing the history of the church in the United States as the history of the people of God, while remarking on the difficulty of making the change from the long-prevailing format of institutional history.[18]

It is only on this basis that we can understand the fortunes of Catholic immigrants in the past. Catholicism in its traditional and often popular molds served both to affirm a first identity, whether Polish, Irish, German, or Czech, and to mediate the second loyalty, that is to the United States, which could be lived without losing contact with the old. In that sense, Catholicism was not seen as a block to being American by Catholics themselves, no more than was being Polish or Irish or Czech. It rather served that cultural and social cohesion and identity without which the transition to survival and eventual advancement in the new world could not be negotiated.

Here we need to be aware of the incipient nature of this history of the people of God, with all its blind spots. Not all immigrants were aided in the same manner and it is useful to compare the devotional Catholicism which Dolan found helpful to Irish, German or Czech immigrants with the less ecclesiastical style of popular religion in which early urban Italian immigrants found relief. In both cases, we have to see what religious identity and practice meant to poor immigrants in terms of helping them accommodate themselves to their status in this new land.

Dolan[19] finds four principal traits in what he dubs devotional Catholicism, by which he means the Catholicism practiced by lay folk, but largely fostered by clergy. The popular practices were such matters as regular mass-going (whatever one did there), devotion to the Sacred Heart, regular confession, and devotions to Mary and the saints within the calendar of the church's year. They included membership in confraternities and sodalities, reading Catholic prayer books and family based devotions. The four traits of this style of Catholicism distinguished by Dolan are: its acknowledgment of the guidance of ecclesiastical authority, its strong sense of sin, its ritual (not necessarily liturgical) structure, and its appeal to the occasional intervention of the miraculous. In a world where poor immigrants had little power, but in which they nonetheless wished to hold a secure place, these factors gave them the confidence of an authority more securely grounded than civil authority, a sound knowledge of good and evil to guide them in their new fields of labor, a well-structured family and parochial life to form an immediate and non-hostile environment, and confidence in a power that could intervene to help them in a world where their own power was grossly inadequate.[20]

This is in contrast with the ways of Italian immigrants, who seem to have kept a popular and tradition based independence of the clergy in their practice of the *festa*.[21] In the extravaganza of the feasts honoring neighborhood Madonnas and saints, poor Italians are deemed by historians to have found ways of overcoming urban pathology, neighborhood isolation, degradation in the view of the outsider, and the rigors of persistent poverty. The setting of the feast was in the family and neighborhood, not in the church as an institution, though from the family setting the values of the feast were transferred to church life. For most clergy (there are always exceptions) it was problematic to build a sense of ecclesial community from such a basis, whereas the devotional Catholicism of Irish or German immigrants was more easily contained within the ecclesiastical structure. Either kind of popular piety nurtured faith, devotion and a communion with God and the saints in times of crisis and in ways that helped people to bring faith and the hope for an improved human life on this continent together.

Unhappily, in its working out of the struggle to show loyalty to both church and republic, this story shows rifts among Catholic groups due to diverse claims to have a monopoly on Catholic identity. As expressed by the historian of American religion, Martin Marty, the problem was that of combining Americanism, Modernism, and that specific ethnic identity to which being Catholic was integral, though diverse in each ethnic group.[22]

As for the place which an interest in ethnicity has for the present moment of church life, Philip Gleason remarks that the interest may not have the fervor of the seventies, but that its importance remains in understanding the life of the church in this country. Indeed, its importance is rendered more urgent because of the waves of new immigrants from all continents.[23] As Gleason notes, there were in the past real differences of viewpoint and policy preference between different ethnic groups. Such differences exist also in the present, but from the past we can learn the danger of shibboleths, as he calls them, that dismiss either the importance of the ethnocentric or the importance of looking for convergence. As we profit from a more critical awareness of the nature of ethnicity, we see that there can be no melting down into a uniform culture. Rather, what is required is a communion in the recognition of the other, and in the ways of communication which allow partners in communion to share the diversity, and indeed to come to communion out of diversity.

THE QUESTION OF THE OTHER

From the past, we have seen the extent to which the church too is implicated in the denial of a place in public and ecclesial life to African-Americans and to Native Americans. We have also recalled the story of those whose religious heritage helped them to make a transition but who entered into conflict with each other, in a denial of legitimate Catholic otherness. In facing the present challenge, we have to consider how much refusal of the other in the past blocks the paths to present communion. It is time therefore to examine the failure of communion by returning to the work of Tzvetan Todorov for a closer analysis, and see from this how much the failure raises the issue of letting the other be other.

ENCOUNTERS WITH THE OTHER

Todorov treats of how the *other* was neglected or refused in the conquest of America, but he takes this as a paradigmatic story to be recounted in the redress of past evils and in mirroring the innate violence of a refusal of the other in our more recent history. Four actions are analyzed by Todorov as paradigmatic for the difficulties and the challenges encountered in intercultural relations.

First, he notes the action of the discoverer, Christopher Columbus, who saw how wonderfully new everything was, but in more senses than one never really knew where he had arrived. He was determined to see everything in terms of a European geography and historiography, and these were the only terms which he had at hand to describe all the marvelous things which held him in awe.

Then there was the action of the conquistador, Hernán Cortes, who mapped the reality correctly in his gathering of data about the land and the people, and who could see the nature of differences between the indigenous peoples and European peoples. This was knowledge in the interests of conquest, to be adroitly used to overthrow the power of the emperor and subjugate the people. What did not fit, Cortes could willingly destroy or leave it to his soldiers to do so. The other, so precisely mapped in this universe, had no place in human relations, was allowed to put no demands on the conqueror, but had to be mapped on a universe of values and priorities already established.

In the third place, the Aztecs, lived in a highly ritualized and controlled universe, where both relations among persons and relations with the earth could be regulated by precise ritual. At times this was bloody and awful, as in the large place given to human sacrifice in their culture, though Todorov rightly asks whether this practice could be any worse than what is done by the society laying claim to knowledge, which defends itself by the massacre of what is known but not appreciated, or

indeed seen as alien to prior interests. The Aztecs had no language or
rite that could account for what was happening to them or for describing European ways. Hence, they were without the power to assimilate
this new experience into their life, and without defense against a more
precise knowledge.

For a fourth example, Todorov turns to a period of some decades
later, by looking at the *Historia de las Indias de la Nueva España*, written
by Diego Duran between 1576 and 1581. He finds this history extraordinarily accurate in its descriptions of both Christian religion and the
religion of the indigenous peoples. It is here that he looks for a reading
of the problems of cultural *métissage*, or the attempt to blend cultures
within Christianity and in the forging of a new society. Duran was
thoroughly opposed to religious syncretism and would not have thought
much of the principle that anything can be adopted from cultural
heritages which is not opposed to the truths of the Christian faith. He
thought, perhaps rightly, that no ritual, no cultural expression, however
large or small, could be assimilated without assimilating something of
the religious beliefs and values of that culture. On the other hand, the
same Duran could draw finely worked analogies on matters religious
between indigenous rites and beliefs and Spanish-Catholic rites and
beliefs. Here Todorov finds that careful and sympathetic understanding
of the other stood as a warning against building a relationship of
métissage, which for Duran could only mean disfigurement (however
attractive in appearance), dislocation, and inner conflict. Taking
Duran's warning into account, today we might find a different response,
since given his time he could not expect the power of Native American
religiosity and religious expression to become the primary medium
through which the response to the gospel and the appropriation of the
gospel in beliefs, rites and ethics could be inherited into their culture.

Thus we have the four paradigms of relation to the other from the
story of conquest: knowledge falsified by prejudgment, knowledge used
in the interests of subjugation, knowledge so tightly bound that it cannot
assimilate what is alien, and knowledge that serves as a warning against
superficial communion. In Todorov's interpretation, these four kinds of
knowing and relating are not simply to be spurned as inadequate. He
contends that they are ever operative when cultures meet. They cannot
simply be dismissed as mistaken but must be allowed to show the
irresolvable perplexities, inherent to a situation where cultures must
need converse. It is the failure to take note of the perplexities or the
attempt to shake free of them in a more liberal openness of heart, that
perverts the encounter, turning into one kind or another of competition
and violence.

We know the carnage that resulted from the failures in the story recounted by Todorov, who also usefully reminds us that it is only in the particular, as in the story of the Mayan woman, that we can let ourselves be grasped by the issues with any force. There is an awesome risk in being "other to" without accepting to be addressed "by the other," without finding a map to locate the other, not as the same as oneself, but as different and as making a demand on oneself by the very right to be distinct and different.

Todorov himself appeals to the thought of Emmanuel Levinas on an ethics of other as a basis of action and indeed of ontology.[24] In other words, with the failure of metaphysical and mythic worldviews, caught in the human subject's incomprehension of its own self, with the collapse of ideologies, and with the loss of maps on which to chart a course, there remains in the human conscience and in the conscience of races, the ethical imperative of assenting to the existence and rights of the other as other. The assent is now exacted in the acknowledgment of having denied not only rights but existence to this other. The other summons one to communion, solidarity, across otherness, but in the very summons judges, reveals the evil of suppressing otherness in self-interest or in the pursuit of some misguided universalism. There can be no invitation to communion, or response to this invitation, except across the bridge of judgment and confession.

Communion and reconciliation across cultures is not a matter of simply acknowledging that the other has rights, but of leaving the other as other, of refusing to impose any similarity upon the other in order to open the way to conversation and communion. But such recognition, conversation and communion is not possible except through the process of letting history and the realities of the present summon us to the bar, questioning the values on whose basis so many of us have won our very existence. The communion is all the more difficult given our submersion in the excess of evil revealed to us through the symbols of Auschwitz, Berlin, Budapest, Saigon and Los Angeles, and through the necessity of living in the shadows of the slave plantations of Virginia and the chaos of Nueva España.

Faced with the impasse of meeting the other face-to-face, the Jewish and the Christian voice address us out of an otherness that is awful and compelling, reminding us that God belongs with the other whose reality has been suppressed and discarded, despised and rejected. God can be known only through the mediation of a servant who is embodied amid the excess of evil, in the rejectedness of the rejected, in the otherness of the not-a-people.

This carries over into the covenant of otherness, the prohibition of false images, that constitutes the basic imperative that Yahweh gave to the people of Israel about the address to God. God's being imaged in any earthly form for worship would deny the divine presence among and in a not-a-people. In somewhat parallel fashion, though most otherly, the French philosopher Stanislas Breton sees in the cross of Christ that fundamental critique of any myth, metaphysics, or religion that would confuse the divine reality and the divine presence with themselves.[25]

For Levinas, whose people suffered the holocaust, the word that heals and reconciles in a time of the excess of evil cannot be spoken except in the prophetic testimony that emerges from the ethical demand of acknowledging the other in the judgment that it passes upon its offenders.[26] It is on this ground that one can engage in the *action pour un monde qui vient*. For Christians, this means embracing Christ in the form of the outcast, the rejected other of our communal lives. It is from this that salvation and communion in one Spirit can come.

This is an extraordinarily new universal viewpoint within which to encompass multiple reality and diversity. It hits up against the tendency in our prevailing European culture to look for ways of making realities converge, whether this be in a perennial philosophy, a turn to the subject, a cultural anthropology, a history of religions, or a sociology of religion. In looking for ways of comprehending the other, or meeting with the other, or even embracing the other, we turn too readily to what we can retrieve from our own very particular, contingent, narrowly constituted cultural memory. How then can we move to a situation in which the demands of the other to be taken as other have priority, and still make the response core to our particular identities, finding such a demand vital to the reconstruction of our particular memories?

ARE THERE COMMON WAGERS?

Beyond this respect for the other as other, and the willingness to let ourselves be judged by the other whom we have refused, there is inevitably the question of whether different cultural groups agree to some common reference in the process of their coming together in communion. This means a kind of commonly accepted wager, one which each group takes from within its own distinctive cultural memory when this is challenged by the other. In the church in this country, formed as it is out of many peoples and cultures, there are two such wagers. The first is civic, the second religious.

I put the civic first, because that is what actually brings people, even Christians, together on the same soil. It is the wager that goes, loosely it must be admitted, under the name of being a U.S. American. It is the wager that communion can be found in a varied (not univocal) retrieval of the hope and purpose expressed in the pursuit of happiness, with a guarantee of freedom and justice for all. The influence of cultures other than Eurocentered, once given their voice, can recast that pursuit in new terms.

For Christians, the second wager is that offered in putting one's faith in Jesus Christ. Such faith has to be recovered as common beyond the particularities of the specific cultural expressions given to it in the course of time, even as these are reconstrued for a better understanding of what was at stake, and indeed what was conceded, in their formulation. The common wager into which all have to be invited in order to seek communion together on the basis of that wager, includes three references. The first is to the memory of Jesus Christ as this comes to us first and foremost in the formulation of the gospels, whatever we have done in our particular cultures to seek to understand and read beneath or through that formulation, and as it is kept alive in Christian worship, in all its diversity. The second is to the power of God's own Spirit living within the church, working through a variety of cultural forms, to bring to life the power of Christ's memory and to bring all believers together in communion. The third reference is to the hope of reconciliation when overshadowed, or overwrought, by the denial of the other and the excess of evil which that brings with it.

PHYSIOGNOMY OF A MULTICULTURAL CHURCH

With such reflections in mind, is it possible to give some tentative strategy for a local U.S. American church that would lead it to self-realization as a communion between communities of diverse cultural expressions? Though only an outline can be offered, it is given in the hope of pointing to important areas of investigation and potential development.

POPULAR DEVOTION AS A LOCUS THEOLOGICUS

Reflection on popular devotion is vital, both in understanding the variety of cultures across the nation and in understanding how the Spirit of God moves among peoples. It belongs, in short, to what is broadly called the incarnation of the gospel or of the church. It has to be taken into account in order to understand the forms in which the Christian memory takes shape, and how it relates people and groups to their own and to surrounding social reality. What this has shown through a study of the past has been recalled. It has to be developed to include a study of the present, where Latin American, Haitian, Laotian or Vietnamese Catholics keep their own folk religions alive, even while letting them be newly shaped by the encounter with the U.S. American way of life.

For Catholic communities, it is in great part the observance and study of popular religiosity which shows how much groups differ in their respective reliance on the written word and on ritual. It is also this which shows how they differ in the priority given either to communion with the earth or to the achievement of communion between human persons. It is particularly important to note such differences in the contrast between groups of European origin and cultures having their roots on other continents, including this one. When the differences are suppressed or remain unacknowledged or undervalued, they lead to the grief and futility inherent to overlooking the irresolvable perplexities inherent in bringing cultures together, or in recognizing that empathy can exist only where diversity is paramount.

LITURGICAL TRAVAIL

Liturgical travail has its own revelations to offer. Here we see the risks either of maintaining an unnecessary ecclesiastical paradigm or of seeking refuge in a mushy and inorganic liturgical polyculture. There are moments when this jumbling is more apparent, as for example when following a black preacher and a gospel choir, there comes the dull recital of a Roman canon. From this very example, we see what happens when the ecclesiastical paradigm persists.

All convergence of diverse cultures in the liturgy, however, is not pointless. In northwest Washington, American-born children of Haitian parents learn the responses of the mass in French, so that they can serve at the altar, even though their own language is a happy usage of English in the neighborhood and of Creole in the home. Rather than simply finding the use of liturgical French amusing, it is better to ask what is the intent of a triple cultural rooting in French Catholicism, Haitian family and American values. The example I have given is one that concerns a threefold focus of the same people. This is quite different to a weekly liturgical jamboree which attempts to bring in features and expressions of every cultural group represented in the region. Answers do not come easily within this difficult struggle, but one can see the need to go beyond the days of one Roman liturgy, and even beyond the attempts to have one universal liturgy for each language, much less a regular mixture of different cultural expressions.

The principal reason for diverse liturgies is not that each culture has its own religious modes of expression, though this is pertinent.[27] It is rather that the memories to be harbored within the memory of Christ's pasch are different, the passages to be negotiated within his passage are different, and the hopes nourished in the hope of his rule are different.

Black Americans and Native Americans cannot celebrate and

hope, except in the memory of their respective holocausts. To them more than to anyone else apply the words of the recent inaugural poem:

> Lift up your faces, you have a piercing need
> For this bright morning dawning for us.
> History, despite its wrenching pain,
>   Cannot be unlived, but if faced
> With courage, need not be lived again.[28]

Irish, Polish, Czech, German, Italian Catholics of the third or fourth generation born in this country, though they have shed deep political or cultural links with the countries of their forebears, retain memories of a difficult transition and of a citizenship won in struggle. Haitians, Vietnamese, Laotians, Guatemalans, Nicaraguans, coming now to this country, remember the travail of their homelands and in negotiating their own passage to a new land, hold out hopes for a passage out of oppression and misery for the countries from which they come.

In the place in northwest Washington to which I have referred, Haitians pray for the success of Father Aristide and for the refugees in U.S. camps, even as they pray for jobs in this country and contract marriages outside their own racial confines. Hill people fleeing from Laos who embraced the faith preached by French and Italian missionaries have more recently fled the hostile environment of Philadelphia for the more open spaces of Washington state, but still find that they keep their faith and their hope alive by lay-led weekly devotional gatherings rather than by churchgoing, even as they write constant appeals to exiled missionaries to come and bring them the sacraments, which they simply do not experience in English language churches.

Because these memories and hopes are so varied, the way in which Christ's memory is kept differs, with a different tonality to the story of his pasch and different ritual movement, prayers and songs that ensue creatively from such a memory. That is the basic ground for different liturgies, which are then celebrated in varieties of aesthetic cultural forms that best embody for a people its memories and hopes.

Some of the tensions which Todorov notes in his work in the encounter between cultures show up strongly in the history of people's religious and ritual expression, whether popular or liturgical. These tensions may be listed as follows: (a) between the independence of cultures and the effort to constitute some kind of cultural fusion, taking bits out of different cultures to mix them together, in the hope that all can reap the greatest benefits of two distinct worlds; (b) between the forms of communication and traditions of belief, knowledge and value that rely primarily on writing, and the communication that is effected principally through ritual or oral literacy; (c) between the precedence given to establishing communication between living human groups, or within human groups, and that given to remaining in communion with the earth or the cosmos and the powers and spirits that inhabit it, however they might be named or imaged; (d) between the desire to identify with the other in sympathetic understanding and common destiny, thus making light of the differences, and the need to keep distinction from the other to the fore, lest worlds and interests be submerged and distorted in some kind of confused and confusing, albeit good-hearted, exchange.

Keeping these tensions in mind serves as a warning against a cultural fusion which does not organically develop from peoples' lives. It is not suggested that the time for segregation is to be given new life in the interests of diversity. Though new rites emerge, hospitality to all-comers has to be the practice of Catholic liturgy. To exercise hospitality, however, is to receive the other as other and to let others see us as other. It is not reducible to the bonhomie of meeting visitors at the door and inviting them to stand up and announce their names. Stories can be shared out of otherness, faith journeys in Christ can be narrated, diverse experiences of the self may be shared in ritual. The diversity manifests both the richness beyond imagining of the forms of humanity and of God's being in the world. It also manifests to each one and to each community the other hidden in the self and not yet imagined or named. In the present, otherness continues to face us with its ultimate diversity and unnameability, leaving final communion as an eschatological hope rather than as something to be reproduced in the conformity of a common rite and universal narrative in which all differences merge into a single structured identity.

Within the circle of the particular community, and from within the circle of hospitality offered to the other, there can never be absent the other who has not been given the power to tell one's own story. The forgotten have to be remembered, the marginal included, the suppressed given voice. The stories and voices and victims heard off-stage have to be invited into keeping the memory of Christ, so that the empathy of faith is not a closed circle of faith-dwellers.

Within such communion in diversity, to prevent isolation and encourage communion within otherness, there need to be periodic (not, however, weekly) celebrations of diversity. These are intercultural rituals that are designed as such, when the church celebrates its manifold richness and its liberating eschatological hope. Such celebration, for example, might very well mark the feast of Pentecost or the common celebration of saints who have become popular across cultures.

For all and in all liturgies, the ultimately unifying eschatological place of hope is the common communion table, where in Christ's body and blood Christians are offered forgiveness of sins, immortality, and a new heaven and earth whose giving lies in the hands of the glorious Christ who for the present time continues to find being in the diversity of many communions.

TRANSITIONS

Passage and transition belong intimately to liturgy, reminding us that more is needed than liturgy or popular devotion to help people negotiate a variety of social and cultural transitions. Neighborhood support systems, educational opportunities, helping with immigration formalities, become the concern of cultural and faith communities, in ways analogous to what we have learned from the stories of an earlier immigrant church. For African-Americans and Native Americans, the churches can provide support systems that allow them to take their own power and find their own voice in expressing their own otherness, despite the past. For new immigrants, there is still the effort to negotiate the dual commitment to being in a new country and remaining faithful to the old. The transition to which people are empowered by the presence of the Spirit in their lives is not, however, one of mere accommodation to the social fabric or the prevailing system of values. Besides expressing the power of the gospel in their own particular cultural expression and practice, they can give new and distinctive expression to the hope and possibilities that come from what this land has to offer.

SOCIAL ETHIC

American Catholics are in constant need of a better defined social ethic, in which the issue of the other is met and dialogue is the means. That this can be at least moderately successful we know from the examples of composing the pastoral letters on the economy and on peace, as we know how badly it can fail from the unhappy effort to negotiate a pastoral letter on the role of women in church and society. At root in the breakdown of dialogue in this last instance there was the falsification of otherness in the adoption of nonverifiable but ideologically tenacious gender differentiations.

The close interaction between cultural expression and economic and political life is of central importance. Peoples cannot be asked to adopt or assimilate a social ethic given to them, but out of the vitality of their own cultural roots and self-expression, out of their own cultural modelling of the world and society, they develop an ethical viewpoint comprising both values and strategies. The economic system and work ethic of U.S. American life is still tributary to European modernity. Sometimes church leadership seems inclined simply to help other peoples find a secure place within this pattern of work and profit, or to fight for their rights according to the model of an ego-centered bill of rights. It is harder to work as a community to effect a change in the public domain, which will reflect how people in their culturally embodied Christian faith see the advent of God's reign in this world.

In forging a social ethic out of diversity, it is time to take up the economic issues raised by the bishops' pastoral on this topic in the form of an ongoing dialogue. The matter of the feminization of poverty, for example, still needs discussion and action, and its roots in several cultures common among Catholics considered. The concerns of new immigrants, health care, and the like, all involve conversing and acting with each other across the boundaries of race, language and culture, not simply to adapt but to make new.

These matters require the kind of ethic that is promoted not so much by teaching as by dialogue and common action. No social ethic is possible in our day without recognizing that it is to be constructed across the bridge of reconciliation. No present ethic is possible for a people who refuse to face the injustices of the past and to see what has carried over into the present out of this. In short, a social ethic must be able to bear the weight of the past, along with the promise of new voices, and construct itself accordingly.

CHURCH STRUCTURES

Diversity in national, diocesan, parish and community organization, and in exercise of ministries, is a must, which means not ceding to the desire for uniform policies. The church as a human community is not best conceived as grouped around one center, but as a communion of communities which in its earthly realization and organization is polycentric. The only sacramental center is the communion table of Christ's body and blood, just as the center of truth is the word of the scripture. Because they all relate to the one Christ who is present among them in sacrament and word, diverse cultural communities seek communion with each other from within the cultural diversity of this one presence, of whose particular form as embodiment of the rejected other a word has already been said.

It is through adequate structure and organization that dialogue and action, joining diverse groups together, can be promoted. Some realities of the past, such as the Interracial Council of an earlier period of church life in this century, still offer helpful models. It is, however, in bringing different communities together, in allowing the interaction of a polycentric church, rather than putting all under one bureaucracy, that the comparative newness would lie. The dialogue may be difficult, especially in facing the heritage of the offense of some groups against others, but its engagement is a necessity without equal.

FUNDAMENTAL PRINCIPLE

Finally, there is a fundamental theological principle which under-girds the application of all the others. At times of critical change, when much has to be put into question if the church is to remain faithful to its mission, some overriding principle that puts all else in focus is needed. This is what Martin Luther did with the principle of the primacy of the Word when he sought to reform the faith in calling much of the still dominant medieval system of practice and piety into question.

What can serve the Catholic Church today in a similar way in renewing its own mission is its faith in the manifold presence of the Spirit and of the living Christ among believers, of all and many different cultures. It is comparable to the vision that Peter had at the houses of Simon and Cornelius when he realized how God had not denied to the Gentiles what had been given to the Jews. As life-force for a multicultural church there is thus the possibility of retrieving the many ways in which Christ and the Spirit are present in the church, all within cultural diversity, beneath or prior to the rituals and institutions which give life its canonical forms. It is at this prior level that we can most truly discover the popular language of religiosity and the ways in which the Spirit works among people of any cultural heritage in bringing them to embrace Christ, within their world. The witness of a life of faith and charity, the exercise of charisms, the telling of stories, mutual rendering of services, a variety of ritual activities, devotional appeals to God, Christ, Mary or the saints, all exist in some measure prior to and beneath, or within the cracks of, canonical language, doctrines, rites and institutions. Too often the canonical has suppressed them, or marginalized them, or even styled them heterodox. Their retrieval counts for much in the recognition of the other, in the sounding of cultural voices, and in the commerce of polycentric communion, as also in the forging of different canonical boundaries and institutions, which can serve this polycentric model of being church.

CONCLUSION

Unity/communion can be assured only in commitment to one another, in the commitment of different cultural groups to support the other in the struggle for a full human life and in the wager of faith. This commitment can be made only in the memory of the stories of victims (holocaust of persons, holocaust of cultures), and in the growing realization of the memory of Jesus Christ as a dangerous memory. Catholic identity has always served people to find their place in secular life, without loosing identity and culture, and in taking their place in the nation forged, *e pluribus unum*. Unhappily, that has often been done over against each other and in rivalry, even within the common appeal to one faith. Today, it has to be tried in commitment to the other, on a new ethical basis, where this, in the memory of the Lord, begins to define our very being, and compels all to hearken to the stories which must not be forgotten, and listen to the voices of those who still live in the shadow of those stories.

This paper concludes with words intended by David Tracy for the global church but applicable to our own polycentric, and world-embracing, reality: "In a parched space and empty time, the conversation must remain critical. The response cannot be one of mere modern liberal guilt, but of Christian responsibility—capable of responding, critically when necessary, to the other as other and not as a projection of ourselves. The result could be a new solidarity in the struggle for the true time of justice and a communal, theological naming of the present in a polycentric world and a global church led by [these] new voices."[29]

Diana L. Hayes

RESPONSE TO
DAVID POWER, O.M.I.

I agree with Professor David Power that the theme encompassed in his title seems to imply that the major concern with which we are confronted is to keep unity rather than addressing the prior need to "work toward pluralism with adequate respect for cultural diversity."[1] Professor Power notes correctly that the question of unity is one that comes much later, after a full and complete discussion and exploration of cultural diversity in all of its diverse meanings. His presentation is divided into five major sections: a) naming the moment; b) remembering from the past; c) ethnicity and religion; d) the question of the other; and, e) physiognomy of a multicultural church. My response is organized along these same lines.

Power begins by noting the challenge of multiculturalism in the introductory section of his paper, defining it as "communion across cultures, within a larger church or society to which all belong."[2] He sees the challenge as "not inculturation and pluralism in churches across the world, but communion within a local church that is facing up to its own inner cultural pluralism."[3] He does so, I would note, in a very tentative and almost fearful fashion without coming to grips completely with the source or nature of that fear. His working hypothesis is that unity (by which I assume he means the above noted communion) "is achieved and maintained through a communion in otherness, developed,...out of an ethic of the other."[4] This ethic is borrowed from Emmanuel Levinas and Johann Baptist Metz which leads to the first of my concerns regarding Power's approach. It seems to be overly centered in the thought and praxis of European theology rather than rooted in the thought and praxis of Americans in all of their cultural and theological diversity. I will discuss this point in greater detail in my response. Suffice it to say, however, that such a beginning seems to already narrow the parameters of discussion, limiting them to avenues and directions which are not reflective of all participants.

· Rather than asking "...how do we begin to find the ways to acknowledge the otherness of the other, and to consider the present in the frank light of the suppression of otherness in the past?"[5] should we not start by examining the language that we use, seeking terms that are less isolated from and extrinsic to actual dialogue? To speak solely in terms of the other without specifically naming those others, regardless of the possible repetitiveness of doing so, is to continue to deny a human face to those who have, as he notes, been rendered invisible and marginalized; whose cultures have not been treated with the respect they are due and whose suitability, therefore, as a fertile bed for the inculturation and fostering of Christianity has been denied.

Naming the Moment. Early in his presentation of a church in search of its mission, Power quotes from the black bishop's pastoral letter[6] on the diversity of blacks. My initial reaction was to see this as an acknowledgement and recognition of blacks' (a significant group of others in this country) ability and authority to name themselves from within their own context in all of its dimensions. Needed is more expression of these heretofore ignored voices in scholarly papers not just by African-Americans or other representatives of these voices but by theologians from other races and ethnicities as well in order for dialogue to truly take place on an equitable basis.[7] For it is not only theologians who are representative of the marginalized who must speak and are empowered to do so, but it is also incumbent upon those who have represented the dominant theological voices to learn of, recognize, and include these voices within their own research and writing as African-American, Asian, Hispanic and women theologians have necessarily done for so long. This should be done not to authenticate or legitimate these voices but to recognize that authenticity and legitimacy which exists at every level of scholarship.

Having presented the black voices, however, the presentation seems to then deny the authority and authenticity first intimated. The passages quoted present the black bishops' understanding of the universality of Catholicism as well as the diversity of the African-American cultural heritage as one which is African, Haitian, Latin American and West Indian.[8] However, they are interpreted as the bishops helping black Catholics to make the cultural and social transitions which the moment, that of the recognition by the church's leadership to hear and respond to the call of new voices, requires.[9] It is stated that the bishops are asking how to mediate between the diverse heritages which exist among black Americans, including those of Catholicism and being American. Yet I read this quite differently. The black bishops are not seeking to help black Catholics as former parishes and pastors helped new immigrants; rather, they are alerting the church, especially the predominantly white Anglo and European dominant group, that they (the latter group) are the ones who need to make this transition. The black bishops' letter cannot be equated with other pastoral letters except perhaps with that of the Hispanic bishops. They have also realized that because their perspective, their frame of reference, their cultural understanding is usually missing or inaccurately reflected in these other letters, they must then speak for themselves. They are, in their letters, asserting the fact that we are not, as blacks or as Hispanics, or even Native Americans, new to the church or to this country, but as Africans have been a part of it from its very beginning and have also been present in the United States, though never truly permitted to see themselves as actually belonging. Therefore, they have an entirely different self-understanding, historical experience and cultural heritage which has made them who they are today, one arising from the reality of centuries-long marginalization within the church.[10] Thus, it is not a question of "what could this new cultural awareness mean for blacks and Native Americans who are looking for their place, if the church can accept solidarity with the American past in which their reality was denied";[11] it is rather a question, first, of when will the church accept this solidarity with peoples who have, historically, always been told what and where their place is in the church and American society. Such peoples are now recovering and discovering their own place, whether they receive officially sanctioned permission or not. Whether the church can or cannot accept this is a moot point. It will have to accept it if it is to remain faithful to the gospel values it has historically proclaimed in a church and society which in the next century, will be one that is predominantly Hispanic as well as Asian, African-American, and Native American, rather than Anglo-Saxon or European.[12]

It is thus necessary in our discussion of this particular moment to look at events in the United States rather than at Europe for self-definition and redefinition. It is no longer viable to look first or solely to European constructs such as those set forth by Jean François Lyotard[13] in which to imagine ourselves. The "turn to the subject" was a European construct which, as noted, failed, for a number of reasons including, perhaps, an inability to define and understand subjectivity in all of its connotations. What is not noted, however, is that the "loss of the subject" is not one that is new to African, Hispanic/Latino, Asian, and Native Americans who have never had the freedom or autonomy to be subjects of their own history but have, instead, always been seen as objects in the histories of others. Therefore, such new awareness on the part of Anglo and Euro-Americans is not wholly applicable to them. It is the framing of a question which is not, in actuality, a question for persons of color, for the poor, or in many cases for women because it restricts and limits. Rather, what is needed is a question that frees and opens the dialogue to new and different perspectives from the margins.

Remembering from the Past. In this section, Power speaks (in Metz's terms) of the retrieval of dangerous memories, those of conquest and oppression while referencing the spiritual holocaust of African-Americans. Here, again, can be seen one of the consequences of referring to sources that speak *about* the other, namely African-Americans, rather than consulting sources that originate from and are delivered in the voices of those faceless and nameless ones. The result is a failure to fully acknowledge the ability of the other to speak for or to provide material worthy of inclusion. To speak in terms of a spiritual holocaust for African-Americans without referring to the actual physical holocaust that took place makes their experience and their interpretation of that experience marginal. It must be remembered and reiterated that this holocaust was, indeed, not only spiritual but physical with millions of lives lost on the voyage to the slave ships, on the middle passage itself, and in the new world. Power relies upon a work by Jon Butler[14] which speaks of this spiritual holocaust, noting, incorrectly, that its results were the permanent destruction of "traditional African religious systems as systems in North America" leaving the slaves "bereft of traditional collective religious practices"; thereby paving the way for a Christianization of the slaves whose "first appearance more closely resembled European expressions of Christianity than might ever be the case again."[15] No! Theories such as these have been long discarded, especially by black historians who have recognized the carryover of many distinctive African religious traditions in the culture of African-Americans, both religious and secular, despite deliberate efforts to destroy them. These new historians have also noted the unique contributions that African slaves made to Christianity, resulting in a transformation of Christianity in new and liberating ways. The religion was Christian, but it was not European: it was black and African.[16]

There is need of a more in-depth and contextualized analysis and presentation of those diverse voices in the culture(s) of the United States which have, historically, been absent, not only from theological discussions, but from most scholarly discourse because they have been relegated to the sidelines as overly pastoral or experiential.

Further development is needed, especially a more complete presentation of the actual stories that should not be forgotten, stories which speak of conquest and violence but, more importantly, also of survival, hope, and persistent faith. Such stories presented in new words and different contexts could provide us with new language for speaking to and with each other about this painful but subversive memory of our past. This is not necessarily the responsibility of the theologians alone, but if we are to truly dialogue on the basis of a shared desire for mutual understanding, it is necessary for all of us to learn the stories of these voiceless and invisible ones. They have for too long a time had to learn the stories of the dominant group to the loss and denial of their own.

Ethnicity and Religion. Power provides an excellent history of the immigrant church in the United States while acknowledging the ethnic experience as a legitimate source of theological reflection.[17] A similar statement regarding the experience of those who did not immigrate willingly or were already present in this land should be added. Is the previous section on remembering the past a presentation of the experience of those marginalized in the church because of race and is it now contrasted with the experience of ethnic Americans in the church? If so, again, it becomes an even greater imperative to locate the experience of the former as a legitimate source of theological reflection despite the constraints placed on the church in its own self-development. The Catholic Church's failure to evangelize the freed slaves after the Civil War, despite the strong recommendations of the Vatican, resulted in the loss of many blacks who were already Catholic and the rejection of those who would have converted to the church. Its preferential option for lapsed ethnic immigrant Catholics instead must be addressed, for this memory has continued impact on black Catholics and would-be converts today.[18]

The fact that this section is strongly grounded in the immigrant experience, revealing its richness, diversity and reemerging self-awareness, is more than likely a reflection of the author's own familiarity with this experience. It confirms the need for scholars to broaden their research sources so that they can adequately present the experience of those with whom they do not share a personal or contextual affiliation and who are still, too often, absent from the dialogues taking place.

The Question of the Other. This section, for me, was the most challenging of Power's presentation. This is due to my inability to comprehend a discussion of the other in terms which never truly name that otherness in its fullness. This is consistent with the way in which theology has been historically developed and presented. It contributes to the denial of face, of humanity, of visibility, to marginalized groups, thereby perpetuating their state of marginality. The discussion of the other is an interesting analysis, in the abstract, which raises several questions of importance for any viable discussion on the issue of multiculturalism and the Roman Catholic Church in the United States.[19]

Is it not imperative that we begin to put human faces on the others so that rather than discussing them from within the safety zone of abstractness, we are forced to confront them in the reality of their suppression and dehumanization? It is so much easier and less grievous to talk of the other as a voiceless, faceless depersonalized entity than to have to deal with the messy details of that other's actual and often painfully human reality.

In discussing the other in terms of the local church, that is, the church in the United States, are there not home-grown voices which can speak to, for, and about the experience themselves? How can and do we enable and empower the others to speak for themselves as other, rather than relying on European and Euro-American interpretations of that otherness? Must we not name ourselves and our fears of the radical and, therefore, subversive differences that they bring? Must we not allow those others whom we fear, more for what has been done to them than for what they have done themselves, to name and claim a heritage and experience uniquely different but equally viable rather than having those who do not share or participate in that heritage do it for them? Is this not why we are experiencing the emergence of liberation and/or liberating theologies in the United States? The others, so long discussed, dissected and analyzed in the abstract and in their own absence, are raising their voices and proclaiming the validity of their own African-American, Asian, Hispanic/Latino and Native American existence as real, as valid, as present in our reality as church and religion. Where and what are the stories of their experience of the church and its myriad manifestations in their lives, in their own voice, in their own language?

How do we create and/or develop a language that is new and uniquely of the United States in which to communicate with each other, breaking down the barrier of old and new hatreds, old and new memories, old and new fears? The language of Todorov and Levinas, of Metz and others is the language of the old world. When do we accept and assume the responsibility of creating new words, new methods, new understandings, in which to express both our otherness and our sameness to one another, in order to build that communion and solidarity to which we are rightly called as followers of Christ? Is it not time, not simply for a new political theology but for a liberating and liberated theology from the underside? Is it not time for a truly contextual theology, even perhaps discordantly polyvocal and polycentric, which lifts up the absent and unheard voices, contexts, and experiences that bring new languages, new understandings, new analyses to new and challengingly different questions?

Physiognomy of a Multicultural Church. It is in the final section of Power's paper that the human voice, in all of its diversity, is finally heard. This section successfully pulls together much of what appeared to be lacking in the earlier sections. However, the absence of a fuller discussion of the issue of racism as a barrier to the emergence of such a church, along with the issues of gender and class and the passing on of the ethos of racism in this society, must be noted critically and addressed.

I thank Professor Power for a presentation that has challenged and stimulated my thinking on this important issue which will continue to confront the Catholic Church in the United States for years to come. His presentation provides an impetus to continue the dialogue that has just begun. It brings to that dialogue many of the problems and concerns that are to be found in the continuing dialogue on the pros and cons of multiculturalism, inculturation, assimilation, integration, and polycentrism. It especially raises those concerns of recognizing and naming the other and empowering the other to name themselves, of retrieving and owning the subversive and dangerous memories of this country's past, and of enabling and empowering those whose cultures have not been recognized as legitimate or fertile seed-beds for the growth of Christianity. Most importantly, the paper calls to our attention that those who have in the past controlled our society and our church in this country, no longer have the luxury to analyze and redefine their theology in order eventually, at a time of their choosing, to acknowledge and accommodate new voices and expressions. Rather, the time has now come and is, actually, overdue for those new voices to articulate their own understandings as paradigms for us all.

As Martin Luther King, Jr. noted in his *Letter from the Birmingham Jail*, power is never given up freely; it must be challenged, pushed, forced, nudged, and coerced to recognize that the other does, indeed, have a human face; those faces and the realities that lie behind them are what we must relate to and with if a living and enlivening multiculturalism is to emerge within our midst.[20]

Peter C. Phan

CONTEMPORARY THEOLOGY AND INCULTURATION IN THE UNITED STATES

John Paul II has emphasized, in almost apocalyptic tone, the urgent need to relate faith and culture: "I have considered the Church's dialogue with the cultures of our time to be a vital area, one in which the destiny of the world at the end of this twentieth century is at stake."[1] To lend focus to my discussion of the topic, I will limit it to the United States of America. In the first part of the essay, I will lay out the theological issues connected with inculturation.[2] In the second part I will survey some recent attempts at inculturating the Christian faith in the United States. In the third section I will broach some of the issues which, in my judgment, still beg for further clarifications and reflections.

INCULTURATION OF THE CHRISTIAN FAITH AND THEOLOGY

THE CONTEXTUAL NATURE OF ALL THEOLOGIES

If the theologian's essential task is taken to be an imaginative and critical mediation between the Christian faith and contemporary culture, then inculturation is inevitably an intrinsic element of the theological method. Of course, such an assertion becomes self-evident only after the concept of inculturation has been elucidated.[3] In general, it may be said that Christian theology as well as mission, as each is carried out in a new land, is marked by the following trajectory: in the first phase, foreign philosophical and theological categories, elaborated in the missionaries' culture, dominate the local catechetical, liturgical and theological scene as these are imported and translated into the indigenous language and employed to communicate the gospel message. Pastorally, this technique can be termed functional substitution, by which a Christian meaning is substituted for a non-Christian one.

Then comes the stage of acculturation in which the Christian faith acquires elements of the host culture which, in its turn, adopts elements of the Christian thought and way of life. Acculturation, as such, is not necessarily cultural alienation. Such borrowing of concepts, symbols, myths and rituals may bring about the enrichment both of the Christian faith and the host culture. However, such a mutual borrowing still operates at a superficial level. Its basic strategy is that of adaptation or accommodation of the foreign religion to a local culture. The Christian faith still remains a sub-culture within the host culture and not infrequently a particular brand of Christianity, in this case, a Eurocentric one, exercises a dominating role on the local church. Not rarely, too, both the Roman bureaucracy and the hierarchy of the local church are suspicious of a more radical measure of adaptation for fear of the loss of Christian identity. The result is ecclesial colonialism.

Lastly, if and when the local church has achieved sufficient autonomy from the sending church, both intellectually and organizationally, and its members, both lay and clerical, have taken over the task of evangelizing not only individuals but their own culture as such, then inculturation begins to take place.[4] By inculturation, then, is meant, in the words of Arij A. R. Crollius, "the integration of the Christian experience of a local Church into the culture of its people, in such a way that this experience not only expresses itself in elements of this culture, but becomes a force that animates, orients and innovates this culture so as to create a new unity and communion, not only within the culture in question but also as an enrichment of the Church universal."[5]

If the above description of the three-step process of inculturation is substantially correct,[6] then there can be no gainsaying that all theologies, which critically and systematically mediate the Christian faith to culture, are necessarily contextual and that inculturation is an essential part of the theological method. Douglas John Hall has made an impassioned plea for the contextuality of all theology:

> Contextuality in theology means that the *form* of faith's self-understanding is always determined by the historical configuration in which the community of belief finds itself. It is this world which insinuates the questions, the concerns, the frustrations and alternatives, the possibilities and impossibilities by which the *content* of the faith must be shaped and reshaped, and finally confessed. Conscious and thoughtful involvement of the disciple community in its cultural setting is thus the *conditio sine qua non* of its right appropriation of its theological discipline.[7]

The reasons for this inevitable contextuality of theology are, according to Hall, threefold: theology is a human enterprise; its task is to speak of the living God and of God's relation to a dynamic creation; and its purpose is to assist the church's confession. As a human construct, theology reflects the sociocultural context of those who make it. As discourse about the living God to a dynamic creation, theology must imitate God's incarnational movement into a particular history; and as a means for the church's confession, theology will be helpful only if it knows from the inside the world to which the church preaches the gospel.[8]

All theologies, then, are necessarily local theologies, ineluctably contextualized, indigenized, on the way to full inculturation. There is no such a thing as Christian faith by itself (*fides qua*), existing pure and unalloyed in the depth of one's heart, in some prelinguistic or alinguistic state. Rather, like any human activity, the act of faith is historically and culturally conditioned, to a certain extent institutionalized, materially based, critically self-reflective, and formulated in terms intelligible to the people of a certain time and place.[9] Theologians, whose task is to mediate the Christian faith to culture, do not stand between a naked faith and culture; rather they stand between a culturally mediated faith of the past, including that embodied in the Bible and the official teachings of the church, and their own cultural context, and attempt to mediate that faith meaningfully to their contemporaries.[10]

Unfortunately, however, this inescapable contextuality of all theologies has not always been recognized, at least by their producers. For instance, nineteenth-century neo-scholastic theology, aided and abetted by the Cartesian notion of rationality and the Enlightenment model of universal reason, made imperious claims to universal validity and normativity, and sought to impose itself upon Christiandom by means of Leo XIII's encyclical *Aeterni Patris* (1879).[11]

Such colonialist pretensions have been rendered inconsequential by the paradigmatic shift in the understanding of culture which Bernard Lonergan described as the change from the classicist to the empirical understanding of culture. The classicist notion of culture views it as a universal and permanent human product normative for all people and all times. The modern, empirical notion of culture regards it as a nexus of meanings constituted by free and responsible incarnate subjects, differing from people to people, and capable of development and decay.[12] Needless to say, such a shift severely undermines the classicist claim for a particular culture's universality and normativeness and encourages the elaboration of local cultural worldviews.

Furthermore, it is generally recognized today that, as Jürgen Habermas and the sociology of knowledge have argued, human cognition is guided by interests that are located culturally, socially, economically, and politically.[13] Armed with such an analysis of human knowledge, liberation theologies of various stripes ruthlessly wield the hermeneutics of suspicion to unmask the oppressive ideologies under-lying the claim to universality of dominant consciousness.

Besides these historical and epistemological considerations, there is also another more practical endeavor that draws attention to the local character of all theologies, namely, Christian mission. In virtue of their calling and work, missionaries are constantly confronted with the task of translating the Christian faith into the idiom of an alien culture. This translation is not merely a linguistic rendering—either by formal or dynamic equivalence—of Greek or Latin or any other European language into the tongues of the peoples to be evangelized.[14] Nor is it confined to clothing the Christian kernel with a different husk, or to change the metaphor, to expressing the Christian substance in another form. Rather, and more radically, it is a planting or earthing of the Christian seed into the new soil of a particular culture, that is, a genuine inculturation.

This model of mission, supported by the worldwide struggle for decolonization, national independence, and economic development since the 1940s, bids farewell to the notion that there exists a universal theology, that is, the European one, to be exported to foreign lands with only cosmetic retouchings. Instead, in addition to the "three-selfs" as the aim of mission (self-government, self-support, and self-propagation), it advocates the construction of local theologies (self-theologizing) in and from the concrete context of a particular culture. Thus, in the recent past, different theologies have been formulated in various parts of the world on the basis of diverse sociopolitical and cultural situations: Latin America with its emphasis (though not exclusive) on social transforma-tion, Africa on plurality of anthropologies, and Asia on interreligious dialogue. As a result, the emerging ecclesial consciousness is one that Rahner has succinctly described as world church, namely, a church that has made the transition from a predominantly Hellenistic and European culture to the cultures of all peoples into which it must be inculturated and its theologies constructed.[15]

The foregoing observations serve to clarify the contextual nature of theology and to stress the need of attending to the cultural context in which theologizing is performed.[16] We now turn to the question of how contextualization of theology has been carried out in recent times.

MODELS OF CONTEXTUAL THEOLOGY

In his recent book, *Models of Contextual Theology*, Stephen Bevans offers a succinct description of the five models in which the contex-tualization of theology has been carried out in recent times.[17] As he sees it, four elements are involved in the inculturation of theology: on the one hand, the gospel message and tradition, and on the other hand, culture and social change.[18] The five models differ among themselves according to the emphasis they place either on fidelity to the first two elements (gospel message and tradition) or adaptation to the second two elements (culture and social change).[19]

The first model, labeled translation model, is the most conservative of all the five. It stresses fidelity to the Christian message. It presupposes that all cultures, despite their diversities, possess the same basic structure and that divine revelation is primarily a communication of truths in propositional form. These truths or meanings, decoded from their cultural-dependent expressions, constitute the supracultural gospel core that can be translated by functional or dynamic equivalence into the idioms and categories of other cultures. Theologizing in cross-cultural perspectives consists mainly in decontextualizing the Christian message and recontextualizing it in the forms of other cultures.[20]

At the opposite end of the spectrum is the anthropological model. It privileges identification with culture and social change. It views divine revelation not as a body of supracultural truths but as a process of God's self-communication taking place in each and every culture. Theologizing in cross-cultural perspectives is not translating a foreign gospel core into the language of another culture but digging deep into the history and tradition of the native culture itself to discover God's grace already actively present therein and naming it in Christian terms. Its starting point is not the gospel message but each culture which is considered as the unique place of divine revelation and the locus of theology. Its primary practitioners are not professional theologians but ordinary people who are not yet contaminated by western culture. This model makes extensive use of the social sciences and interreligious dialogue to unveil the word of God present in each culture as a dormant seed to be brought to full growth.[21]

The third model, termed praxis model, privileges neither fidelity to the Christian identity nor identification with culture but social and cultural transformation in the light of the gospel message. Its starting point is neither the gospel nor critical analysis but praxis, that is, reflected-upon action and acted-upon reflection in light of a rereading of the Bible and Christian tradition. This circular and spiralling process of transformation of unjust structures is theologizing in a cross-cultural manner.[22]

The fourth model, called the synthetic model, combines the best insights of the first three models. On the one hand, with the second and third models, it recognizes the role of culture in the formulation of the Christian message and the necessity of fostering social transformation in light of the Christian message. Hence, it starts with a careful study of a particular culture to discover its basic system of symbols. On the other hand, with the first model, it stresses the need to maintain fidelity to the Christian tradition which it views as a series of local theologies and with which it remains in constant dialogue. In addition, it emphasizes the necessity for people of one culture to learn from other cultures. Hence, it holds both the uniqueness and complementarity of all cultures since one's cultural identity is shaped by a dialogue between one's cultural traditions and those of other peoples. Such a dialogue between one's own culture (including popular religiosity) on the one hand and other peoples' cultures as well as previous local theologies on the other hand will produce mutually enriching results in all conversation partners.[23]

The last model, called the transcendental model, approaches the issue of contextual theology, starting not from culture as such, but from the subject doing theology. The theologian is one who is converted—intellectually, morally, and religiously—that is, a self-transcending subject who falls in love with God unrestrictedly.[24] Though the emphasis is on the individual's personal conversion, such a subject is not an isolated person but is a member of a definite cultural community. Furthermore, practitioners of this model are convinced that despite cultural differences, the human mind, driven by an irrepressible desire to know, operates in identical, transcultural ways. As Bernard Lonergan has shown, there is in human knowing an unrevisable and universal fourfold pattern of experiencing, understanding, judging, and deciding.[25] To the extent that a theologian carries out the theological task in authentic conversion in a particular cultural context, she or he, so this model claims, is doing genuine contextual theology.[26]

At this point it is my concern neither to evaluate the strengths and the weaknesses of each of these models nor to assess the accuracy of Bevans' description of the theologians he selects as exemplification of these models.[27] Rather, my interest consists, in the first place, in identifying, by means of Bevans' account, possible ways of inculturating theology and, secondly, in highlighting the theological issues and problems connected with the project of inculturating the Christian faith. To the latter task I now turn.

THEOLOGICAL ISSUES POSED BY INCULTURATION

From the preceding discussion it is clear that inculturation goes much deeper than translation, adaptation, accommodation, and acculturation of the Christian faith to the local culture. Because of its radical nature, it poses unsettling challenges to theology as we know it, in terms of both method and content. I will concentrate here on some of the challenges regarding theological method.

1. What is the starting point of contextual theology: Where does one begin, with the gospel message or the analysis of culture?

2. Whatever starting point is adopted, can the gospel message be isolated from the Hebraic, Hellenistic, Roman, and, in general, western cultures in which it has been embedded in such a way that one can speak of a supracultural gospel core?[28] If it can, what is it?[29]

3. While recognizing that the analysis of culture must encompass all forms of culture, high as well as popular, and that it must identify the forces shaping the identity of a particular culture as well as the factors contributing to social change, the question remains: what are the tools with which to analyze culture? Should theologians rely on the philosophical, functionalist, ecological, Marxist-dialectical, structuralist, or semiotic analysis of culture?[30]

4. Since culture is not static but is constantly changing, in what sense can one speak of cultural identity? Furthermore, since a particular culture is often made up of various racial, ethnic, national, and linguistic groups, can one meaningfully speak of a Hispanic, Asian, or African culture or perspective? Should gender too be regarded as a component of culture?[31]

5. What are the sources of contextual theology? Of course, scripture and tradition continue to function as normative for Catholic theology; but what role should be assigned to other materials retrieved through cultural analysis, such as symbols, myths, rituals, popular religion, sacred texts of other religious traditions and so on? Should these be regarded as "the very sources of the theological enterprise, along with and equal to scripture and tradition,"[32] or should they be made subordinate to the twin Christian source, scripture and tradition?

6. Implied in the last issue is the question about the relationship between the local cultural tradition and the Christian message. What are the criteria by which fidelity to the Christian message and Christian identity can be judged?[33]

7. Almost all descriptions of inculturation have so far emphasized the transformation of a local culture by the Christian faith and even the necessity for the Christian faith to correct and reject certain elements of culture, if these are found contrary to it. Two questions, however, arise. First, if inculturation does not limit itself to the first two levels of culture but must reach and transform its third level,[34] does it not alter the culture itself so radically so as to produce a new culture? Secondly, contextual theologians often speak of the enrichment of the Christian message by inculturation. Are there not instances in which the local culture contradicts a particular church doctrine and tradition, and for the better?[35]

8. A large number of contextual theologians insist that the primary

agent of contextual theology is the local community of believers, in particular the common people. Local theology is addressed primarily to the community of believers, and not to the academy. The role of experts and professional theologians is not thereby abolished but significantly reduced; it consists mainly in listening, interpreting, and giving voice to the experience and reflection of the community and relating it to those of other communities, past and present.[36] In practice, who makes up this local community whose experience is foundational for contextual theology? Also, to what extent should theologians in the academy participate in the local community in order to discern its experience? What level of linguistic and theological sophistication must be used to express it? Is it realistic to expect academic theologians to produce tomes in line with the *Summa Theologiae, Schriften zur Theologie,* or *Method in Theology* and at the same time be intelligible to the people of the community, whoever they are? If not, is it advocated that there be produced two kinds of theological works, one which is academic but which is not local, and the other which is local but shorn of all scholarly sophistication? Or is local theology a *haute vulgarization* of academic theology?

9. If a particular country is composed of many ethnic groups such as the United States of America, should each ethnic minority group develop its own contextual theology, side by side with the contextual theology that is elaborated from the experience of the majority? If so, how can the theology of one ethnic group speak to that of another ethnic group and to the theology of the majority? What forms of dialogue should take place among them? Are there common categories with which to articulate the distinctive experience of each group?

The mention of multiculturalism or cultural pluralism brings me to the second part of this essay, namely, the survey of some recent attempts at inculturating Christian theology in the United States.

CONTEXTUAL THEOLOGIES IN THE UNITED STATES

In a genuine sense of the word, the process of inculturation in the American Catholic Church can be said to be as old as the church itself. As far as the church's inculturation into the nation is concerned, there is a consensus among historians and sociologists that the American Catholic Church has gone through four phases after the colonial period (1492–1790)[37]: (1) the republican era (1790–1852), dominated by such figures as Archbishop John Carroll and Isaac Hecker and characterized by an extensive effort at Americanizing the church by means of the civic virtues of democracy; (2) the immigrant phase (1850–1908), led by clerics such as Bernard McQuaid, William O'Connell, and George

Mundelein, marked by an intentional withdrawal from public affairs (exacerbated by Leo XIII's condemnation of "Americanism" in 1899), and concerned with building a heavily clerical Catholic subculture, promoting a distinctive Catholic public agenda (e.g., parochial schools), while leaving the laity free in economic and political arenas; (3) the maturing phase (1908–1960), characterized by the upward mobility and gradual penetration of Catholics into the middle class and their success in all areas of society and peaking with the election of John F. Kennedy as President; (4) the post-Vatican II phase, termed creative inculturation (1960–), marked by identity crisis and by what David J. O'Brien terms the evangelical style. This style, exemplified by the Catholic Worker movement of Dorothy Day and Peter Maurin, rejects both the republican style as too secular and the immigrant style as too self-centered. Instead it seeks an inculturation style, both personal and public, by means of a radical commitment to the gospel, expressed in profound religious faith and prayer, and yet at the same time engaged in the sociopolitical and economic transformation of American society. This style, O'Brien argues, is recently embodied in the American bishops' two letters on war and peace and the economy.[38]

If inculturation had been a central concern of the American church since its inception, it has occupied the attention and engaged the efforts of mainstream Catholic theologians only recently. The Catholic Theological Society of America made contextualization of theology the theme of three of its annual conventions: in 1981 (the local church), in 1986 (Catholic theology in the North American context), and in 1990 (inculturation and catholicity).[39] The College Theology Society chose the topic of ethnicity, nationality and religious experience for its 1990 annual meeting.[40] Moreover, during these conventions, there often were seminars devoted to Asian, African-American, Hispanic/Latino, and Native American theologies. Finally, there has been a concerted effort by a group of theologians to retrieve the philosophical and religious heritage of the United States, with its experiential, affective, aesthetic, and pragmatist traits, to develop a distinctively North American, non-ethnic theology.[41]

Within the restricted confines of this essay it is impossible to examine, even cursorily, all the current efforts at theologically inculturating the Christian message into the American culture mentioned above. I will present only three such attempts, namely, the African-American, Hispanic/Latino, and Asian. The reasons for this choice are both theological and pastoral. Theologically, these ethnic groups, who are mainly composed of the lower middle class and poor, present the most vocal and powerful challenge to the white, overly Americanized church to be truly prophetic in its commitment to justice. Pastorally, from the demographic point of view, the single most significant change in the American church is the dramatic growth of its new ethnics membership. It is projected that by the year 2020, Hispanics/Latinos will constitute the majority of Roman Catholics in the United States, not to mention the dramatic growth of Catholic Asians and African-Americans.[42]

My concern here is not to present a full survey of the origins and development of each of these three ethnic theologies, but to discern their common methodology, their basic themes, and their contributions to theological inculturation.

BLACK THEOLOGY

The phrase black theology emerged sometime in the late sixties, perhaps for the first time in the preparatory process of a report presented in the fall of 1968 by the Theological Commission of the National Conference of Black Churchmen, or in the writings of Albert B. Cleage, Jr., and his followers.[43] M. Shawn Copeland has pointed out that black theology is "a global theological movement among peoples of African descent on the Continent and in the diaspora including the Caribbean and Latin American as well as the United States."[44]

The development of black theology can be divided, according to Copeland, into four phases: The first phase, 1964–1969, is dominated by the encounter and confrontation between the civil rights movement, the secular black power movement and African-American Christianity.[45] It is marked by "The Black Manifesto," adopted by the National Black Economic Development Conference on April 26, 1969, by the June 13, 1969 statement by the National Committee of Black Churchmen entitled "Black Theology," and by James Cone's book *Black Theology and Black Power* (1969). Its salient feature is an attack against the white ecclesiastical and theological establishment. In the second phase, 1970–1976, black theology received serious scholarly evaluation by a small group of seminary and university professors, both black and white, but still remained marginalized in mainline church and academy. The third phase, 1977–1989, black theology entered into dialogue with other theologies, in particular African and Latin American liberation theologians and feminist theologians. Two memorable events marked this phase: first, the Detroit Conference on Theology in the Americas in 1975, and secondly, the meeting of the Black Theology Project in Atlanta, Georgia, 1977.[46] In its fourth and current phase, black theology is called "to put forward a critical mediation of the Christian gospel which takes into full account the biases of racism, sexism, class exploitation, and human objectification in a capitalist system of production as well as the psychological and affective realities which suffuse the dramatic pattern of human living."[47]

In reaction to Joseph R. Washington, Jr., who asserted that black congregations are not churches but religious societies to be integrated into the mainstream of American religion and that the black church has no theology,[48] black theology has developed since the late sixties. But black theology is not a school, much less a monolithic system of thought. Although James Cone, whose prolific writings are influential, is often taken as the representative of black theology, by no means is his theology irenically accepted by the majority of black theologians.[49] For instance, there is no agreement that black theology is essentially a liberation theology. Contrary to James Cone, J. Deotis Roberts and Major Jones argue that its primary goal should be reconciliation of all races, including black and white.[50] Furthermore, there is no consensus on the nature of black religion and black theology as such. Charles Long argues that black religion is unique, rooted as it is in "blackness" and African culture, and cannot therefore be elaborated in the categories of white Christian doctrine.[51] Cecil Cone, James Cone's brother, on the other hand, maintains that there is a black religion and a black theology, but rejects his brother's identification of black religion and black theology with black power because he wants to rehabilitate the institutional black church as an instrument of black liberation.[52] Gayraud Wilmore agrees with Cecil Cone that there is a black religion and black theology, but is critical of James Cone's narrowly Christian interpretation of them, because he wants to appeal to non-Christian black nationalists.[53] William Jones criticizes contemporary black theology's inadequate solution to the problem of black suffering because of its adherence to classical theism.[54] Finally, from a Roman Catholic standpoint, Edward K. Braxton is critical of James Cone's negative evaluation of western, white theology and strongly urges that blacks should be open and attentive to any classics, irrespective of the race of their authors.[55]

Despite these significant differences, black theology does possess fundamental common elements, both in methodology and basic orientations, that would qualify it as one of the most articulate and enriching contextual theologies in the United States.

It is rooted in the foundational experience of African-Americans, namely, chattel slavery and its pervasive consequences in all areas of their lives. Recently it has also drawn from the womanist experience, that is, the experience of oppression by black women who suffer a "double jeopardy" or even "triple jeopardy."[56]

Besides drawing on the Bible[57] and the writings of past black thinkers and activists (e.g., W.E.B. Dubois, Henry M. Turner, Martin Luther King, Jr., and Malcolm X), black theology makes extensive use of social analysis and even Marxist categories to convey its message of liberation.[58] It also engages in a reinterpretation of cultural history, highlighting the cultural achievements of blacks.[59] It mines the rich black spiritual tradition embodied in sermons, folktales and music (the spirituals and the blues).[60]

Black theology has conducted a fruitful dialogue with other forms of liberation theologies, in addition to feminist theology, especially African (South Africa in particular), Latin American, and Asian, and in this way has enlarged its vision of liberation beyond racism and sexism.[61]

Beyond these methodological innovations, black theology has also developed distinctive themes in theology, e.g., the liberating God (James Cone), theodicy (William Jones), the black Messiah (Albert Kleage Jr.), black religion (Gayraud Wilmore and Cecil Jone), liberation and reconciliation (Deotis Roberts), agape ethics (Major Jones), Marxist-based revolutionary theology (Cornell West), church-based social ethics (Theodore Walker, Jr.), black theology from the Roman Catholic perspective (Edward Braxton, Toinette Eugene, Jamie Phelps, Diana Hayes, Shawn Copeland).[62] All these theologians and many others have contributed in shaping an African-American theology, genuinely contextualized into the particular cultural situation of the U.S. and at the same time attempting to achieve some measure of universality by dialoging with other forms of theology developed in the third world.

HISPANIC/LATINO THEOLOGY

Younger than black theology but rapidly developing, Hispanic/Latino theology is bound to gain greater national attention as Hispanics are projected to constitute the majority of U.S. Catholics in the next two decades.[63] The American Catholic hierarchy is conscious of the rising importance of the Hispanic phenomenon and has attempted to come to grips with it in two documents, the 1983 pastoral letter *The Hispanic Presence* and the 1987 *National Plan for Hispanic Ministry*.[64]

One important event for the development of Hispanic theology is the foundation in 1988 of the Academy of Catholic Hispanic Theologians of the United States (ACHTUS).[65] The organization intentionally and successfully recruited members from women and from various national groups comprising the Hispanic population. It also wanted to differentiate U.S. Hispanic theology from the Latin American liberation theology, even though there are common traits between the two, because it wants to attend to its particular social location in the United States. Lastly, it wants to foster an ecumenical dialogue with Hispanic Protestant theologians, through collaboration with the group *La Comunidad* and *Apuntes*, until recently the only journal for Hispanic theology in the United States.[66]

The history of contemporary U.S. Hispanic theology began with Virgil Elizondo, a priest of the Archdiocese of San Antonio, founding president of the Mexican-American Cultural Center in the same city, and a prolific and internationally known theologian.[67] For about twenty years, from the late 1960s to the late 1980s, he was the sole, highly visible U.S. Hispanic theologian. But he is now followed by a new generation of well-trained and well-published theologians who are dedicated to developing a distinctive Hispanic theology contextualized into the cultural situation of the United States. What follows is no more than a survey of the methodology and salient themes of this new theology.

As with all contextual theologies, Hispanic theology starts with a cultural and social analysis of the Hispanic community in the United States. Culturally, U.S. Hispanics are characterized by what Elizondo terms *mestizaje* and Justo González, being in exile.[68] This condition does not refer simply to the physiological fact that Hispanics, like many other peoples, are a mixed race composed of many bloods. Rather, it bespeaks the violent forging of a new people born out of the intercourse between the Iberian conquistadors and the vanquished Amerindian women, and the domination of the ancient Amerindian religion by medieval European Catholicism. As a consequence of this double conquest, the mestizos are forced to live as foreigners in their own land. As Elizondo puts it, Mexican-Americans suffer from an unfinished or undefined identity. Their Spanish is too anglicized for the Mexicans, and their English is too Mexicanized for the Anglo-Americans. For Mexicans, Hispanics are too close to the United States, and for Anglo-Americans they are too close to Mexico. The mestizo reality is feared and rejected by both racial groups that produce it because it blurs the identity-constituting boundaries between them. This is the peculiar situation of U.S. Hispanics which Elizondo describes with the term *el rechazo* (rejection). Its hyphenated character cannot be adequately understood by an analysis of either group. *Mestizaje*, then, is a symbol of biologico-cultural oppression, exploitation, and alienation. On the other hand, it also contains a seed for creating a new reality and a new culture, provided it is not reabsorbed into either of its parent. Hence, it is a foundational *locus theologicus* for U.S. Hispanic theology.

As far as social analysis is concerned, some Hispanic theologians, like Latin American liberation theologians, make use of Marxist-dialectical analysis of society in terms of class conflicts and find its interpretation of certain elements of the Hispanic social and economic situation in the United States persuasive. However, they are well aware of the limits of such a method, particularly its failure to deal with the reality of the second and third generations of Hispanic immigrants. On the other hand, they find the functionalist method of social analysis also unsatisfactory because it tends to stress the assimilation of Hispanics into U.S. society and ignores the structural causes of ongoing discrimination and injustice against them. A new method, called *investigación acción participativa*, is being developed to study more adequately the Hispanic situation.[69]

More than any other contextual theology, Hispanic theology is an ecclesiocentric theology, in the sense that it is deeply rooted in the Hispanic experience of church rather than in the academy. It is a church experience that is strongly sacramental, and yet steeped in popular devotions; community-oriented (e.g., *Encuentro Nacional Hispano de Pastoral*, basic ecclesial communities, various apostolic and spiritual movements, and parish renewal programs) and yet non-clerical. Indeed, one of the distinctive characteristics of the Hispanic church is that since its beginnings it developed in spite of the scarcity of priests. The laity has always exercised a key role in the life of the church: sacristans who functioned as parish administrators, *rezadores* who led funeral prayers, *mayordomos* who were in charge of parish finances, and catechists responsible for religious instruction.

There is, however, another sense in which Hispanic theology is ecclesiocentric, and that is, it is self-consciously structured according to the *pastoral de conjunto*, a pastoral strategy that brings together and calls into action all levels of the community.[70] Theologically, this entails that Hispanic theology, as *teología de conjunto*, is based on the praxis of Hispanics; that it does not speak *for* or *to* the people, but *with* the people; that it must be inclusive of all people and express solidarity with their life of faith and struggle for self-determination.

In particular, because Hispanic theology is rooted in the Hispanics' experience of *mestizaje* and *rechazo* and is in solidarity with them, it must start from the existential option for the poor. This means that central to its methodology is the relation between theory and praxis. Roberto Goizueta, who has written extensively on this issue, warns U.S. Hispanic theologians not to yield to the anti-intellectual temptation of renouncing theory in favor of praxis reducing, as the later Karl Marx and some Latin American theologians have done, praxis to *poiesis*. He sees in Hispanic popular devotions a unique contribution of Hispanic culture toward elucidating the relationship between theory and praxis insofar as their inherently communal and aesthetic dimensions demand subversive sociopolitical praxis. Furthermore, he cautions Hispanic theologians not to follow post-modernity's premature rejection of the Enlightenment's demand for rationality, lest their Hispanic theology be marginalized by Anglo theologians as no more than Hispanic advocacy theology, devoid of intellectual rigor and therefore irrelevant to the theological enterprise as such.[71]

Another noteworthy development in Hispanic theology is the emergence of women's voices. As I have mentioned, from its very beginning, ACTHUS sought to recognize the work of Hispanic female theologians. Currently approximately twenty-five percent of U.S. Hispanic theologians are women.[72] They seek to develop a *mujerista* theology, that is, a theology which has as its point of departure the experience of Hispanic-American women in the dominant Anglo-Saxon culture, facing oppression and discrimination from both a sexist world as women and a racist world as Hispanic.[73] It is interesting to note that the apparitions of Our Lady at Tepeyac in the form of a member of the vanquished race and a pregnant woman function as the foundational event for Hispanic theology, as a symbol of struggle for justice and new life, just as the Exodus is the paradigmatic event for Latin American theology.

Finally, Hispanic theology has begun to develop some Christian themes from a Hispanic perspective: biblical hermeneutics,[74] the liberative dimension of popular religion, [75] the Trinity,[76] anthropology,[77] ecclesiology,[78] pastoral ministry,[79] catechetics,[80] and spirituality.[81] Of course, the current production of Hispanic theology is nowhere near that of Latin American theology or black theology, but these writings do mark an auspicious beginning of the "Border Theology," heralding original and lasting contributions to theological inculturation in the United States.

ASIN THEOLOGY

ASIAN THEOLOGY

The youngest and the least known form of contextual theology is Asian theology in the United States, whereas inculturation has been a pervasive and constant concern of the Asian churches in general.[82] There are many reasons for this tardy development, chief among which are the still relatively small number of Asian Christians in the United States and Asians' general lack of interest in academic disciplines other than the empirical and scientific.

There are two notable Asian Christian theologians, both Protestant, actively working in the United States with deep interest in the project of inculturation: Kosuke Koyama, a Japanese, currently Professor of Ecumenics and World Christianity at Union Theological Seminary in New York City; and Choan-Seng Song, a Taiwanese, currently Professor of Theology at the Pacific School of Theology. Since Stephen Bevans has already discussed Kosuke Koyama as a synthetic contextual theologian,[83] I will focus on Choan-Seng Song.[84]

Describing the condition of Asian Christian theology, Song compares it to the fat man in the Filipino folk-tale, "The Gungutan and the Big-Bellied Man," in which the Big-Bellied Man is forced by the

Gungutan to act out his feigned dream and in the process is transformed into a handsome athletic young man:

> Christian theology in Asia has been overweight, like that big-bellied man. It could hardly walk or run with its huge belly of undigested food—a belly crammed with schools of theology, theories of biblical interpretation, Christian views of cultures and religions, all originating from the church of the West and propounded by traditional theology. It became more obese when the vast space of Asia, with its rich cultures, vigorous religions, and turbulent histories, began to compete for room in that already over-loaded theological belly. The result is painful indigestion. Our chief concern must be how to cure its indigestion, reduce its weight, and regain its agility and dynamic to win the hand of theology authentic to the Asian mind.[85]

The remedy Song prescribes is the revitalization of the theological imagination whereby one gains freedom to perform the following tasks: a critique of western theology; a radical commitment to the praxis of liberation in church and society; a comprehensive socio-cultural analysis of the Asian situation in order to identify its challenges; making an inventory of Asian resources for doing theology; and a theological reformulation of basic Christian doctrines.

Song's first published book, *Christian Mission in Reconstruction*, intimates the future direction of his theology. He sees Christian mission rotted in the twin doctrines of God's creation and incarnation. Corresponding to God's creative act, Christian mission must be exercised in four areas: culture, history, society, and politics. Corresponding to God's act of self-emptying in the incarnation, Christian mission must not be concerned with its own self-aggrandizement but must work for the sake of humanity.

It is also in light of the nature of Christian mission as manifesting the redemptive presence of Christ in the world through actions for peace and justice that Song reexamines the sacraments, in particular the eucharist. For him, the battles between Catholics and Protestants regarding the sacraments have been waged wrongly as ecclesiastical, confessional, and liturgical issues; rather they should be viewed as mission-oriented themes. They are words-in-action for socio-political liberation. Furthermore, they should be seen within the sacramental nature of the universe in which anything is potentially sacramental because the world is created by God and redeemed by Christ. Using the biblical image of the Exodus, Song goes on to elaborate at great length the sociopolitical dimension of Christian mission to promote freedom both in the church and in the society at large.

A discussion of Christian mission in Asia cannot but deal with the presence and function of Asian religions. Song believes that in a dialogue with Asian religions, the universality of Christ must be proclaimed; the grace manifested in these religions must have something to do with the grace of God in Jesus Christ, whether recognized or not. But Song does not subscribe to the theory that non-Christian religions are nothing but *praeparatio evangelica* or *praeparation incarnationis*, according to which they have no intrinsic salvific value and therefore are set aside after the incarnation. Rather, he holds that "the Word of God which was present in the beginning of the creation and has become present in Jesus Christ has always constituted the basis of man's spirituality."[86] Finally, Song urges Christian mission in Asia to abandon what he calls morphological fundamentalism, that is, the churches in Asia must make a serious effort at erasing denominational barriers (in church polity, liturgy, and theology which are inherited from western denominations), proselytism, and missionary elitism (the idea that some are missionaries while the majority are not).

Song's two basic themes, namely, inculturation of Christianity through cultural imagination and sociopolitical activity, recur in his later works, but with a notable difference. Whereas in his first book, there were but sporadic references to Asian literature (most of the footnotes cite European and North American authors), in his later works the use of Asian sources increases dramatically. This is of set purpose. He now wants to develop a third-eye theology. The expression "third eye," derived from Buddhism, refers to the power to perceive hitherto unprecedented regions concealed from us through our ignorance. Asian theology needs to break away from the predominantly Latin and German theology (Song speaks of the Latin and Teutonic captivity of western theology) in order to develop that third-eye power to grasp the meaning of reality from the Asian perspective.

An Asian Christian theology, according to Song, proceeds not from abstract and universal principles but from two basic facts: love and suffering, the former because the biblical God acting in history is defined as *agape*, and the latter because of the Buddha's insight that life is suffering and of the immense suffering of masses of Asian peoples. Theology, which has its beginning in the "heartache of God,"

> should not begin with the study of God. Rather it should start with the study of humanity, the study of people and the world, in short, the study of God's creation. Human beings with all their problems—social, political, psychological,

ecological, or whatever—are subject matters of theology. The world with all its ideology, organizations and structure, religions, arts and poetry, provides themes for a living theology. The whole universe with all its problems and issues calls for theological analysis and interpretation.[87]

Following his own methodological counsel, Song devotes large sections of his works to a sociocultural analysis of Asia and Asian religions. This analysis serves as the background for the theological process of passing from the ethno-religious exclusivism (which Song calls centrism) of Judaism and Christianity to the movements of nations and peoples of Asia. Such an act, which is termed transposition, will disclose the presence of God in this vast part of the world outside of the Judeo-Christian traditions.

In his *The Compassionate God*, Song shows how centrism is one of the main obstacles to the building of an Asian theology. Accordingly, to achieve the transposition his first step is to locate the forces of the Old Testament that drew Israel out of its centrism and set it in relation to other nations. The second step is to examine Jesus' attempts to liberate his own people from their ethno-religious centrism. The third step is to explore the ways in which God is redemptively present in the suffering of Asian peoples under poverty, oppression and injustice. Only in this way can an authentically Asian theology be crafted.

In shaping this ethnic theology, Song makes extensive use of a great variety of stories, poems, folktales, novels, artistic drawings, both classical and contemporary, from all parts of Asia. Prominent also are the sayings and teachings of religious sages, as well as the doctrines of Asian religions. He meditates on the grief and hope of a Vietnamese young war widow, explores the sacramentality of a bowl of rice, reflects on ancestor worship, fathoms the depth of Japanese *haiku* (seventeen-syllable poems), unleashes the liberative power of Taiwanese and Korean folksongs, celebrates the poems of an imprisoned Filipino revolutionary, explicates the import of anti-Reagan and anti-Deng Xiaoping cartoons, and unfolds the critical transcendence of mask dance.[88]

Of particular interest is Song's elaboration of political theology on the basis of the Chinese folktale of Lady Meng whose husband was sacrificed by Emperor Ch'in Shih Huang-ti during the construction of his protective ramparts. Because she had dared to curse his cruelty and injustice, her bones were ground into powder at the Emperor's order, but they were turned into little living fishes and thus became a symbol of resistance and victory.[89]

In developing his Christology Song keeps asking himself whether Jesus has not been waiting for the past two thousand years to hear something different about himself from the parts of the world now called the third world, especially Asia. To answer this question Song combs the stories of sufferings and oppression of Asian peoples to construct a political and feminist Christology which identifies Jesus with the crucified people, men and women.[90]

It is true that Song has not developed his theology from the context of Asians in the United States and with the express purpose of helping them inculturate the Christian faith into the American culture. Rather, he is interested in showing how the Christian message can be inculturated into Asian countries. But his theology, steeped in the humus of Asian culture and religions, enlivened by a rich imagination, driven by a fierce prophetic conscience, and graced with a poetic style, offers precious examples as to how contextual theology should be done, no matter what cultural contexts may be. Nurtured by the Reformed tradition, with a heavy emphasis on the word of God and the cross of Christ, his texts are crafted like multi-colored tapestries, weaving biblical narratives with Asian cultural and religious threads, and intricately crisscrossing with the twin patterns of inculturation and sociopolitical liberation. One may wish that Song had not dismissed metaphysics so quickly and that he had mined more extensively the philosophical ore of Asian religions in elaborating his theology of God and the world. But his is, no doubt, a contextual theology at its boldest and most thought-provoking.[91]

INCULTURATED THEOLOGY: FURTHER QUESTIONS

In this final part I will briefly summarize the main common features of the three contextual theologies that are being constructed in the United States. In this way, one can gain a glimpse of a possible shape that a contextual theology for North America may assume. I will conclude by drawing attention to some of the questions and challenges that such a contextual theology still has to face.

The three contextual theologies are founded on a broad study of the local culture in and for which they are articulated. This study focuses on the local people's history; their *Weltanschauung* embodied in symbols, myths, and rituals; their moral and religious values.

Such a study identifies a key experience which serves as a lens through which the community's culture is interpreted: slavery for African-Americans, *mestizaje* and *rechazo* for Hispanics, suffering for Asians. Furthermore, under the impact of feminist theology, all three theologies have recently become aware that women have suffered more from these injustices.

This history of racism, colonization, and pauperization compels these ethnic theologians to be hermeneutically suspicious of the western dominant theology which they regard as their oppressors' ideological tool to perpetuate the racist, classist, and sexist structures of both church and society. Hence, following Latin American liberation theology, they propose praxis in favor of the poor and the oppressed as the first moment of the method of contextual theology. There is, then, in these contextual theologies an intimate link between inculturation and the struggle for justice.

Theological hermeneutical reflections follow this praxis. In this second phase, the first step for contextual theologians is to retrieve resources from their own cultures, often forgotten or suppressed, from Negro spirituals and blues to folktales, popular devotions and non-Christian sacred texts, in order to unveil the opaque or hidden presence of divine grace in their culture.

The next step is for contextual theologians to reformulate key Christian doctrines in light of the foundational experiences of their people's history and by means of the resources discovered at the third level of culture, namely, the level of culture as a total and coherent system of meanings. This task of reformulation comprises not only a rereading of the sacred scripture but also a recasting of systematic and moral theology.

Such is, in brief, the methodology of contextual theology as exemplified in African-American, Hispanic/Latino, and Asian theologies. This somewhat straightforward outline of the three contextual theologies in the United States should not, however, obscure the formidable challenges still facing them, in spite of their evident and hard-won successes. I will mention some of them.

Still unresolved is the question of which analytical tools contextual theologians should make use of in order to study their cultures. Of course, no cultural analysis is neutral or value-free, whether functionalist or dialectical. As we have seen, all three theologies make extensive use of the dialectical method of social analysis, and quite understandably so, given the conflictual nature of their current cultural situation. However, as Aloysius Pieris has argued, an Asian theology that makes an exclusive use of the Marxist tools of social analysis will remain un-Asian and ineffective until it integrates the psychological tools of introspection which sages of various religions have discovered. Marxism, he points out, is unable to appreciate the religious dimension that Asian cultures attribute to poverty and therefore fails to acknowledge the revolutionary impact of voluntary poverty.[92] Similarly, Marxist analysis tends to dismiss popular devotions as opium for the people, as expressions of false consciousness, and misses its potential for social resistance and transformation. The same thing should be said of its failure to understand the character of civil religion in American society. Even if the semiotic approach is taken as the most adequate method of cultural analysis, it is too complex for theologians to learn to make fruitful use of it. At any rate, to date, no theologian of any of the three contextual theologies has produced, to my knowledge, a theology based on a comprehensive study of his or her culture.

All three contextual theologies emphasize that the primary agents of inculturation are the people themselves and that contextual theologians do not speak for, about, or to the people but with them. While such rhetoric about the role of the people or community is certainly to be commended, it is not yet clear how in the concrete theologians speak with the people, at least in the United States. Certainly, it means more than just physical company or even psychological empathy. It presumably implies political and economic solidarity with the victims of oppression. It also means lending a voice to their feelings and aspirations. But here lurks a temptation to which intellectuals are known to have succumbed, namely, to impose upon the people their own categories and concepts which have little to do with the people themselves. Furthermore, the majority of U.S. theologians work in the academy, which is a world *sui generis* with its own language, ethos and requirements about hiring, retention, tenure and promotion. To what extent and in what ways should and can contextual theologians be immersed in the world of the people, so that as intellectuals they can articulate the interests of the people and bring about their hegemony?

There exists a painful anomaly in the Roman Catholic attempt at inculturation of the faith in the United States as well as in all other parts of the world. On the one hand, if inculturation of the Christian faith must reach the third and deepest level of culture, and on the other hand if, as currently is the case with the Roman Catholic Church, it is not allowed to express itself on the second and third levels of culture which are being regulated by canon law imported from the sidelines and quite alien to it, then two possibilities result. Either there arises an unbearable tension if not contradiction between the different levels of culture that threatens to destroy its integrity and unity, or inculturation in all areas of church life, from liturgy to catechesis to theology, will remain no more than skin-deep and theologians' learned discourses on inculturation are not much more than wishful thinking.[93]

Contextual theologies must come to grips with the fundamental question of identity of the Christian faith within diversity, unity within plurality. That issue, it would seem, must be approached on the basis of an adequate communion ecclesiology and the related theology of the local church. There is, however, another solution to the problem, namely, dialogue between the ethnic theologies and the dominant theology and dialogue among the ethnic theologies themselves. On the one hand, then, ethnic theologies must go beyond the protest stage in which accusations of colonialism, imperialism, abstractionism, racism, sexism, and classism are hurled at the western white theologians and must be willing to show that they and mainline theology can learn from each other. On the other hand, a truly fruitful conversation among the three contextual theologies in the United States must be an ongoing project. As we have seen, African-American theology has attempted to do so with African and South American liberation theology; unfortunately, little two or three way traffic has been established among the three contextual theologies themselves.

Connected with the previous point is the issue of globalization of theology. So far, contextual theologies have paid a lot of attention to the problems posed by modernity and its impact upon local cultures and local theologies. However, as Robert Schreiter has pointed out,[94] concomitant with the rise of ethnic consciousness, there is also the phenomenon of globalization, caused by the growth of economic unions (e.g., the European community), the end of the east-west determination of geopolitics, the rise of economic power in Asia, high-speed travel, electronic communications, and the emergence of a new global capitalism. In this climate of global culture, which undermines the importance of nation-states and ethnic groups, there is talk of a global or universal theology.[95] To reconcile the demands of a contextual theology with those of a global theology, to negotiate a path from the particular to the universal, and to fashion new symbols of hope for this emergent world culture constitute some of the most exacting and exciting challenges for theology today.

Finally, no fruitful inculturation can be obtained unless there is available an accurate and rich knowledge of the history of the local culture and the local church. With perhaps the exception of African-American theology, there is still a long way to go in the case of Hispanic theology and much more so in the case of Asian theology. Even basic sociological data regarding Asian Catholics are not yet available. It is clear, therefore, that inculturation of theology can only be carried out as an interdisciplinary enterprise, and it is encouraging that it has taken very auspicious first steps.

Roberto S. Goizueta

RESPONSE TO PETER C. PHAN

Rather than attempt to summarize Professor Phan's discussion of theological inculturation, I would like to limit my response to the concluding section of the paper, in which a series of questions or challenges are set forth. I would like to offer some preliminary reflections on one question which is of particular import for U.S. Hispanic theologians specifically.

The first question raised by Professor Phan is that of social analytical mediation: If theology is always informed by its sociohistorical context, and if, therefore, the theologian must be able to self-consciously appropriate that context, what hermeneutical tools or methods will he or she use to understand the context? More specifically, what, if any, should be the mediating role of a Marxist-dialectical analysis?

This issue is of particular moment for U.S. Hispanic theologians for at least two reasons: It is the issue upon which U.S. Hispanic theology has, from the beginning, staked out its own particular identity in relation to Latin American liberation theology; and it is a methodological issue which, maybe more than any other, reveals the diversity of what we call the U.S. Hispanic community (a point perceptively raised by Phan where he discusses the limits of dialectical social analysis in addressing the context of second and third generation Hispanics). In other words, whether in relation to Latin American liberation theology or in relation to our own communities, the question of social analysis has historically surfaced, at least initially, as an implicitly divisive element directly tied to the question of self-identity.

This is not to suggest that such division is necessarily detrimental, since, for example, it has made possible the process of contextualization itself. As we U.S. Hispanics have become increasingly conscious of the fact that we are not Latin Americans, the question of identity has implied a methodological and epistemological distancing from the Latin American context: our context is not their context and our history is not their history. Hence, there is a certain inevitable ambivalence in

131

our approach to the issue of social analysis, which symbolizes both identity and separation.

One might argue that, methodologically and historically, what first distinguished U.S. Hispanic theology from Latin American liberation theology was the former's emphasis on the priority of culture over class as determinative of theological context and social location. It would, on the one hand, be overly simplistic to suggest that liberation theologians as a whole have ever dismissed the significance of culture as a determinant of theological context. While acknowledging its importance for Latin America, theologians such as Juan Carlos Scannone and Enrique Dussel (both Argentinian and, thus, influenced early on by Peronist populism) have always also acknowledged the limitations of Marxist class analysis, as have virtually all of their Latin American colleagues, and this has become increasingly true in recent years.[1] On the other hand, it is equally true that Latin American liberation theologians have historically emphasized a socioeconomic mediation of praxis.

Throughout the 1960s and 1970s, U.S. Hispanic pastoral workers, intellectuals, and social activists were very much influenced by Latin American liberation theology.[2] With the support and encouragement of Latin American theologians like Gustavo Gutiérrez, however, U.S. Hispanics began to develop a theology within our own context.[3] As Allan Figueroa Deck observes, the implications of this new methodological self-consciousness were evident from the outset: "While seldom if ever critiquing the emphasis on economic, structural, and social class analyses of their Latin American counterparts and their passionate calls for socioeconomic and political transformation, U.S. Hispanic theologians have gravitated toward *cultural* analysis, especially to popular culture as epitomized by popular religiosity."[4] The lack of a socioeconomic emphasis, he continues, "is notable and a contrasting feature with much Latin American theology."[5]

This quote from Allan Figueroa Deck reveals a further ambiguity, namely, the connotations which the terms cultural analysis and social analysis have taken on within Latin American liberation theology and U.S. Hispanic theology, and in the dialogue between these two theological movements. The origins of this ambiguity lie in Marxist social analysis itself, more specifically, in the anthropological and sociological dualism that underlies Marx's distinction between base, or structure, and superstructure. Indeed, that distinction is precisely what leads many Marxists, as Phan correctly observes, "to dismiss popular devotions as opium for the people as expressions of false consciousness." Once the economic mode of production and class relations become anthropologically formdational, culture becomes relegated, as consciousness, to the superstructure and, thus, divorced from the economic base: cultural expressions and practices become, by definition, mere ideological epiphenomena.

While few if any U.S. Hispanic theologians would find the substance of Marxist social analysis adequate to our experience, the ongoing debate concerning the primacy of class or culture as a determinant of social location and the U.S. Hispanic preference for cultural analysis over Marxist social analysis presuppose a nevertheless Marxian separation of society (understood as the economic order) and culture. While Marx privileged the socioeconomic, and therefore social analysis, we, as Deck observes, have tended to privilege the cultural; yet both views presuppose an external relationship between class and culture, or between civil society, on the one hand, and cultural symbols and practices on the other. In turn, an implicit opposition is set up between social analysis and cultural analysis, or social theory and cultural theory. The present debates over social analysis versus cultural analysis presuppose Marx's separation of society and culture, which in turn presupposes Marx's identification of society or civil society with economic production and economic relationships. Conversely, culture becomes everything that is not explicitly economic. Those critics who emphasize class are forced, by this paradigm, to relativize culture and, conversely, those who emphasize culture are forced to relativize class.

I would like to address this complex issue by examining the class-culture dichotomy in Marx and its influence on U.S. Hispanic theological method, while suggesting possible avenues toward alternative, more wholistic forms of social analysis. This analysis will be a necessarily cursory, initial attempt to address Professor Phan's profound challenge from my own particular perspective as a U.S. Hispanic theologian.

MARXIST SOCIAL ANALYSIS

The dichotomy between class and culture, or between social analysis and cultural analysis, is not yet present in the so-called early Marx. John Brenkman has noted that, in the early Marx, both economic production and culture are forms of material-social practice: "In every historical epoch, human life is social activity and social existence. The material interchange with nature and structured social interaction are two sides of the same process...."[6] Just as economic relationships are always social relationships mediated by culture, so too is culture always mediated by productive labor (as in the production of art, artifacts, cultural symbols, tools, clothing, food, liturgical symbols like bread and wine, institutions, etc.).[7]

The view of the socioeconomic and the cultural as two dimensions of human activity that are always both material and social later gives way, in Marx, to a view of culture as consciousness, by definition opposed to real human activity, that is, production.[8] Culture is no longer a set of material-social practices but is now a symbolic realm separated from and determined by production.[9] Henceforth, debates over the priority of socioeconomic categories or cultural categories would presuppose Marx's framework in which culture and production are only externally related. The irony, of course, is that that very framework was intended as a critique of the idealist reification of consciousness. In the final analysis, however, one cannot subvert a dichotomy by simply turning it on its head.

The separation of the socioeconomic and the cultural is retained, moreover, in some subsequent attempts, within the Marxist tradition itself, to redress the perceived economism of Marx. Even Antonio Gramsci, whose notion of ideological hegemony countered reductionist interpretations of class, nonetheless contended that all social groups, or classes, take their original identity from their role in the process of production.[10] Later, Herbert Marcuse would argue for the importance of culture, specifically art, in the process of social transformation: art has an affective, transformative power that derives from the contradiction between the unity implicit in the work of art and the divisiveness of social reality. Yet his argument for privileging the aesthetic over the economic itself presupposes a dichotomous, external relationship between the two; indeed it is that very dichotomy, that is, the radical otherness of art, which lends art its power as an instrument of critique.[11] Another critical Marxist of the Frankfurt School, Jürgen Habermas, likewise fails to bridge the inherited gap. Though Habermas certainly stresses the role of capitalism in eroding and distorting cultural practices, the critique of capitalism itself is isolated from the hermeneutics of culture, through which cultural practices are preserved and transmitted.[12] Anthony Giddens and Robert Wuthnow have taken Habermas to task for separating the symbolic-expressive activity of culture from the instrumental activity of labor.[13]

It thus seems that even the most critical of Marxists remain trapped within what amounts to a conceptualist reification of both economy and culture. Once these concepts are reified and set in mutual opposition, the only point of contention remains that of priority: Which category should take precedence as a determinant of social location, class or culture? Even the suggestion that the two condition each other itself presupposes that two separate and opposed entities called class and culture do in fact exist and can, thus, relate to and condition each other. Meanwhile, outside the Marxist camp the polarization between socioeconomic analysis and cultural analysis remains in force, as evidenced by "the completely formal treatment of economic problems and the theoretical isolation of economics from the rest of the social sciences among non-Marxists."[14]

A more subtle consequence of the dichotomy between the socioeconomic and the cultural has been the often implicit assumption that those who favor class analysis, or social analysis, are the true political radicals while those who favor cultural analysis are closet liberals unwilling to attack the real roots of injustice. Unfortunately, in an intellectual environment where society and culture are set in mutual opposition, such a polarization becomes almost inevitable. As with all dichotomies, the rejection of one pole invariably leads to an embracing of the opposite pole, even if unwittingly. Is it possible, for example, that the current concern for multiculturalism and cultural diversity is simply an equal and opposite reaction to the patent failures of Marxist social analysis? Does the option for multiculturalism represent, then, a tacit renunciation of the struggle for socioeconomic justice? (The problem with putting all one's social analytical eggs in a single basket is that, if it falls apart, instead of weaving another basket one may simply give up on baskets altogether). Is it possible that, disillusioned and frustrated by the failure of socioeconomic approaches to liberation (read, Marxist social analysis), we have given up on the socioeconomic altogether in favor of a multiculturalism that demands not a preferential option for the poor but a much less threatening openness to otherness?

The preferential option for the poor, as enunciated by Latin American liberation theologians, the Latin American bishops, the U.S. bishops, and, indeed, the pope, demanded of us a radical change in lifestyle; multiculturalism (as the term is currently used in the popular media) does not. It only demands an open mind and, at the most, an open heart. Solidarity with the poor, now defined as the culturally marginalized, can be effected simply through consciousness raising rather than through a practical identification with the struggles of the poor. One can become open to other cultural perspectives without ever having to leave one's home. Is multiculturalism the middle-aged yuppie's attempt to recover his or her long-forgotten political commitment without having to surrender the economic gains he or she has made in the interim? Has multiculturalism become the radicalism of a middle class suffering from sheer political exhaustion?[15] Could it be that our society's present concern for cultural diversity is masking an underlying despair, a despair over our inability to make any appreciable progress in the struggle against poverty and, more importantly, a despair over our inability to take the difficult personal and social steps entailed in a preferential option for the poor? In short, is multiculturalism simply a culturalism as reductive as Marx's economism, but one much more self-serving?

U.S. HISPANIC THEOLOGY AND SOCIAL ANALYSIS

The only way to avoid being forced into one of these camps, either the culturalist or the economicist, is to move toward a reintegration of cultural analysis and socioeconomic analysis by developing mediating categories and methodologies which avoid a too restrictive categorization of human types of behavior or experience. For U.S. Hispanic theologians, specifically, such categories would prevent an idealization of cultural practices such as popular religious devotions. The ability to interpret popular religiosity as a cultural-economic practice, and to analyze it as such, would prevent us, for example, from overlooking the fact that in many of our communities (and certainly in the Cuban American community to which I belong) the extent to which religious practices remain European can vary greatly, often precisely along class lines, with the upper classes exhibiting a religiosity very similar in some cases to high church Iberian Catholicism. These differences are inherited from a Latin American Catholicism that, as Justo González points out, has never been monolithic.[16]

While the vast majority of U.S. Hispanics remain poor, the significance of these difficulties for U.S. Hispanic theology will only increase as the assimilation of Hispanics into the United States middle class increases. Though the popular religious worldview may indeed be common to all Latinos, the concrete manifestations of that worldview differ not only according to one's cultural subgroup, for example, Mexican, Cuban, Puerto Rican, but also according to socioeconomic differences. Moreover, even when the prevalence of popular religious practices, such as devotions to the crucified Jesus, seems to cut across class lines, those practices may function quite differently in different contexts, empowering the poor, on the one hand, while legitimating the power of the wealthy on the other.

Our ability to develop a critical reflection on U.S. Hispanic popular religiosity will thus depend on our ability to understand those practices as cultural-economic practices, what other scholars have called poietic praxis,[17] or material-social practice.[18] Just as economic structures are always at the same time cultural structures (witness the differences between Japanese and United States capitalism), so too are cultural structures and expressions always economic in that they are produced within a particular economic system and utilize the products of that system.[19] Practical human relationships are mediated by things, or products, which in turn acquire meaning in and through those very relationships. Religious symbols, for instance, are at the same time cultural and economic products: for example, as real bread and, hence, the product of someone's labor, eucharistic bread has both a religious, sacramental meaning and an economic meaning.[20] When we break bread with others we are thus engaging in an act that is at the same time cultural and economic. The relationship between the two is not linear, or even dialectical, but organic. The distinction between them is relevant, "not as a classificatory device, but as an analytic distinction highlighting different *dimensions* of behavior."[21]

If U.S. Hispanic theologians are to help develop such a cultural-economic analysis, we must root our analytical categories neither in Marxist social analysis nor in an economically innocent cultural analysis but in the historical experience of our own communities. In this light, it is interesting to note that U.S. Hispanic theology, with its emphasis on cultural analysis, has not yet taken seriously many of the insights arising out of the Chicano movement, with its greater emphasis on socioeconomic analysis.[22] In comparison with the impact of Martin Luther King, Malcolm X, and the black civil rights movement on black theology, the impact of Cesar Chávez's activism was explicitly rooted in a spirituality and theology.

What can we learn, for instance, from the colonial analysis of some Chicano scholars, whose point of departure is the Chicano context as one of internal neocolonialism?[23] They suggest that such an analysis would necessarily be integrative; "to be colonized means to be affected in every aspect of one's life: political, economic, social, cultural, and psychological."[24] These scholars would distinguish their analytical approach from social scientific approaches that focus on either class or culture.[25]

It is significant that, insofar as U.S. Hispanic theologians have developed analytical categories also prevalent in Chicano studies, these have been explicitly cultural and racial: for example, *mestizaje*. Important as the notion of *mestizaje* is for understanding the U.S. Hispanic theological context, exclusive focus on *mestizaje* would tacitly exclude socioeconomic dimensions as determinants of our historical context. In Professor Phan's words, *mestizaje* is a symbol of biologico-cultural oppression, exploitation, and alienation. Like popular religiosity, *mestizaje* is a common experience of all Latinos. Yet, also like popular religiosity, *mestizaje* manifests itself quite differently among different Latinos. And like popular religiosity, those differences are often linked to socioeconomic differences. As Phan indicates, a nascent social scientific methodology which seeks to overcome this dualism is that of *investigación-acción participativa*, or participatory action research.[26] This method is being developed among third-world social scientists critical of both Marxist and functionalist schools. In some ways, participatory action research is the social scientific analogue of Paulo Freire's pedagogical method, striving to empower the poor to develop their own social scientific analyses. Consequently, this method shares both the strengths and the ambiguities of Freire's method; among the latter I would include Phan's concerns about the nature of the relationship between the intellectuals and the people. Orlando Fals Borda documents how Colombian social scientists attempting to implement this method ended up imposing their own Marxist class analysis on the experience of the people and then presumptuously calling the analysis popular science.[27] This experience reveals a weakness of participatory action research; despite its criticisms of Marxist social analysis, its ideology continues to be dialectical materialism.[28]

Nevertheless, participatory action research ascribes the totalitarian tendencies of both Marxist analysis and functionalist analysis to their common assumption that only an intellectual elite or vanguard can do social scientific analysis, which in turn assumes "that the people are incapable of systematizing their own thought—that is, of building their own science."[29] According to proponents of participatory action research, Phan's question, "What does it mean to be with the people?" presupposes the very theory-praxis dichotomy which they have rejected. Such a question could not be asked and answered in the abstract: "How far this...can go from any given situation cannot be usefully speculated about in the abstract....In this sense there is no theory of how participatory action research may, if at all, bring about macrostructural change by itself or through the processes that it generates."[30] Yet, one may ask, isn't the very presupposition that there can be no antecedent theory itself a theory which functions as the researcher's methodological starting point and which, as such, pre-supposes the very theory-praxis dichotomy it has ostensibly rejected? In sum, participatory action research shows promise in its desire to expand the notion of scientific analysis to include the popular wisdom of the poor, yet it remains susceptible to the very elitism it abjures.

What becomes clear in the end is the extent to which all of us are heirs to the post-Enlightenment anthropologies and epistemologies underlying both Marxist analysis and functionalist analysis, both social analysis and cultural analysis. It may be that U.S. Hispanic theologians can draw on the insights and integrative orientation of such movements as *chicanismo* and participatory action research. At the same time, we must remain attentive to the questions raised by Professor Phan concerning the process of contextualization. Those questions may function both as warnings and as catalysts for creativity in formulating methodologies for understanding more accurately the context from which we theologize. In what we have come to call our postmodern world, we can no longer look exclusively to western social science and theology. That is both the challenge and the promise of our task. It is a challenge presented not only to U.S. Hispanic theology but to so-called contextual theologies as a whole. Consequently, third world, feminist, and critical western theologians must work together so that, together and each from within the particularity of our own context, we may help move theology beyond the destructive dichotomies of modernity.

Bishop Enrique San Pedro, S.J.

THE PASTOR AND THE THEOLOGIAN

The title of this paper might mislead some into thinking that I have given in to the easy temptation of borrowing an ancient and well-tested genre: the so-called literary joust.[1] From the Sumerian and Babylonian literatures there have come to us several pieces belonging to what scholars classify as contest literature; in them two contestants would argue the merits of each one, leaving usually to a god the task of settling the question with a final verdict. We are somewhat familiar with this form from the story of Cain and Abel in the book of Genesis, where a distant echo is found of the Sumerian poem Dumuzi and Enkimdu.[2] The genre has well defined elements; it also offers the distinct advantage of fine-tuning the dispute in an entertaining vein. In a way it might be considered a worthy forerunner of the platonic dialogue and even of the medieval scholastic *disputatio*.

Be that as it may, my intention is not to engage in a debate, but rather to explore in an irenic mode the relationship between these two very important callings and functions in the church, namely, those of the pastor and theologian. The task assigned to me has been to answer the question: What does the pastor expect from the theologian? This question could be answered facetiously in a very short statement by saying that as a shepherd in the church I expect the theologian to be truly Catholic. I would hasten to add that I likewise expect the pastor to be Catholic. It should be obvious, therefore, that the answer I will attempt to sketch requires some understanding of the nature of being Catholic, as well as the function and charism of the theologian and the pastor in the church. Hence, this paper will explore these three topics as necessary premises to a correct answer.

140

WHAT IS CATHOLIC?

It is not my intention to define the nature of Catholicity in some sort of thesis; I would rather share with you some basic principles that allow me, existentially as it were, to determine what is Catholic, doctrinally as well as pastorally speaking. Although I do not pretend to be original to any special degree, I must confess that the identification of these principles as basic guides in the task of distinguishing what is Catholic from what is the fruit of my own search and meditations.

The principle of paradoxical balance. I consider this principle the most fundamental one, and in a way the easiest test to detect what is Catholic. It must be said also that by its very nature it is the most difficult one to live by and to put into practice in doctrinal matters as well as in pastoral praxis. I would dare to say that properly understood and correctly applied it constitutes the clearest and safest beacon to guide us through the stormy seas of Catholic thinking and living.

According to this principle any Catholic doctrine, any Catholic praxis is characterized by an extremely difficult and delicate balance of two propositions (in pastoral praxis we would speak of actions, programs, attitudes) that although not contradictory in themselves, do appear as very difficult to reconcile with each other.

I do not know any article of our Catholic faith that is not a concrete example of this principle. Suffice it to mention only a few as examples to which, I trust, many more could be added: the doctrine of the Trinity, the relationship between scripture and tradition, the sharing in Christ's unique priesthood by all the baptized in the universal priesthood of the sacrament of holy orders; and in the practical order, the preferential option for the poor and the universal pastoral care of all and everyone, the fostering of sincere and respectful ecumenical and interreligious dialogue and faithful obedience to the mission of the church to preach the good news to all.

This principle touches the very heart of what is Catholic. It is a well-known fact that from its earliest usage by Christian authors the word "Catholic" has two main meanings (another example of the same principle): namely, the universality and totality of the church, but also her authenticity and perfection in the possession of the whole truth in her union with Christ.[3] This second meaning is the one that opposes Catholic to heretical, words that contain an implicit but necessary reference to the principle under discussion. It is precisely because the tension of the paradox becomes unbearable that the heretic chooses one of the terms of an article of Catholic faith over another, destroying thus its delicate balance.[4] Examples are abundant and easy to find; more important is the awareness of the universal character of this principle, of its inherent difficulty, and most of all of the absolute need of the presence and guidance of the Holy Spirit to be able to sail through this Christian Scylla and Charybdis.[5]

The principle of Incarnation. This principle is in itself another example of the previously discussed one. It could be enunciated thus: in the present economy God saves us through man (in its generic meaning) and in a human manner. Although as enunciated this principle is restricted to the present economy and supposes therefore the need of salvation, it does not preclude that to communicate with us in another hypothetical economy God could use a different approach. I see here a substantial difference between these two principles; the former is in my opinion absolutely necessary given the mysterious nature of the central tenets of our faith, the latter on the other hand is not only conditioned by our present existential situation, but also by God's own salvific will.

Theologically speaking, the principle of Incarnation is also fundamental. It is one of the oldest tests of orthodoxy (and I would add consequently, of orthopraxis), as clearly proclaimed by the first letter of John: "Thus will you recognize the spirit of God: every spirit that acknowledges Jesus Christ comes in the flesh is from God; but any spirit that does not acknowledge Jesus is not from God."[6]

This principle rules out any form of gnosticism, that insidious and perennial cancer of sound theological thinking. It opposes also the common temptation of angelism, and of a *Deus ex machina* mentality, not so rare, especially in practical matters.

To this same principle belongs the sacramental dimension of Catholic thought and life; for without the symbolic efficacy of the sacraments neither the doctrine nor the praxis of the Catholic Church can be properly understood.[7]

The paschal principle. This principle affirms the truth that the cross of Jesus is the instrument chosen by God to achieve our redemption, and simultaneously that the transit of the Lord, the paschal mystery, is not complete without the glory and triumph of his resurrection. It contains, therefore, three main assertions or elements: the necessity of the death of Jesus on the cross for our redemption, the necessity of his resurrection, and the necessity for each one of us to share in his cross and resurrection.

Few principles are so clearly stated in the New Testament and foreshadowed in the Old Testament. From the unmistakably clear injunction of Jesus, "If anyone wishes to come after me, he must deny himself, take up his cross daily and follow me,"[8] to the practical consequences so forcefully drawn by St. Paul, "I have been crucified with Christ."[9] Also, "those who belong to Christ have crucified their flesh with its passions and desires."[10] "We who were baptized into Christ

Jesus were baptized into his death. We were indeed buried with him through baptism into death, so that, just as Christ was raised from the dead by the glory of the Father, we too might live in the newness of life."[11]

The practical aspect of this principle does not need to be argued. It would be, however, a serious mistake to think that there are no significant implications for theological thought and research in it. The intemperate outbursts of St. Paul in his letters to the Corinthians and the Galatians should warn us against this dangerous misconception. Did he not write to the Corinthians: "The message of the cross is foolishness to those who are perishing, but to us who are being saved it is the power of God...we proclaim Christ crucified, a stumbling block to Jews and foolishness to Gentiles?"[12] Did he not admonish them concerning the resurrection: "If Christ has not been raised, your faith is vain; you are still in your sins?"[13] And to the Galatians, did he not share with them that passionate *cri du coeur*: "May I never boast except in the cross of our Lord Jesus Christ, through which the world has been crucified to me, and I to the world?"[14]

The risen Lord of the Lukan narrative also clearly indicates the central position of this principle in the apostolic kerygma when he chides the disciples on their way to Emmaus: "Oh, how foolish you are! How slow of heart to believe all that the prophets spoke! Was it not necessary that the Messiah should suffer these things so as to enter into his glory?"[15]

Therefore, no true Christian living, no sound Christian theology is possible if the basic attitude is the one decried by St. Paul in his letter to the Philippians: "For many, as I have often told you and now tell you even in tears, conduct themselves as enemies of the cross of Christ."[16] Similarly, the clear and public profession of our faith in the risen Lord is necessary both theoretically and practically: "If Christ has not been raised, then empty is our preaching; empty, too, your faith."[17]

It is not my intention to enter here into a concrete and detailed account of the consequences for theology derived from this principle. Anyone familiar with the contemporary theological and pastoral landscape knows how difficult it is to live by it.

The soteriological principle. This principle is primarily pastoral, although it is doctrinally founded and has, too, theological ramifications. It is best defined by that old legal dictum of the church's jurisprudence: "*Salus animarum suprema in Ecclesia lex esto.*"[18]

The principle has positive as well as negative implications. It requires from all of us, but especially from the pastor and the theologian, to avoid destructive and scandalous attitudes, behavior, utterances. We all know that some of the harshest sayings of Jesus are reserved for those who scandalize his little ones: "Whoever causes one of these little ones who believe in me to sin, it would be better for him if a great millstone were put around his neck and he were thrown into the sea."[19] St. Paul echoes faithfully this warning of the Master with his characteristic poignancy: "It is good not to...do anything that causes your brother to stumble."[20] "I urge you...to watch out for those who create dissensions and obstacles, in opposition to the teaching that you learned; avoid them. For such people do not serve our Lord Jesus Christ but their own appetites, and by fair and flattering speech they deceive the hearts of the innocent."[21] And writing to the Corinthians he sets down with forceful bluntness this principle in its negative aspect: "If food causes my brother to sin, I will never eat meat again, so that I may not cause my brother to sin."[22]

As mentioned before, there are also positive implications of this principle. We are not called only or even in the first place to avoid evil; the true Christian call is to perfection. It goes without saying that this task to achieve perfection cannot be understood as a strictly individual and isolated effort; it is a common undertaking in which everyone bears a share of the burden for the universal good. For this reason we find so often in the Pauline literature the exhortation to build the church. In the letter to the Romans we read: "Let us then pursue what leads to peace and to building up one another;"[23] and again, "We who are strong ought to put up with the failings of the weak and not to please ourselves; let each of us please our neighbor for the good, for building up."[24] One final quote from First Corinthians will give us the insight into the rationale for this Christian duty: "Knowledge inflates with pride, but love builds up."[25]

The somatic principle. This last principle is intimately related to the previous one. It shares with it the priority of the pastoral dimension without excluding doctrinal or theological implications. Its classical expression is found in the great Pauline texts dealing with "the body of Christ."[26]

There are three things contained in the Pauline analogy that have some bearing on our subject. It should be clear in the first place that the unity of the church is not uniformity, but the result of a variety of members. Second, this variety exists for the sake of its organic totality and well-being; thus the different gifts and functions, although good in themselves, are meaningless if they do not contribute to the common good.[27] Moreover, the authenticity and justification of any such function must be gauged by its contribution to the commonweal of the whole body, the church. Third, the unity and variety of the members is warranted by the Spirit, the giver of the gifts, the guarantor and sponsor of the church's unity.[28]

Consequently, it should be evident that no member can have any legitimate claim against the good of the body of Christ which is the church; and on the other hand the good of the body validates the claims of the individual members, and confirms the authenticity of the gifts.

WHAT IS CATHOLIC THEOLOGY?

It is not my purpose to deal here with the difficult question of the possibility and nature of theology as a scientific endeavor of the human intelligence; it has been thoroughly researched in recently available literature.[29] My goal is much more modest; I will simply underscore three aspects or characteristics of theological reflection that are especially important to answering the question before us.

Fides quaerens intellectum. This Anselmian definition of theology brings to our attention the first important characteristic; the relationship between faith and theology. By definition the object of theology is the content of faith. Although taken in very general terms this assertion is true of any theology (Muslim, Hindu, etc.). It contains, nonetheless, a specific element when applied to Christian theology; an element that constitutes the central problem of any Christian theological enterprise, namely, the fact that the core of our faith is the revelation of the mystery of God, as the Second Vatican Council reminded us in the dogmatic constitution *Dei Verbum*.[30] It should be evident, therefore, that we are faced here with a difficult problem inherent in Christian theology. I see in it one more example of the first principle of paradoxical balance discussed earlier.

In the definition of Anselm, however, the word *fides* should not be taken to mean exclusively the content of our faith, but also the assent of faith. In scholastic language, theological reflection is related to faith not only as *fides quae*, but also as *fides qua*.[31] In other words, nobody can be a true Catholic theologian by simply applying to the content of the Christian faith the scientific method proper to theology, albeit in the most rigorous manner,[32] without the opening to God who reveals himself, that St. Paul calls the *oboeditio fidei*,[33] and which the Second Vatican Council explains as that attitude by which "man freely commits his entire self to God, making 'the full submission of his intellect and will to God who reveals', and willingly assenting to the revelation given by him."[34]

This first characteristic tells us, therefore, that the task assigned to a truly Christian theology can never be outside the realm of faith, not only because its proper object is necessarily related to God's revelation, but also because it cannot be properly accomplished from the outside.

It is possible indeed to apply from the outside the theological reflection to Christian theology and in this instance it would be part of the discipline of comparative religion.[35]

Ecclesial dimension of the theological reflection. This second characteristic is intimately related to the first one in as much as the Christian faith is essentially oriented toward the formation of the community of believers. In other words the church as the people of God, as the body of Christ is the necessary consequence and complement, at least in the present salvific plan of God, of individual faith. The Second Vatican Council affirms explicitly in the dogmatic constitution on the church that God "has willed to make men holy and save them, not as individuals without any bond or link between them, but rather to make them into a people who might acknowledge him and serve him in holiness."[36]

Thus it follows that the necessary and proper locus of Catholic theological reflection must be the community and communion of believers.[37]

I do not deem it necessary to spell out in detail what it means to engage in theological work from within the church. It will be enough for me to note two or three of the most important consequences of this dimension of theology.

In the first place this dimension requires an inner attitude of love and loyalty that Ignatius of Loyola so beautifully expressed in his *sentire cum ecclesia* and in the rules for this purpose found in the Spiritual Exercises.[38] To my knowledge Henri de Lubac's *Meditations sur l'Eglise* are one of the most outstanding examples in our time of this heroic love. The loyalty and love for the church of true Catholic theology does not preclude the service to her of honest criticism that must, however, be done always from within the communion, and according to the rules of charity.

It follows also that the true exercise of this ecclesial reflection must be based upon a clear consciousness of its intrinsic limitations. I am not speaking only or even in the first place of the limitations proper to the human condition, but rather of the limitation that brought Jesus to praise the Father: "for although you have hidden these things from the wise and the learned you have revealed them to the merest children."[39] I am speaking of the limitations that touch the essence of the Christian message, the foolishness of the cross, "for it is written: 'I will destroy the wisdom of the wise, and the learning of the learned I will set aside.'"[40] Without this clear consciousness no Christian theology is possible.

Finally, it also follows that theology in the church must be practiced with a true spirit of collaboration. This is perhaps not the best way to express what is also a necessary attitude, namely the one that flows from the somatic principle as examined above. What that attitude requires is the joyous acceptance of the variety of spiritual gifts and the recognition that they are given to us for the common good within the reality of the body of Christ which is the church.

Pastoral dimension of the theological reflection. I call attention to this last characteristic of Catholic theology. By requiring it to have a pastoral dimension the fact is underscored that theology as a function and a service in the church can never be exclusively a barren intellectual exercise.[41]

Although this pastoral dimension of theological activity touches somehow the scholastic dispute concerning its speculative or practical character, it goes beyond the question of the nature of theology as a branch of scientific knowledge.[42] The adjective "pastoral" indicates the intrinsic, essential orientation of theology, if it is to be truly Christian, toward the fulfillment of hope and love in the life of the community of believers. In a very true sense the credentials and credibility of theological activity that wishes to be faithful to its Christian vocation must be measured by its kerygmatic character, that is, by its service to the announcement of the good news of salvation.[43] The well-known dictum of Dibelius concerning the origin of the gospels, *An Anfang war die Predigt*, is true also of theology, certainly not in the sense of its literary forms and rhetorical qualities, but in the deeper one of its goal and orientation. Indeed a theology that does not foster the growth and deepening of the faith, hope and love not only of its practitioner, but of the Christian community in general, is not worthy of its name, and decidedly not of the designation Catholic.

What is a shepherd in the church? Although I have formulated the question in the concrete, a shepherd, it might be better to develop the theme in the abstract, asking what is the pastoral office or charism in the church. This will have the distinct advantage among others of keeping balance with the previous theme where we asked, "What is Catholic Theology?"

It is a truism to say that the word pastoral in itself brings us to the ancient occupation of shepherding. As in many other instances the realities of our daily lives usher us into the world of divine salvific reality. It seems, therefore, opportune to outline first the biblical data concerning pastoral care, and then discuss its concrete exercise in the church.

The shepherd in the Bible. It is beside the scope of this discussion to enter into the archaeological, socioeconomic, historical or cultural details of the role and occupation of shepherds in ancient Israel or in Jesus' times.[44] I may safely assume that all of us are familiar with them. For my purpose it will be enough to note the transference from the historical and socioeconomic reality to the revealed relationship of God with his people.

We all remember the great classical texts of the Old Testament that present to us the God of Israel as the true and faithful shepherd of his people, especially in sharp opposition to the unfaithful human shepherds that lead the people astray.[45] We are even more familiar with the synoptic and Johannine gospel passages where Jesus attributes to himself the divine Old Testament prerogative of being the good and true shepherd of the people.[46] It is remarkable, then, that we would find this prerogative applied to some in the church. Among the several texts that witness to this shift, the episode in John's narrative where the risen Lord entrusts to Simon Peter the pastoral care of his flock occupies a place of honor, and rightly so.[47] It is worth noting in this pericope the strong, indeed the necessary relationship established between the public though very humble profession of love of Peter and the bestowal upon him of the pastoral task.

Pastoral service to the People of God. The Second Vatican Council in its Dogmatic Constitution on the Church (*Lumen Gentium*) stated that "the bishops received the charge of the community, presiding in God's stead over the flock of which they are shepherds in that they are teachers of doctrine, ministers of sacred worship and holders of office in government."[48] Similarly in the decree *Christus Dominus* on the Pastoral Office of Bishops in the Church we read "The bishops also have been designated by the Holy Spirit to take the place of the apostles as pastors of souls and, together with the supreme pontiff and subject to his authority, they are commissioned to perpetuate the work of Christ, the eternal pastor. For Christ commanded the apostles and their successors and gave them the power to teach all peoples, to sanctify men in truth and to give them spiritual nourishment. By virtue, therefore, of the Holy Spirit who has been given to them, bishops have been constituted true and authentic teachers of the faith and have been made pontiffs and pastors."[49]

I have quoted these two texts at length because they contain an excellent description of the pastoral office as the church understands it. Although the quoted texts speak of bishops, it should be noted that the constitution *Lumen Gentium* adds explicitly "with priests and deacons as helpers";[50] similarly the Decree on the Ministry and Life of Priests reminds us that "The function of the bishops' ministry was handed over in a subordinate degree to priests so that they might be appointed in the order of the priesthood and be co-workers of the episcopal order for the proper fulfillment of the apostolic mission that had been entrusted to it by Christ."[51]

There are three main conclusions to be drawn from these conciliar texts pertaining to the theme of this paper.

It should be clear in the first place that the pastoral office in the church includes as an essential element the service of teaching. This consideration brought Karl Rahner to state explicitly that "every priest, even more so every bishop must be a theologian."[52] The object, of course, of this teaching is none other than the salvific truth as declared in the first letter to Timothy: "[God] wills everyone to be saved and to come to knowledge of the truth";[53] the truth contained and taught in holy scripture "for the sake of our salvation,"[54] in the words of the dogmatic constitution *Dei Verbum*.

It follows also that the knowledge of salvific revealed truth and its doctrinal research and development (theology), are not ends in themselves, but are subordinated to salvation and consequently to the sanctification of the church and her members. This consequence which flows from the characteristics of the pastoral office coincides with what was said above concerning the pastoral dimension of theological reflection. It does not detract, however, from the legitimate autonomy of theology as a branch of scientific endeavor; it merely underlines the fact that as a service and a charism it cannot be divorced from the first and main purpose of the church, which is salvation through the announcement of the good news, and the establishment of the community of believers.[55]

A third consequence is the distinction between the apostolic (pastoral) charism and theological activity, in their relationship to the revealed truth. The specific service of the pastoral office in the church is to safeguard, warrant and promote ecclesial communion. Since an essential component of this communion is unity of faith based on the revealed word of God, whose interpretation "has been entrusted to the living teaching office of the church alone,"[56] it follows that the relationship of pastoral office to revealed truth is the one just described. On the other hand, the task of theologians is very similar to the one assigned to exegetes by the constitution *Dei Verbum*, that is, "to work, according to [the] rules [of their discipline], toward a better understanding and explanation of the meaning of [the revealed truth] in order that their research may help the church to form a firmer judgment."[57]

THE PASTOR AND THE THEOLOGIAN

We come finally to the question that gave origin to these reflections: What does the pastor expect from the theologian? Although the question has been implicitly but sufficiently answered, yet it might be advisable to summarize our findings in a few conclusions.

The teaching office. We have seen that the pastor and the theologian share some type of teaching ministry. We have seen likewise that this ministry in the church must be subordinate to the main end and goal of the church's activity: the proclamation of the good news of salvation and the establishment of the Christian community.[58]

The pastor then expects from the theologian an attitude of conscious acceptance of these data. Moreover, the difference in nature of both teaching ministries must be acknowledged and respected. Whereas the teaching authority of the theologian is based primarily on the quality of the doctrine and the soundness of the scientific method; that of the pastor, specifically the bishop (including of course the bishop of Rome, the pope), is based, on the contrary, on the grace of and call to the apostolic office, not excluding, of course, the necessary doctrinal preparation.

In other words, the pastor expects the theologian not only to engage seriously in the carrying out of the theological task, but also as a loyal member of the faith community to acquiesce to the action and guidance of the Holy Spirit, who puts some as overseers "to shepherd the church of God."[59]

Evangelization and inculturation. This might be the most important service that the pastor may solicit from the theologian. Although not an easy task, it is certainly within the province of theological activity. It is, besides, an aspect of the church's mission of paramount importance as the pastoral constitution *Gaudium et Spes*,[60] the apostolic exhortation *Evangelii Nuntiandi*,[61] and the recent encyclical *Redemptoris Missio*[62] of John Paul II have made abundantly clear.

What is asked of the theologian is a twofold undertaking: on the one hand the message of the gospel must be translated into the language of the culture, in such a manner that its integrity and purity would not be imperiled or compromised in any way. Paul VI expressed clearly the importance and difficulty of this task when he wrote in the apostolic exhortation *Evangelii Nuntiandi*: "Evangelization loses much of its force and effectiveness if it does not take into consideration the actual people to whom it is addressed, if it does not use their language, their signs and symbols....But on the other hand evangelization risks losing its power and disappearing altogether if one empties or adulterates its content under the pretext of translating it."[63]

On the other hand, the theologian must also help to evangelize the culture. In the same exhortation Paul VI lamented "the split between the gospel and culture"; this, he said, "is without a doubt the drama of our time."[64] To attain this goal the theologian must be very familiar with the culture, but must also be willing to analyze it with a keen eye illumined by the gospel in order to discover those elements that "have to be regenerated by an encounter with the gospel."[65]

Professional responsibility. This third conclusion touches a point that could be used as an example of the evangelization of culture. In our present cultural perception the freedom of speech, the right to instant and complete information is given such priority and importance that it is often portrayed as overriding any other consideration.

A truly responsible theologian would gauge very carefully not only the weight and value of his/her theological research, whether it is a simple hypothesis or a probable opinion, or again a more solid one; but also, and even more so, the pastoral consequences of an immature, hasty, or indiscriminate broadcasting or publication.

It is too unbecoming to spread among the general public theological theories and opinions, even solid ones, that oppose or contradict commonly held doctrinal positions without offering at the same time the necessary explanations. To destroy without constructing is not responsible behavior.

Let the great Augustinian rule of conduct also be our guide in this matter: *In necessariis unitas, in dubiis libertas et in omnibus caritas*; remembering, however, that the universal character of love binds us in a very special way to be concerned for the least of our brothers and sisters.

Edward Branch

RESPONSE TO
BISHOP ENRIQUE SAN PEDRO, S.J.

When one asks the question how theologians can aid pastors, it seems to me one is asking for responses to felt needs. The pastor as bishop serves a local church gone global and public. His institutional persona feels a "blessed rage for order." The grass roots pastor is, however, treading water at best in an undulating sea of paradigm shifts and sociological change. He needs trusted allies in the dialogues and confrontations that take place without benefit of common meaning and symbol as ethnocentric and econocentric communities are called into exchange. He needs help with an articulation of the experience of new popular religion and new propositional religion.

Bishop San Pedro speaks to the question from above, urged on by his responsibility for institutional stability and the values it embodies and protects. The grass roots pastor, on the other hand, cries out from below seeking light in the midst of the experience of keenly felt threats to personal worldviews whether his own or his constituents'. The perspective of our traditional western theologies is from above: God speaks and people hear. Theologies from below, black and other liberation theologies, begin from another perspective: we cry and God hears. Bishop San Pedro speaks to the question from above, as it were, from the perspective of institutional imperatives seated in long-standing tradition. While the approach is true, good, and of value, it needs the balance of a perspective from below, a call to address the sources of what Joseph Donders[1] terms a non-bourgeois theology. Such would, among other things, free one to listen to others, to be instructed, freed and even led by the so-called under-developed minorities (who happen to be the majority in the church) and in the process discover true identity and a common source of unity.

The bishop's presentation begins with an encouraging reflection. The question what is Catholic theology is apt. The response, however, while providing institutional parameters does not provide for present pastoral needs. There is a felt need to replace a propositional faith with an articulation that honors the experience of an emerging global church. The experience that the ecclesiology of Avery Dulles[2] attempts to respect does not appear to be acknowledged here. The author's task description for the academy by implication does not aptly reflect the total clientele served. The need for order must be balanced by the need for community.

I take no exception to the identifying principles. They are useful as far as they go: Catholic theology characterized by the paradoxical principle by which it accepts a tension of opposing interests and concepts as a normal state of affairs; the incarnational principle that God's action is by means of human agents; the paschal principle that lifts up the necessity of the cross in every Christian life; the soteri-ological principle by which relationship is drawn between church law and salvation; and the somatic principle which confirms the notion that the good of the body (the whole church) before the individual and the community validates the claims of the members and their gifts.

It is timely as well for Bishop San Pedro to remind us of theology's description as faith seeking understanding. The confirming of the Catholic theologian's role in the church is a faith task operating from within, as opposed to a strictly scientific approach as is the case for some scholars of comparative religion. The description of doctrinal and ecclesiastical parameters and tasks is clarifying and may in some quarters provide a corrective.

The grass roots pastor, however, seeks the need for theology at a different level. This local pastor contends daily with a panic shared with the people. The old props appear out of place and where they are employed they are not helping people sense a valued place in the cosmos or their own community; in some cases not even in their homes and primary relationships. Defining and directing themselves by propositions and duties is not providing wholeness or relatedness in a fast shrinking world. In the new global village there are other approaches to reality which seem sensible, helpful, and even healthy. As David Tracy so well states in this introduction to Mary Durkin Greeley and Andrew Greeley's work:

> They know that the Church of our childhood memories, the Church where doctrinal propositions and ethical norms often seem to be the heart of the matter was but one moment in a wider richer history of spirituality, imagina-tion, story and community.[3]

From below we need theologians to augment and articulate this consciousness of a wider, richer history, a spirituality, an imagination that is at the heart of a healthy Catholic identity. To speak of Catholic identity is to ask theologians to walk with Greeley in calling up our characteristically analogical imagination. In all our confusion we depend on theological reflection to carry us back to what is most secure and settling, our common valuing of space, time, silence, people, story, prayer, and sacramentality.[4] Then we can with confidence, enter into conversation with others.

A second role of the theologian as Bishop San Pedro states is to proclaim the good news and establish Christian community. That community is crying out to be globally pollinated. Joseph Donders' reflection referenced above is the fruit of his East African experience. He asks the theologian of the west to begin with the experience of the people. He asks that non-western visions and ways of seeing reality be allowed to speak to us of who God is and who we are. As an example he cites the contrast in point of view between our very familiar Cartesian philosophical principle, "I think therefore I am," and African philosophies that begin with the base principle, "I relate therefore I am." Popularly stated, "I am because we are." This communal basis for self-reflection calls into question our individualistic and personalist approaches to experience. It is a counterpoint to our western penchant for separating the secular from the sacred which leads at times to structures that respond to individual agendas rather than communal need. This is a balance from below or from the outside with which the church needs to be evangelized. Theologians need this vision in order to help us with our own self-vision.

The pastor needs the theologian to be in conversation with the whole church, not just the western church. Latin quotations and dicta are symbolic and even sacramental of a particular hegemony which is often oppressive. To cite Hispanic and Native American wisdom literature is to model a comfort with the rainbow we are. This habit prepares the pastor to welcome difference as freedom. The pastor needs the theologian to assist, for example, in the encounter with Africa which will bring back together the secular and the sacred. Donders maintains that this religious margin that we in the west have evolved is a primary reason for the development of independent African churches and, one might add, the rise of such fundamentalist communities as the Church of God in Christ. The latter boasts the most rapid growth among black churches according to the recent black church study by Franklin and Mamya. Not a few of these converts are Catholics.

I am excited and encouraged by the author's celebration of Paul VI's emphasis on evangelization and inculturation. He invokes *Evangelii nuntiandi* to call theologians to the task of evangelizing and being evangelized by cultures. Pastors from below depend on theologians to accompany them with the fruit of their carefully cultivated relationships into the threatening waters of the domestic, prophetic cultures to be evangelized and cultures that will evangelize us. I would ask Bishop San Pedro to call theologians into conversation not only with South American liberation theologians who are distant, but also with North American anawim who are near. Not the least of these ought to be the scholars of the African-American experience. We need this conversation to take place as assiduously as we have carried on Anglican and Lutheran dialogues.

In his work, *Troubling Biblical Waters*, Cain Hope Felder invites us into such conversation as he proclaims a new role in evangelization for the black church.

> Perhaps the Black church with her long history of being regarded as "the least of these" may claim and exercise a leadership that can emerge only out of a commitment to the suffering witness of Jesus who though poor made many rich. We are at a curious juncture where the Black church vocation...includes a word of survival for the whole human family.[5]

The grass roots pastor needs desperately to enjoy eavesdropping status on conversation between Roman Catholic and black church theologians as well as other so-called minority theologians. It is out of such conversation that a black Catholic identity can emerge to evangelize our Roman church in the light of Felder's vision. A view from below will enable theologians to help pastors listen to C. Eric Lincoln's call to hear the black church's moral voice evangelizing the mainstream in the midst of what Gunnar Myrdal terms our American dilemma.

In my view, Bishop San Pedro raises up traditional emphasis on institutionally focused parameters for the work of the theologian. While this is valued and necessary, there are grass roots imperatives occasioned by our social and spiritual history which must be highlighted as well if the academy is to help the pastor usher in the kingdom of God today. The theologian can help the pastor focus on that Catholic imagination which is at the heart of our unity. Help us, theologians, to do by baptism and ordination what you do by profession: be at once institution and person. Help us to reformulate and reinterpret space, time, silence, story, and sacrament in a meaningful way from below, not for but with the *anawim*.

NOTES

Self-Identity in a Multicultural Church in a Multicultural Context

1. This is a collage poster prepared by Dean Williams for the Seattle Production Center's "Festival Sundiata," 16–18 February 1991–10th Anniversary Celebration of African American Culture, History & Art, Jazz, Gospel, Dance, Theatre, African & Caribbean Music & Blues.

2. See Hans Konig, *Columbus: His Enterprise* (New York: Monthly Review Press, 1976); Tzvetan Todorov, *The Conquest of America*, trans. Richard Howard (1982; New York: Harper & Row Publishers, 1984). For an insightful discussion of this work by Todorov, see José Piedra, "The Game of Critical Arrival," *Diacritics* 19, 1 (Spring 1989):34–61. See also, Bartolomé de Las Casas, *The Devastation of the Indies: A Brief Account*, trans. Herma Briffault (1552; New York: The Seabury Press, 1974); Miguel Leon-Portillo, *The Broken Spears: The Aztec Account of the Conquest of Mexico* (Boston: Beacon Press, 1962); Bernal Díaz del Castillo, *The Conquest of New Spain*, trans. J.M. Cohen (1560; Baltimore, MD: Penguin Books, 1963); Eric Williams, *From Columbus to Castro: The History of the Caribbean*, 1492–1969 (New York: Vintage Books, 1984); Robert Conrad, *Children of God's Fire: A Documentary History of Black Slavery in Brazil* (Princeton, NJ: Princeton University Press, 1983).

3. This is not a catalogue of the contents of my personal library. I mention here some of the authors whose work has helped me to think through issues, to clarify my questions more carefully and more critically, to shape and state my positions more concretely. Most of these men and women are not theologians, but their works have given me crucial assistance in framing the task of theologizing in a multicultural context. Lest the reader grow alarmed: I do read and study theological works.

4. Cornel West, "The New Cultural Politics of Difference," in *Out There: Marginalization and Contemporary Cultures*, ed. Russell Ferguson, et al.

(Cambridge, MA: MIT Press in association with the New Museum of Contemporary Art, 1990) 19–36; also, Stuart Hall, "New Ethnicities," *Black Film/British Cinema, ICA Document* 7, ed. Kobena Mercer (London: Institute of Contemporary Arts, 1988) 27–31.

5. See Hervé Carrier, "Understanding Culture: The Ultimate Challenge of the World-Church?" in *The Church and Culture Since Vatican II: The Experiences of North and Latin America*, ed. Joseph Gremillion (Notre Dame, IN: University of Notre Dame Press, 1985) 14.

6. Edward Tylor, *Primitive Culture* (London: John Murray, 1871) I, 1.

7. Charles H. Craft, *Christianity in Culture: A Study in Dynamic Biblical Theologizing in Cross-Cultural Perspective* (Maryknoll, New York: Orbis Books, 1979) 45–46.

8. Alfred L. Kroeber and Clyde Kluckhohn, *Culture: A Critical Review of Concepts and Definitions* (New York: Vintage Books, 1952) 357, cited in Craft, *Christianity and Culture*, 46.

9. Cornel West, *Prophesy Deliverance! An Afro-American Revolutionary Christianity* (Philadelphia: The Westminster Press, 1982) 29.

10. Ibid.

11. I am indebted to Dr. Marina Herrera for reminding me of the deep Spanish influence in the west and southwest of the U.S. See James Hennesey, *American Catholics: A History of the Roman Catholic Community in the United States* (New York: Oxford University Press, 1981) 9–22; Cyprian Davis, *The History of Black Catholics* (New York: Crossroad Publishing, 1990) 28–34.

12. Frantz Fanon, *Wretched of the Earth* (New York: Grove Weidenfeld, 1963) 233.

13. Cited in Roy Harvey Pearce, *Savagism and Civilization: A Story of the Indian and the American Mind* (1953; Berkeley: University of California Press, 1988) 51; see Dee Brown, *Bury My Heart at Wounded Knee: An Indian History of the American West* (1970; New York: Bantam Books/Holt, Rinehart, & Winston, Inc., 1971); Vine Deloria, Jr., *Custer Died for Your Sins: An Indian Manifesto* (New York: The Macmillan Company, 1969), idem, *We Talk, You Listen: New Tribes, New Turf* (New York: Macmillan, 1970); Francis Jennings, *The Invasion of America: Indians, Colonialism, and the Cant of Conquest* (Chapel Hill: University of North Carolina Press, 1975); James S. Olson and Raymond Wilson,

Native Americans in the Twentieth Century (1984; Urbana and Chicago: University of Illinois Press, 1986).

14. Oscar Handlin, *The Uprooted*, 2nd rev. ed. (1951; Boston: Little, Brown and Company, 1973) 31.

15. Ibid., 31–33.

16. The precise numbers of Africans who were captured, who died in the infamous Middle Passage or in ways related to their embarkation may never be known; nor can scholars determine the exact numbers of those enslaved. See Philip Curtin, *The Atlantic Slave Trade: A Census* (Madison: University of Wisconsin Press, 1969); Joseph E. Holloway, ed., *Africanisms in American Culture* (Bloomington and Indianapolis, IN: Indiana University Press, 1990).

17. See Holloway, "The Origins of African-American Culture," 1–18, especially, 2–13; Albert Raboteau, *Slave Religion: The "Invisible Institution" in the Antebellum South* (Oxford: Oxford University Press, 1978) 5–7; Martha Washington Creel, *"A Peculiar People": Slave Religion and Community-Culture Among the Gullahs* (New York: New York University Press, 1988) 29–50; Walter Rodney, *A History of the Upper Guinea Coast, 1545–1800* (Oxford: Clarendon Press, 1970) 32–33, 65–67.

18. Immanuel Wallerstein suggests that "peoplehood is not merely a construct but one which, in each particular instance, has constantly changing boundaries. Maybe a people is something that is supposed to be inconstant in form. But if so, why the passion? Maybe because no one is supposed to comment upon the inconstancy. If I am right, then we have a very curious phenomenon indeed—one whose central features are the reality of inconstancy and the denial of this reality," in Etienne Balibur and Immanuel Wallerstein, *Race, Nation, Class: Ambiguous Identities* (1988; London/New York: Verso Press, 1971) 77.

19. Handlin, *The Uprooted*, 31.

20. Handlin, *The Uprooted*, 31; see Richard Sennett & Jonathan Cobb, *The Hidden Injuries of Class* (1972; New York: Vintage Books/Random House, 1973); cf. Nathan Glazer and Daniel Patrick Moynihan, *Beyond the Melting Pot: The Negroes, Puerto Ricans, Jews, Italians, and Irish of New York City* (Cambridge, MA: MIT Press, 1964).

21. Richard Rodriguez, *Hunger of Memory: The Education of Richard Rodriguez* (1982; 1983; New York: Bantam Books, 1988) 1–18.

22. Bernard Lonergan, *A Second Collection*, eds., William F.J. Ryan and Bernard J. Tyrrell (Philadelphia: Westminster Press, 1974), especially, "The Transition from a Classicist World-View to Historical-Mindedness," 1–10, "The Absence of God in Modern Culture," 101–116, "Theology and Man's Future," 135–148, "The Future of Christianity," 149–163.

23. This struggle is frequently enjoined at the crossroads of language. Four observations: (1) There is the authorial decision regarding language. The bilingual or multilingual author must decide which language in which to write. For instance, in 1977, Kenyan Ngugi Wa Thiong'o, author of more than several dozen novels and plays, declared that English would no longer serve as the vehicle for his work. The last novel Ngugi wrote in English was *Petals of Blood*, although he continued to write explanatory prose in English up until 1986. His last work in this language was *Decolonising the Mind: The Politics of Language in African Literature* (1986; London/Nairobi: James Currey/Heinemann, 1989). Ngugi now writes in Gikuyu and Kiswahili. (2) Hispanic, Latina/Latino writers face a similar decision: Shall they write in their rich, particular cultural-linguistic adaptations of Spanish or in the so-called standardized English of the United States? Either choice brings challenges—both languages are languages of the conqueror. Ada Maria Isasi-Diaz and Yolando Tarango pose one solution in their *Hispanic Women: Prophetic Voice in the Church* (San Francisco: Harper & Row, 1986). Isasi-Diaz and Tarango use both English and Spanish in their text, thus making it accessible for Spanish readers who choose not to or do not read American English. (3) Blacks in the United States know these agonies intimately and all too well. To a certain extent, literacy has always been a site of struggle for the descendants of the enslaved Africans. Blacks were forbidden to learn to read and to write. Enslaved African women and men caught attempting to learn to read were severely flogged; those caught attempting to write often lost a thumb or finger to the slave-master's cruelty. (4) Finally, consider the courageous example of black South African students. On July 16, 1976, the Soweto Students Representative Council held a meeting to protest the compulsory use of Afrikaans, the language of white supremacy in South Africa, as the medium of their education. As they marched to a mass rally scheduled for the Orlando stadium, the students were confronted by police. At the end of the day, 100 brave young black children had been killed.

24. Archives of the Congregation for Propagation of the Faith. Rome, Scritture riferite nei Congressi, I: America centrale dal Canada all'isthmo di Panama, 1673–1775, fols. 442rv, 443r, Charles M. Whelan, O.F.M. Cap., to Nuncio at Paris, New York, January 28, 1785, cited in Hennesey, *American Catholics*, 75.

25. Henry Werner Bowden, "Foreword," *To Promote, Defend, and Redeem: The Catholic Literary Revival and the Cultural Transformation of American Catholicism,* 1920–1960 by Allan Sparr (Westport, CT: Greenwood Press, 1990) ix.

26. Ibid.

27. For some representative discussions, see Pontifical Commission Iustitia et Pax, *The Church and Racism: Towards a More Fraternal Society* (Vatican City, 1988); Gregory Baum and John Coleman, ed., *The Church and Racism* (Edinburgh/New York: T. & T. Clark Ltd/Seabury Press, 1982).

28. Cyprian Davis, *The History of Black Catholics,* 33.

29. Ibid.

30. See United States Catholic Conference, *Cultural Pluralism in the United States* (Washington, D.C., 1980); Philip Gleason, *Speaking of Diversity: Language and Ethnicity in Twentieth-Century America* (Baltimore and London: The Johns Hopkins University Press, 1992) especially, chapter 11.

31. See David J. Bosch, *Transforming Mission: Paradigm Shifts in Theology of Mission* (Maryknoll: Orbis Books, 1991); Robert J. Schreiter, *Constructing Local Theologies* (Maryknoll: Orbis Books, 1985). Also, see *Gaudium et Spes,* "The Pastoral Constitution on the Church in the Modern World" (Second Vatican Council, December 7, 1965) in Joseph Gremillion, compl., *The Gospel of Peace and Justice: Catholic Social Teaching Since Pope John* (Maryknoll: Orbis Books, 1976). I will be quoting from this below.

32. *Gaudium et Spes,* #53.

33. Kroeber and Kluckhohn, *Culture: A Critical Review of Concepts and Definitions,* 357, cited in Craft, *Christianity in Culture,* 46.

34. *Webster's New World Dictionary of the American Language,* 2nd College Edition (New York: Simon and Schuster, 1982).

35. See Joseph Devlin, *A Dictionary of Synonyms and Antonyms* (1938; New York: Popular Library, Inc., 1961): Difference: separation, disagreement, dissent, discord, estrangement, variety, distinction, dissimilarity, dissimilitude, variation, variance, divergence, contention, dispute, disparity, inequality, unlikeness, discrimination, diversity, discrepancy.

36. Iris Marion Young, *Justice and the Politics of Difference* (Princeton, NJ: Princeton University Press, 1990) 157.

37. Ibid., 98; see Max Horkheimer and Theodor W. Adorno, *Dialectic of Enlightenment*, trans. John Cumming (1944; 1969; New York: Continuum Publishing, 1972) especially, 120–167.

38. Young, *Justice and the Politics of Difference*, 99.

39. Hazel V. Carby, "The Politics of Difference," *Ms. Magazine* (September/October 1990); 84; cf. idem, "The Multicultural Wars" in *Black Popular Culture*, ed., Gina Dent (Seattle: Bay Press, 1992) 187–199.

40. Ibid., 85.

41. Balibar and Wallerstein, *Race, Nation, Class*, 21.

42. Anthony Giddens, *Modernity and Self-Identity: Self and Society in the Late Modern Age* (Stanford: Stanford University Press, 1991) 5.

43. For helpful discussions of modernity, see Daniel Bell, *The Cultural Contradictions of Capitalism*, especially 3–30; Peter Faulkner, *Modernism* (London: Methuen & Co. Ltd., 1977); and Anthony Giddens, *Modernity and Self-Identity*, especially, 10–34; Cornel West, *Prophesy Deliverance!*, especially, 47–65; T.S. Eliot, *Christianity and Culture: The Idea of a Christian Society and Notes Towards the Definition of Culture* (1940; 1949; New York: Harcourt, Brace & World, Inc., 1968) especially 24–35; and James Evans, "African-American Christianity and the Postmodern Condition," *Journal of the American Academy of Religion* 58,2 (Spring 1990): 207–22, especially, 209–213.

44. Giddens, *Modernity and Self-Identity*, 53.

45. Tina Plaza, "In El Paso, Looking Latin Is a Crime," *Progressive Magazine* 57, 4 (April 1993): 18, 20; see Robert Gooding-Williams, ed., *Reading Rodney King: Reading Urban Uprising* (New York: Routledge, 1993).

46. Elaine H. Kim, "Home is Where the Han Is: A Korean American Perspective on the Los Angeles Upheavals," *Social Justice* 20, 1–2 (Spring and Summer 1993): 1–21.

47. Ibid., 8.

48. Ibid.

49. Ibid., 9.

50. Ibid., 16.

51. Ibid.

52. Ibid.

53. Ibid., 10.

54. Ibid., 11.

55. Lourdes, Torres, "The Construction of the Self in U.S. Latina Autobiographies," in Chandra Mohanty, et al., ed. *Third World Women and the Politics of Feminism* (Bloomington and Indianapolis, IN: Indiana University Press, 1991) 275; see also Daniela Gioseffi, ed., *On Prejudice: A Global Perspective* (New York: Doubleday/Anchor Books, 1993); Cameron McCarthy and Warren Crichlow, ed., *Race, Identity and Representation in Education* (New York: Routledge, 1993); and Theresa Perry and James W. Fraser, ed., *Freedom's Plow: Teaching in the Multicultural Classroom* (New York: Routledge, 1993).

56. Torres, "The Construction of the Self," 276.

57. Trinh T. Min-ha, "Cotton and Iron," in *Out There: Marginalization and Contemporary Cultures*, 332.

58. For a statement of the responsibilities and struggles of insurgent intellectuals, see Bell Hooks and Cornel West, *Breaking Bread: Insurgent Black Intellectual Life* (Boston: South End Press, 1991).

59. "Aztec Poem," in *Poems of the Aztec People*, trans. Edward Kissam and Michael Schmidt (Ypsilanti, MI: Bilingual Press, 1983), cited in Renny Golden, et al., ed., *Dangerous Memories: Invasion and Resistance Since 1492* (Chicago: Chicago Religious Task Force on Central America, 1991) n.p.

Response to M. Shawn Copeland

1. *Church and Cultures: New Perspectives in Missiological Anthropology* (Maryknoll: Orbis Press, 1989).

2. Bartolomé de las Casas, *Historia de las Indias* (Santo Domingo: Sociedad Dominicana de Bibliofilos, 1987), 2.3.4:441–42.

3. Letter to Diego Colón, governor and Viceroy in Santo Domingo from King Ferdinand V, the Catholic. As quoted by Luis N. Rivera Pagán,

Evangelización y Violencia: La Conquista de América (San Juan, Puerto Rico: Editorial Cemi, 1990), 399. My own translation from Spanish original.

4. This has been defined as the ability to understand and have empathy with peoples from different cultures. Cf. David W. Augsburguer, *Pastoral Counseling Across Cultures* (Philadelphia: The Westminster Press, 1986).

5. "Traveler, there is no way to make one walk." Translation by the editor.

The Theology of the Local Church: State of the Question

1. I have described these developments and supplied extensive bibliographies in "The Local Church and the Church Catholic: The Contemporary Theological Problematic," in *The Jurist* 52 (1992) 416–447; and in "Subsidiarity in the Church: The State of the Question," *The Jurist* 48 (1988) 298–349.

2. Pius XII, *Mystici Corporis*, AAS 35 (1943) 211–12.

3. This theological validation is carried forward when *Christus Dominus* gives a theological and not merely canonical definition of a diocese as "a portion of the People of God which is entrusted for shepherding to a bishop with the cooperation of the presbyterate, so that in union with its pastor and assembled by him through the Gospel and the eucharist in the Holy Spirit, it may constitute a particular Church in which the one holy catholic and apostolic Church of Christ exists and acts" (*CD* 11).

4. Here I borrow several paragraphs from the first article cited in footnote 1.

5. "Draft Statement on Episcopal Conferences," *Origins,* 17 (1987–88) 735. For a critique of this text, see Joseph A. Komonchak, "Introduction: Episcopal Conferences under Criticism," in *Episcopal Conferences: Historical, Canonical, and Theological Studies*, ed. Thomas J. Reese (Washington: Georgetown University Press, 1989) 1–22, and "The Roman Working Paper on Episcopal Conferences," Ibid., 177–204.

6. See *Origins* 22/7 (25 June 1992) 108–12.

7. See Hermann J. Pottmeyer, "Kirche als Communio: Eine Reformidee aus unterschiedlichen Perspektiven," *Stimmen der Zeit* 210 (September 1992) 579–89; Robert W. Jensen, "Some Contentious Aspects of

Communion," *Pro Ecclesia* 2 (1993) 133-37; and the responses to the Letter from Orthodox, Methodist, Reformed, and Anglican perspectives in *Catholic International* 3 (September 1992) 767-76.

8. Pope John Paul II, Speech to the Roman Curia, 20 December 1990; *AAS* 83 (1991) 746.

9. This is a rather different interpretation of the Pentecost assembly than that proposed by the Congregation. But it has behind it the views of such theologians as Louis Bouyer, Henri de Lubac, J.M.R. Tillard, and Herve Legrand. In addition, both Bouyer and Tillard propose the thought-experiment of imagining that some catastrophe has reduced the church to a single community of believers gathering around a bishop to celebrate the eucharist. (Nothing in Christ's promises prevents one from imagining that what happened, say, to the church in North Africa, could not happen on a worldwide scale.) In that case, this one little community of the faith would be at once the local and the universal church, the heir of Christ's promises and the bearer of his mission to the world.

10. Pope John Paul II, Address to the Roman Curia, 21 December 1984, *AAS* 77 (1985) 503-14.

11. *Origins*, 16 (1986) 476.

12. Pope John Paul II's 1985 Encyclical, *Slavorum Apostoli*, esp. #16-20, contains a powerful illustration of the encounter of gospel and a single culture.

13. For this reason, as Herve Legrand has argued, territorial divisions of the church—as into parishes, dioceses, regional and national groupings—are not merely a matter of administrative efficiency but have theological value. Everyone in a place is welcome. Where this territorial assembling in one place is neglected in favor of primarily intentional reasons for gathering (e.g., ethnicity, race, gender, economic status, political orientation, etc.), there is a great danger that the integration of diversity into unity in Christ, which is the very definition of catholicity, will cease to count.

Response to Joseph A. Komonchak

1. Yale University Press, 1990, 174.

2. 20 December, 1984 (*AAS* 77 [1985]).

3. Text in *Origins*, 16 (1986) 476.

4. Ibid.

A Multicultural Church? Theological Reflections from Below

1. My views on culture (and on its components and consequences) have been shaped, especially, by two authors, Peter L. Berger and Antonio Gramsci. In spite of their philosophical differences, Berger and Gramsci seem to share some foundational intuitions on the roles of conscience and reality-building that can greatly affect and enrich the theological enterprise. They are certainly not the only thinkers to address these and parallel issues, but they have seemed to me to better articulate the issues more relevant to those socially below. This paper has clearly been influenced by Berger and Gramsci, but I do not claim to be repeating what they said. From Berger's long list of publications, see, *The Social Construction of Reality*, with T. Luckmann (New York: Doubleday/Anchor, 1967); *The Sacred Canopy* (New York: Doubleday/Anchor, 1969); *A Rumor of Angels* (New York: Doubleday/Anchor, 1970); and *The Heretical Imperative* (New York: Doubleday/Anchor, 1980); *The Precarious Vision* (New York: Doubleday, 1961); "Marriage and the Construction of Reality," with H. Kellner, *Diogenes*, 46:2 (1964) 1–24; and "Reification and the Sociological Critique of Consciousness," *History and Theory*, 4:2 (1965) 196–211. A fine synthesis and analysis of Berger's thoughts on culture may be found in R. Wuthnow, et al., *Cultural Analysis: The Work of Peter L. Berger, Mary Douglas, Michel Foucault and Jürgen Habermas* (London: Routledge & Kegan Paul, 1984). For a strong reaction against Berger, see, J.M. Gonzalez Garcia, *La sociologia del conocimiento hoy* (Madrid: Ediciones Espejo, 1979). I have read Antonio Gramsci's complete works in Portuguese translations, and it is these that I use here. From Gramsci's bibliography, see, *Os intelectuais e a organização da cultura* (Rio de Janeiro, ed. Civilização Brasileira, 1979. [Transl. of *Gli intellettuali e l'organizzazionne della cultura*]); *Cartas do cárcere* (Rio de Janeiro: Ed. Civilização Brasileira, 1978 [Transl. of *Lettere dal carcere*]); *Maquiavel, a politica e o estado moderno* (Rio de Janeiro: Ed. Civilização Brasileira, 1980 [Transl. of *Note sul Machiavelli, sulla politica, e sullo stato moderno*]); *Concepção dialética da história* (Rio de Janeiro, ed. Civilização Brasileira, 1981 [Transl. of *Il Materialismo storico e la filosofia di Benedetto Croce*]); *Literatura e vida nacional* (Rio de Janeiro, ed. Civilização Brasileira, 1978 [Transl. of *Letteratura e vita nazionale*]). For fine syntheses and analyses of Gramsci's thought, see, H. Portelli, *Gramsci y el bloque histórico* (Mexico: Siglo XXI Editores, 1980), and, idem, *Gramsci y la cuestión religiosa* (Barcelona: Editorial Laia, 1977). Also, L. Gruppi, *O conceito de hegemonia em Gramsci* (Rio de Janeiro: Edições Graal, 1980);

C.N. Coutinho, *Gramsci* (Porto Alegre: L&PM Editores, 1981); M.A. Manacorda, *El principio educative en Gramsci* (Salamanca: Ediciones Sígueme, 1977); and, C. Buci-Glucksmann, *Gramsci e o estado* (Rio de Janeiro: Editora Paz e Terra, 1980).

2. See A. Gramsci, *Concepção dialética da história*; also, L. Gruppi, *O conceito de hegemonia em Gramsci*.

3. *Praxis* and *poiesis* will be italicized throughout in order to refer to the meanings articulated in my discussion. See N. Lobkowicz, *Theory and Practice: History of a Concept from Aristotle to Marx* (Notre Dame: University of Notre Dame Press, 1967); F. Taborda, *Cristianismo e ideologia* (Sao Paulo: Ed. Loyola, 1984); C. Boff, *Teologia e prática: Teologia do político e suas mediações* (Petrópolis: Ed. Vozes, 1978); R. Bernstein, *Beyond Objectivism and Relativism: Science, Hermeneutics, and Praxis* (Philadelphia: University of Pennsylvania Press, 1985); and, H.G. Gadamer, "Hermeneutics and Social Science," in, *Cultural Hermeneutics*, 2 (1975) 307–316.

4. See his three programmatic articles: "*Nosotros*: Toward a U.S. Hispanic Anthropology," in *Listening, Journal of Religion and Culture*, 27:1 (1992) 55–69; "U.S. Hispanic Theology and the Challenge of Pluralism," in A.F. Deck, ed. *Frontiers of Hispanic Theology in the United States* (Maryknoll: Orbis Books, 1992) 1–22; and, "Rediscovering Praxis: The Significance of U.S. Hispanic Experience for Theological Method," in R.S. Goizueta, ed. *We Are a People!: Initiatives in Hispanic American Theology* (Minneapolis: Fortress Press, 1992) 51–78.

5. This point is thoroughly explained by Gramsci, especially through his analyses of "hegemony" and of the "historical block." Berger, although not discussing this issue directly, implies as much in his discussions of "plausibility." See the pertinent bibliography in note 1, supra.

6. The reflection on these issues can and should be enriched by the thought of Emmanuel Levinas and Juan Carlos Scannone. The latter, especially, has consistently reflected upon the meaning of these cultural (and sociological) issues for theology. By Levinas, *L'Humanisme de l'autre homme* (Montpellier: F. Morgana, 1972); and, *Totalite et infini* (The Hague: Martinus Nijhoff, 1971). By Scannone, *Evangelizacíon, cultura y teología* (Buenos Aires, ed. Guadalupe, 1990); *Teología de la liberación y doctrina social de la Iglesia* (Buenos Aires, ed. Guadalupe, 1987); *Teología de la liberación y praxis popular* (Salamanca, ed. Sígueme, 1976); and, *Sabiduría popular, símbolo y filosofía* (Buenos Aires, ed. Guadalupe, 1984).

7. By socialism I mean (throughout this paper) non-Leninist socialist

thought. In my view, real socialism was not directly involved in establishing and running the former communist states. Leninist communism did not take real socialism seriously, although there might be some shared philosophical categories and analytical methodologies, given the fact that orthodox Leninism developed from a strand within the broader socialist thought. Even some well-known Marxist thinkers were considered dangerous and unacceptable in the former Leninist states.

8. It would be extraordinarily naive (and inaccurate "wishful thinking") to assume that the collapse of the Leninist states of eastern Europe implies the clear victory of capitalism. Real socialism, after all, had also been perceived as inimical by the former Leninist states. State Leninism might be dead in most places (and unfortunately, not everywhere), but the questions and issues raised by real socialism are still very much with us. The victory of capitalism seems to have been celebrated, understandably, in some quarters of the planet. Most of the third world (both within and beyond the first world) has not been as jubilant or as certain that the questions raised by real socialism are dead. In any case, the demise of state Leninism may not be interpreted as the triumph of the first world.

9. This, I would argue, is much more an ecclesiological, doctrinal datum than a historical one.

10. This, obviously, is doctrinally unacceptable to Christianity, and yet, the valiant and sustained critique of this assumption has been missing within and from much of the church. The occasional prophetic document cannot undo the established connivance implied in the efforts spent legitimizing the economy as the real, everyday force behind truth and history.

11. See C. Boff, *Teologia e prática*, 377–389, esp. 378.

12. A fruitful discussion with Alasdair MacIntyre might be interesting in reference to these questions. See his *After Virtue: A Study in Moral Theory* (Notre Dame: University of Notre Dame Press, 1981) and, *Whose Justice? Which Rationality?* (Notre Dame: University of Notre Dame Press, 1988).

13. This issue is discussed by Gramsci in his analyses of the historical block. In my view, the best synthesis of his thought on this is H. Portelli's *Gramsci y el bloque histórico*. For these issues, 70–118.

14. See Berger, *The Sacred Canopy*, 84–87, 93, 95. Also, M. Olivetti, "El problema de la comunidad ética," in J.C. Scannone, ed., *Sabiduría*

popular, símbolo y filosofía, 209–222. Implied in Gramsci, see, *Os intelectuais e a organização da cultura*, 117–128.

15. Indeed, scholars from below who raise serious questions concerning the misinterpretation of their cultures, inherent in the epistemologies underlying dominant methodologies, are quickly dismissed as ultimately insignificant or as too politicized. An accusation of "too political" is grounds for dismissal or persecution of a non-dominant interpretation, and yet the fact that the establishment of the dismissal-provoking nature of that label (political) is, in itself, an act of power (and, therefore, also a political act) does not seem evident to the dominant. See Gramsci, *Literatura e vida nacional*, 15–19, 29–31, 168–171; and *Concepção dialética da história*, 64-90.

16. See Portelli, *Gramsci y el bloque histórico*, 45–48, 70–73, 93–143.

17. See Berger and Luckmann, *The Social Construction of Reality*, 92–128.

18. One example of this, in the reverse, is the case of Catholic evangelization in sixteenth-century Mexico. See my "Trinitarian Monotheism and the Birth of Popular Catholicism: The Case of Sixteenth-Century Mexico," in *Missiology*, 20:2 (1992), 177–204.

19. *Mestizaje*, as used here, is more the mix of cultures than of races (the latter understood biologically). I do not know of anyone who has theologically worked on the concept of *mestizaje* more than Virgilio Elizondo. See his *Mestizaje: The Dialectic of Cultural Birth and the Gospel* (San Antonio: Mexican American Cultural Center, 1978), 3 vols.; *The Future Is Mestizo* (Bloomington: Meyer-Stone Books, 1988); *Christianity and Culture* (San Antonio: Mexican American Cultural Center, 1975); *La Morenita: Evangelizer of the Americas* (San Antonio: Mexican American Cultural Center, 1980); and, *Galilean Journey: The Mexican-American Promise* (Maryknoll: Orbis Books, 1985). Practically all other U.S. Hispanic Catholic theologians make extensive use of *mestizaje* in their work, in diverse ways, following Elizondo's contributions.

20. Clodovis Boff's *Teologia e prática* is a very powerful argument in favor of a serious methodological dialogue between theology and the social sciences. Two other works on this same subject, that deserve very close attention by Euro-American theologies, are—R. J. Schreiter, *Constructing Local Theologies* (Maryknoll: Orbis Books, 1985); and, G. Gutierrez, "Teología y ciencias sociales," in *Páginas*, Separata 4 (1984), 4–14.

21. Very pertinent to any discussion of ecclesiological models is Berger's treatment of "institutionalization" and Gramsci's explanations on the

relation between structure and superstructure in the "historical block." See Berger and Luckmann, *The Social Construction of Reality*, 45–92; and, R. Bodei, "Gramsci: Vontade, hegemonia, recionalização," in F. Ferri, ed. *Política e história em Gramsci* (Rio de Janeiro, ed., Civilização Brasileira, 1978) vol. 1, 71–116. I have found H. Portelli's *Gramsci y la cuestíon religiosa* to be invaluable for a cultural and sociological understanding of the origins and implementations of ecclesiological models, especially within the Catholic Church.

22. Although not directly dealing with ecclesiology, one example of a theological piece that failed to observe its own culturally-bound symbolizations, blind spots and biases, and thereby resulted in a "dismissing" critique of Latin American theologians, is J.P. Meier's "The Bible as a Source for Theology," in *Proceedings of the Catholic Theological Society of America*, 43 (1988), 1–14. J. Nilson's response to Meier, *ibid.*, 15–18, rightly points to the shortcomings.

23. The text of Chalcedon's definition is in the *Acta Conciliorum Oecumenicorum*, vol. II, II, i (Berlin: 1922) 129–30. The English translation is by Albert C. Outler, John H. Leith, ed. *Creeds of the Churches* (Atlanta: John Knox Press, 1982, 3rd ed.), 35–36.

24. See, for example, M. de França Miranda, *Libertados para a práxis da justiça* (São Paulo, ed., Loyola, 1980) 37–46.

25. I would suggest that cultural analysis might be fruitfully incorporated (methodologically) into such theological areas as soteriology, anthropology and grace, and, of course, christology.

26. See H. Portelli, *Gramsci y la cuestión religiosa*, 101–107, 141–162.

27. I have insisted on this in other places. For example, "Trinitarian Monotheism and the Birth of Popular Catholicism"; and also, "The Vanquished, Faithful Solidarity and the Marian Symbol: A Hispanic Perspective on Providence," in J. Coultas and B. Doherty, eds. *On Keeping Providence* (Terre Haute: St. Mary of the Woods College, 1991) 84–101; and, "The God of the Vanquished," in *Listening, Journal of Religion and Culture*, 27:1 (1992), 70–83.

28. The imposition of at least one model clearly happened with the forced evangelization of the Americas, starting at the end of the fifteenth century. The idea that evangelization is bound to ecclesiological imposition, although not original to the western hemisphere, seems to have been assumed (by those with ecclesiastical and social power) as true, self-evident and valid in the Americas since 1492. Those

ecclesiastically and socially vulnerable seem to have responded with a strong doubt. The persistence of popular Catholicism is an important indication of this resisting doubt. For the early colonial period, see, L.N. Rivera Pagán, *Evangelización y violencia* (San Juan: Editorial Cemí, 1991); and for the late colonial and post-colonial periods, my "Popular Religion among Latinos," J. Dolan, A.F. Deck and J. Vidal, eds. *History of Hispanic Catholics in the U.S.* (Notre Dame, University of Notre Dame Press, forthcoming) vol. 3. Virgilio Elizondo's *Galilean Journey* is eloquent in addressing this issue from the perspective of the Mexican American.

29. This discussion can be enriched by dialogue with Gramsci's concepts of the "organic intellectual" and the "traditional intellectual." See Portelli, *Gramsci y el bloque histórico*, 93–118.

Response to Orlando Espín

1. "The Refusal of Women in Clerical Circles," in *Women in the Church*, ed. Madonna Kolbenschlag (Washington, DC: Pastoral Press, 1987) I:51–63.

2. See, for example, Ada Maria Isasi-Diaz and Yolanda Tarango, *Hispanic Women: Prophetic Voice in the Church* (Minneapolis: Fortress Press, 1992) 3–9.

3. Sally McFague, *Models of God.* (Philadelphia: Fortress Press, 1978) 34ff.

4. David Power, *The Sacrifice We Offer.* (New York: Crossroad, 1987), especially chapters 2 and 5.

5. Commentators on the Hans Urs von Balthasar's *The Glory of the Lord: A Theological Aesthetics* tend to accord greater ontological density to the bride-bridegroom metaphor than does von Balthasar himself. See, for example, Sara Butler, "The Priest as Sacrament of Christ the Bridegroom," in *Worship* (November 1992) 498–517; also, Elizabeth Picken, "If Christ Is Bridegroom, the Priest Must Be Male," in *Worship*, (May 1993) 269–278.

6. See Elizabeth Johnson, *She Who Is* (New York: Crossroad, 1992) who finds in the doctrine of the Trinity the ontological basis for an ecclesiology of mutual relations of equality.

7. "It has always been my contention that popular religiosity is a privileged vehicle for Hispanic cultures. Popular religiosity has been, and still is, the least 'invaded' cultural creation of our peoples, and a locus for our most authentic self-disclosure." See "Grace and Human-

ness" in Roberto S. Goizueta, ed. *We Are a People* (Minneapolis: Augsburg Fortress, 1992) 148.

8. Isasi-Diaz and Tarango, ibid.

9. Anticipation of an inclusive eschatological *mestizaje*, symbol of God's gracious future, is not the central focus of this presentation. Elsewhere in his writings, Espín uses the term historically to designate the new culture generated by the mingling of Spanish and Native American cultures; see Roberto Goizueta, ed. *We Are A People*, 133, n.2.

10. "An Adventuresome Hypothesis: Women as Authors of Liturgical Traditions," in the *1993 Proceedings* of the North American Academy of Liturgy (Valparaiso, IN); also "Principles of Feminist Liturgy," in *Women's Liturgy Handbook*, ed. Janet Walton and Marjorie Proctor-Smith (Nashville: Abingdon Press, 1993).

Communion within Pluralism in the Local Church: Maintaining Unity in the Process of Inculturation

1. The term is used by Anscar Chupungco, *Liturgical Inculturation: Sacramentals, Religiosity, and Catechesis* (Collegeville: The Liturgical Press, 1992) 47–51.

2. Johann-Baptist Metz, "Unity and Diversity: Problems and Prospects for Inculturation," *Concilium* 204 (1989): 79–87.

3. Tzevan Todorov, *La Conquête de l'Amérique. La Question de l'Autre* (Paris: Ed. du Seuil, 1982).

4. What is presented is scarcely more than an outline, such as allowed within the dimensions of a paper. It is at least hoped that a strategy is offered for more adequate reflection.

5. *"What We Have Seen and Heard ." A Pastoral Letter on Evangelization from the Black Bishops of the United States* (Cincinnati: St. Anthony Messenger Press, 1984) 4.

6. Ibid., 31.

7. "Without wishing to decide immediately whether we are dealing with facts or signs, it seems difficult to refute the available evidence of the defaillancy of the modern subject. No matter which genre it makes hegemonic, the very basis of each of the great narratives of emancipation has, so to speak, been invalidated over the last fifty years. All that is real is rational, all that is rational is real: 'Auschwitz' refutes

speculative doctrine. At least that crime, which was real, was not rational. All that is proletarian is communist, all that is communist is proletarian: 'Berlin 1953, Budapest 1956, Czechoslovakia 1968, Poland 1980' (to mention only the obvious examples) refute the doctrine of historical materialism: the workers rise up against the Party. All that is democratic exists through and for the people, and vice versa: 'May 1968' refutes the doctrine of parliamentary liberalism. If left to themselves, the laws of supply and demand will result in universal prosperity, and vice versa: 'the crises of 1911 and 1929' refute the doctrine of economic liberalism. And 'the 1974–9 crisis' refutes the post-Keynesian adjustments that have been made to that doctrine." *The Lyotard Reader*, edited by Andrew Benjamin (Oxford and Cambridge, Mass.: Blackwell, 1989) 318.

To Lyotard's sad list, we may add the failure of the doctrine of the community of democratic nations, as symbolized in Vietnam 1968–75, Sarajevo 1992, and Mogadishu 1992, equalled by the failure of proletarian democracies as symbolized by Moscow 1991.

8. Vatican II, *Lumen Gentium* 1.

9. The word is coined to indicate a tendency to revert to practices and values of a previous era.

10. Jon Butler, *Awash in a Sea of Faith. Christianizing the American People* (London and Cambridge, Mass.: Harvard University Press, 1990) 129–130: "Those who molded and imbibed slavery also produced the single most important religious transformation to occur in the American colonies before 1776: an African spiritual holocaust that forever destroyed traditional African religious systems as *systems* in North America and left slaves remarkably bereft of traditional collective religious practice before 1760. The supreme irony of this holocaust was that it paved the way for a remarkable post-1760 slave Christianization, whose first appearances more closely resembled European expressions of Christianity than might ever be the case again. Together the rise of Christian absolutism and the creation of an African spiritual holocaust demonstrates how and why, despite its vagaries, renewed Christian activity in eighteenth-century America could powerfully reshape New World society, European and African alike." The chapter is entitled, "Slavery and the African Spiritual Holocaust." Butler is not suggesting that enslavement was necessary to the evangelization of African peoples. He is simply describing what came about, with all its cruelty to black people and blindness to African culture. It was evangelization at a terrible and shocking price.

11. On the common opposition of Catholics to abolition and their support of the South at the time of the Civil War, see David O'Brien, *Public Catholicism* (New York: Macmillan, 1989) 64–70.

12. For Catholics in particular, see Cyprian Davis, *The History of Black Catholics in the United States* (New York: Crossroad, 1990). The same author summarizes the concerns and qualities of African-American spirituality in his entry under that heading in *The New Dictionary of Catholic Spirituality*, edited by Michael Downey (Collegeville: Liturgical Press, 1993) 21–24.

13. Jay P. Dolan, *The American Catholic Experience* (New York: Doubleday, 1987) 55.

14. Further on, Dolan remarks: "Of all the obstacles to conversion, none loomed so large and remained so persistent as the Indians themselves. They had their own ethical and religious beliefs, their own traditions concerning work and community living, and this religious and cultural system proved to be a formidable opponent for the missionary." Ibid., 68.

15. Ibid., 101–124.

16. For a survey of the investigations necessary for tracing the historic relation between culture and religion among Hispanics, see Allan Figueroa Deck, *The Second Wave: Hispanic Ministry and the Evangelization of Cultures* (New York: Paulist, 1989) 26–53. On some specific devotions, see C. Gilbert Romero, *Hispanic Devotional Piety. Tracing the Biblical Roots* (Maryknoll: Orbis, 1991). On Mexican-Americans in particular, see Virgil Elizondo, *Galilean Journey: The Mexican-American Promise* (Maryknoll: Orbis, 1983).

17. David Tracy, "Ethnic Pluralism and Systematic Theology; Reflections," *Concilium* 101 (1977): 91.

18. Philip Gleason, *Keeping the Faith. American Catholicism Past and Present* (Notre Dame: University of Notre Dame Press, 1987) 200–201.

19. *The American Catholic Experience*, 221–240.

20. One could elaborate on this in the story of Irish Catholicism by showing how in the interests of adaptation to milieu, a more folkloric and popular religiosity, largely independent of ecclesiastical control, was replaced both at home and in America by this more contained piety. See Patrick Corish, *The Irish Catholic Experience. A Historical Survey* (Dublin: Gill and Macmillan, 1985) 151–225.

21. See Regis A. Duffy, "Devotio Futura: The Need for Post-Conciliar Devotions?" in *A Promise of Presence*, edited by Michael Downey and Richard Fragomeni (Washington, D.C.: Pastoral Press, 1992) 163–183. Duffy refers to Robert Anthony Orsi, *The Madonna of 115th Street: Faith and Community in Italian Harlem, 1880–1950* (New Haven: Yale University Press, 1985).

22. Martin Marty, *Modern American Religion*, vol. 1, *The Irony of it All 1893–1919* (Chicago & London: University of Chicago Press, 1986) 130–149.

23. On the place which an interest in ethnicity has for the present moment of church life, Philip Gleason has this to say: "By the mid-1980s, the revival of ethnicity was over as a surge of popular sentiment and as a self-conscious "movement." Scholarly interest in ethnic history continues, however, and so do the realities of ethnic interaction in contemporary society and politics, with the Hispanics gaining greater visibility on the political, social, and religious scene and with Asians becoming a significant element. It would be unfortunate if the pendulum swung in the opposite direction, although the unbalanced interpretations advanced by spokesmen for the ethnic revival require correction. With respect to American Catholic understanding of past and present, what we must try to do is free ourselves from stereotypes both old and new." *Keeping the Faith* , 56–57.

24. For two pertinent short essays by Levinas, see Emmanuel Levinas, *Collected Philosophical Papers*, translated by Alphonso Lingis (Dordrecht & Boston: Martinus Nijhoff Publishers, 1987) 153–186.

25. Stanislas Breton, *Le Verbe et la Croix* (Paris:Desclée, 1981).

26. For a helpful overview of Levinas' thought as it applies to this question, see Luc Crommelinck, "Du souci pour l'être au souci pour l'autre. La pensée d'Emmanuel Levinas." *Lumen Vitae* 1992/3: 300–310.

27. For apposite reflections on what is involved in the development of new rites, see Diana L. Hayes, "An African American Catholic Rite: Questions of Inculturation, Collegiality, Subsidiarity," *The Living Light* 28 (Winter 1992): 35–48.

28. Maya Angelou, *On the Pulse of the Morning: The Inaugural Poem* (New York: Random House, 1993). No pages numbered.

29. David Tracy, "On Naming the Present," *Concilium* 1990/1, 83.

Response to David Power, O.M.I.

1. Power, "Communion Within Pluralism in the Local Church."

2. Ibid.

3. Ibid.

4. Ibid.

5. Ibid.

6. "What We Have Seen and Heard." A Pastoral Letter On Evangelization from the Black Bishops of the United States (Cincinnati: St. Anthony Messenger Press, 1984) 4.

7. It should be noted that in the final version of his paper, Professor Power has included references to writings by Hispanic Americans, African-Americans and others. My comments herein refer to the earlier version to which I responded at the symposium itself.

8. Power.

9. Ibid.

10. See Cyprian Davis, *The History of Black Catholics in the United States* (New York: Crossroad, 1990).

11. Power.

12. In his revised paper, Professor Power addresses this issue more along the lines of my critique noting, for example, that black Catholics are seeking "to find their own voice and define their own identities...free from Eurocentric modes of thought, power and expression: and noting that Catholicism itself played a role in the denial of this effort in the past."

13. Power, referring to *The Lyotard Reader*, Andrew Benjamin, ed. (Oxford and Cambridge, Mass.: Blackwell, 1989), 318.

14. See pp.10–11 referring to *Awash in a Sea of Faith. Christianizing the American People* (London and Cambridge, Mass.: Harvard University Press, 1990), the chapter entitled "Slavery and the African Spiritual Holocaust."

15. Butler, 129–130 as quoted in Power, footnote 10.

16. See Albert Raboteau, *Slave Religion* (NY: Oxford, 1978); Joseph

Holloway, *Africanisms in American Culture* (Bloomington: Indiana University Press, 1990); Dwight Hopkins and George Cummings, *Cut Loose Your Stammering Tongue* (Maryknoll, NY: Orbis, 1993) and Hopkins, *Shoes That Fit Our Feet: Sources for a Constructive Black Theology* (Maryknoll, NY: Orbis, 1993); Diana L. Hayes, "Black Catholic Revivalism: The Emergence of A New Form of Worship" *in The Journal of the Interdenominational Theological Center*, Vols, XIV, Fall 1986/Spring 1987, 87–107, among others on this point.

17. Power.

18. The reference to works by Jay Dolan and Philip Gleason needs to be supplemented with those of Cyprian Davis, cited above, and the U.S. Catholic Historical Society's issues on black Catholics, vols. 5/1 (1986) and 7/2, 3 (1988).

19. Note that these questions arise solely from my own encounter with the paper I am responding to rather than with the work of Tzevan Todorov upon which this section is heavily based. (See Power.)

20. See, *A Testament of Hope: The Essential Writings of Martin Luther King, Jr.,* James Melvin Washington, ed. (San Francisco: Harper and Row, 1986), 292.

Contemporary Theology and Inculturation in the United States

1. Letter to Agostino Cardinal Casaroli, on the occasion of the creation of the Pontifical Council for Culture, *Osservatore romano* (English edition), June 28, 1982, 7.

2. In this essay I will be discussing inculturation only with respect to systematic theology and leave aside other important aspects of the issue such as inculturation on the one hand and theology of the local church, mission, liturgy, pastoral practice, spirituality, and interreligious dialogue on the other. For the theology of the local church, see J.-M. R. Tillard, *Church of Churches: The Ecclesiology of Communion*, trans. R.C. De Peaux (Collegeville, MN: The Liturgical Press, 1992); *Proceedings of the Thirty-Sixth Annual Convention* of the Catholic Theological Society of America, ed. Luke Salm (1981) whose theme is the local church, with important essays by Michael Fahey, Joseph Komonchak and Robert Schreiter; Patrick Granfield, "The Local Church as a Center of Communication and Control," *Proceedings of the Thirty-Fifth Annual Convention* of the Catholic Theological Society of America, ed. Luke Salm (1980) 256–263. For mission, see David Bosch's magisterial work, *Transforming Mission: Paradigm Shifts in Theology of Mission* (Maryknoll,

N.Y.: Orbis Books, 1991), especially 447–57; Leonardo Boff, *New Evangelization: Good News to the Poor*, trans. Robert Barr (Maryknoll, N.Y.: Orbis Books, 1991); Kenneth Boyack (ed.), *The New Catholic Evangelization* (New York: Paulist Press, 1992); Mary Motte and Joseph R. Lang (eds.) *Mission in Dialogue* (Maryknoll, N.Y.: Orbis Books, 1982); James A. Schere and Stephen B. Bevans (eds.), *New Directions in Mission & Evangelization: Basic Statements 1974–1991* (Maryknoll, N.Y.: Orbis Books, 1992). For liturgy, see David Power, *Culture and Theology* (Washington, D.C.: The Pastoral Press, 1990); Mary Collins, *Renewal to Practice* (Washington, D.C.: The Pastoral Press, 1987); Anscar J. Chupungco, *Cultural Adaptation of the Liturgy* (New York: Paulist Press, 1982). For pastoral practice, see Gerald A. Arbuckle, *Earthing the Gospel: An Inculturation Handbook for the Pastoral Worker* (Maryknoll, N.Y.: Orbis Books, 1990); Peter Schineller, *A Handbook on Inculturation* (New York: Paulist Press, 1990). For spirituality, see Anthony Bellagamba, *Mission & Ministry in the Global Church* (Maryknoll, N.Y.: Orbis Books, 1992), especially 93–146; A. Retif, *La Missione: Elementi di Teologia e Spiritualitá Missionaria* (Turin: Edizioni Missioni Consolata, 1965). For Interreligious dialogue, see Peter C. Phan (ed.), *Christianity and the Wider Ecumenism* (New York: Paragon House, 1990); Tosh Arai and Wesley Ariarajah (eds.), *Spirituality in Interfaith Dialogue* (Maryknoll, N.Y.: Orbis Books, 1989).

3. For the history of the term "inculturation," see Arij Roest Crollius, "What Is So New About Inculturation?" *Gregorianum* 59 (1978) 721–38, reissued in Arij Roest Crollius and Théoneste Nkeramihigo (eds.) *Inculturation*, vol. 5 (Rome: Editrice Pontificia Universitá Gregoriana, 1984), 1–18; and Aylward Shorter, *Toward a Theology of Inculturation* (Maryknoll, N.Y.: Orbis Books, 1988) 3–16. In general, inculturation is distinguished from enculturation and acculturation. *Enculturation*, which is a sociological concept closely related to that of socialization, denotes the process whereby the individual is inserted into his or her own culture through formal and informal teaching and learning. There is an analogy between this process and the insertion of the Christian faith in a new culture. *Acculturation* is the encounter between two cultures or among cultures. Such an encounter is a dynamic and diachronic process and unavoidable today given the fact that the world has become a global village. Acculturation may lead to a mere juxtaposition of unassimilated cultural expressions by which the two cultures operate side by side, or one culture is practiced in its integrity together with selected elements of another culture or both cultures are practiced together (a form of "double belonging"). Acculturation may also lead to syncretism, by which elements of one culture are mixed with those of another so that one, if not both, loses basic identity and

structures. There are, of course, parallels between this process of acculturation between two cultures and the process whereby the Christian faith enters into a new culture, with the same dangers of juxtaposition and syncretism. See Robert Schreiter, *Constructing Local Theologies* (Maryknoll, N.Y.: Orbis Books, 1985) 144-58.

4. For a brief survey of the process of inculturation in the Christian church, see Aylward Shorter, *Toward a Theology of Inculturation* 137-76; Gerald Arbuckle, *Earthing the Gospel* 10-25.

5. "What Is So New About Inculturation?" *Inculturation*, vol. 5, 15-16. Aylward Shorter defines inculturation as: "[T]he ongoing dialogue between faith and culture or cultures. More fully, it is the creative and dynamic relationship between the Christian message and a culture or cultures." See *Toward a Theology of Inculturation* 11. Marcello De Carvaho Alzevedo describes it as: "[T]he dynamic relation between the Christian message and culture or cultures; an insertion of the Christian life into a culture; an ongoing process of reciprocal and critical interaction and assimilation between them." See "Inculturation and the Challenges of Modernity," in Arij A. R. Crollius (ed.), *Inculturation*, vol. 1 (Rome: Editrice Pontificia Università Gregoriana, 1982) 11.

Besides the term "inculturation" other terms have been used to describe this process of critical interaction and exchange between the Christian faith and cultures such as contextualization, indigenization, transposition, and incarnation. There are some disadvantages in these terms. *Contextualization* seems to suggest that inculturation is the task of only missionary lands and not of already well-established churches of the west whereas such a task is an urgent necessity of the west as well as other parts of the world; *indigenization* or *localization* historically connotes the recruitment of local people for the priestly and religious life; *transposition* (Pope Paul VI's preferred term) suffers from extrincisism; and *incarnation* encourages the wrong view that inculturation is a one-time and one-way affair, whereas it is an ongoing process affecting both the local culture and the church. To eschew these deficiencies, the neologism "inculturation" (recognized as such by Pope John Paul II) or better still "interculturation" (recommended by Bishop Joseph Blomjous) is used. For a discussion of these terms, see Aylward Shorter, *Toward a Theology of Inculturation*, 10-16, 79-83; Peter Schineller, *A Handbook on Inculturation*, 14-27 and Gerald Arbuckle, *Earthing the Gospel* , 17-20.

In this essay I use inculturation and contextualization interchangeably.

6. My second and third steps correspond to the first and second stages of evangelization as outlined by Pope Paul VI in his *Evangelii Nuntiandi*,

no. 63, in which he refers to the three phases of evangelization as assimilation, transposition (the pope's term for inculturation), and proclamation.

7. *Thinking the Faith: Christian Theology in a North American Context* (Minneapolis: Augsburg, 1989) 84. By "contextuality" Douglas means what is connoted by inculturation.

8. See ibid., 93–110. Stephen Bevans gives both external and internal reasons why theology must be contextual today. External reasons include a general dissatisfaction with classical approaches to theology among contemporary philosophers and theologians, the oppressive nature of these approaches insofar as they ignore other voices and experiences than their own, the growing autonomy of local churches, and the shift from the classicist to the empirical understanding of culture. Among internal reasons are the incarnational nature of Christianity, the sacramental nature of reality, and the new theology of revelation which sees it as an ongoing interpersonal self-communication of God to humans of all times. See his *Models of Contextual Theology* (Maryknoll, N.Y.: Orbis Books, 1992) 5–10.

9. For a brief and lucid discussion of this historically conditioned character of human knowledge, see David Kelsey, *To Understand God Truly: What's Theological About A Theological School* (Louisville, KY: Westminster/John Knox Press, 1992) 115–29.

10. See Robert Schreiter, *Constructing Local Theologies*, 75–94. Schreiter suggests that church tradition is a series of local theologies.

11. For a detailed study of this neo-scholastic theology's attempt to impose itself upon the universal church, see Gerard McCool, *Catholic Theology in the Nineteenth Century: The Quest for a Unitary Method* (New York: The Seabury Press, 1977).

12. See Bernard Lonergan, *Method in Theology* (London: Darton, Longman and Todd, 1972) xi. Lonergan's two other essays are very important on this theme: "Theology in its New Context" and "Belief: Today's Issue" reprinted in *A Second Collection*, ed. W.F.J. Ryan and B. J. Tyrrell (Darton, Longman and Todd, 1974) 55–67 and 87–99, respectively. Lonergan took the year 1680 as the dividing line marking this momentous cultural shift: then it was that Herbert Butterfield placed the origins of modern science, that Paul Hazard the beginning of the Enlightenment, and Yves Congar the birth of Roman Catholic dogmatic theology.

13. See, for instance, Jurgen Habermas, *Knowledge and Human Interests* (Boston: Beacon Press, 1971) and Peter Berger and Thomas Luckmann, *The Social Construction of Reality: A Treatise on the Sociology of Knowledge* (New York: Doubleday, 1967).

14. For a detailed discussion of this task of translating the Christian message, see Charles H. Kraft, *Christianity in Culture: A Study in Dynamic Biblical Theologizing in Cross-Cultural Perspective* (Maryknoll, N.Y.: Orbis Books, 1979).

15. See Karl Rahner, "Basic Theological Interpretation of the Second Vatican Council," *Theological Investigations*, trans. Edward Quinn (New York: Crossroad, 1981) 77–89.

16. This need of inculturating the church, and hence of theology, has been recognized by recent teachings of the hierarchical magisterium, especially by the Second Vatican Council (e.g., *Ad Gentes, Gaudium et Spes*), Paul VI (e.g., *Evangelii Nuntiandi*) and John Paul II (e.g., *Catechesi Tradendae*). For an analysis of their positions on inculturation, see Joseph Gremillion (ed.), *The Church & Culture Since Vatican II: The Experience of North and Latin America* (Notre Dame, IN: University of Notre Dame Press, 1985); Aylward Shorter, *Toward a Theology of Inculturation*, 179–238; Herve Carrier, *Gospel Message and Human Cultures from Leo XIII to John Paul II*, trans. John Drury (Pittsburgh, PA: Duquesne University Press, 1989); Paul Surlis, "The Relation between Social Justice and Inculturation in the Papal Magisterium," in Arij A.R. Crollius (ed.) *Inculturation*, vol. 8 (Rome: Editrice Pontificia Università Gregoriana, 1986) 11–40. Also deserving attention is Part II of the final document of the Third General Conference of Latin American Episcopate (CELAM) at Puebla, Mexico, January 27–February 13, 1979. On May 20, 1982, John Paul II established the Pontifical Council for Culture. In December, 1987, the International Theological Commission issued a document entitled "Faith and Inculturation."

17. This work is a further elaboration of his earlier articles, in particular, "Five Approaches to the Indigenization of Theology," in *The Kingdom of the Word*, Philippine SVD Festschrift (Manila: Catholic Trade School, 1976) 112–37; "Contextual Theology in the Philippines: A Preliminary Report," *Philippiniana sacra* 14 (1979) 36–58; "Notes on Christ and Local Community in the Philippine Context," *Verbum SVD* 21 (1980) 303–15; and "Models of Contextual Theology," *Missiology: An International Review* 13, 2 (April, 1985) 185–202. In this last article Bevans speaks of six rather than five models: the translation model, the anthropological model, the praxis model, the synthetic model, the

semiotic model, and the transcendental model. In his later book he combines the synthetic and the semiotic models together.

It would be an interesting exercise to compare these models of inculturation with the five models that H. Richard Niebuhr identifies in his classic *Christ and Culture* (New York: Harper and Row, 1951). Obviously all the five models of inculturation would reject the "Christ against Culture" approach; the translation model would be close to the "Christ above Culture" approach; the anthropological model to the "Christ of Culture" approach; the praxis model, the synthetic model and the transcendental model to the "Christ the Transformer of Culture" approach, though each with its own distinct emphasis and accent.

18. To emphasize that culture is constantly changing, Bevans makes social change a factor separate from culture. Others, e.g., Robert Schreiter, speak only of three elements, namely, the gospel message, the church, and culture. See his *Constructing Local Theologies*, 22–24. Furthermore, insofar as inculturation is seen as a process, three poles are seen as interacting with each other in a hermeneutical circle: the Christian message, the situation, and the pastoral agent. See Peter Schineller, *A Handbook of Inculturation* , 61–73. Gerald Arbuckle prefers to use the image of "earthing" for the process of inculturation in which the evangelizer, under the action of the Holy Spirit, is the sower, the gospel is the seed, and culture is the earth. See his *Earthing the Gospel*, 2–4.

19. Robert Schreiter already discerns three basic models of local theologies and discusses their strengths and weaknesses: translation models (e.g., Charles Kraft); adaptation models (e.g., Placide Tempel's *Bantu Philosophy*, Charles Nyamiti, Paul VI, and Vincent Donovan); and contextual models (ethnographic theologies and liberation theologies). Obviously there are discrepancies between his categorization and Bevans'. For example, Vincent Donovan, who is the author of many books on mission among which *Christianity Rediscovered* (Maryknoll, N.Y.: Orbis Books, 1978) is regarded by Bevans (correctly, in my view) as exemplifying the radical anthropological model rather than the middle-of-the-road adaptation model. Furthermore, Bevans' categories are, in my judgment, more nuanced and representative than Schreiter's.

20. See *Models of Contextual Theology*, 30–37. Bevans presents two proponents of this model, David J. Hesselgrave and Pope John Paul II, 37–46.

21. See ibid., 474–54. Bevans focuses on the works of Robert E. Hood and Vincent Donovan as representatives of this model (54–62).

22. See ibid., 63–71. Examples of this model Bevans found in the writings of Douglas John Hall and Asian feminist theologians (72–80).

23. See ibid., 81–88. The works of Kosuke Koyama and Jose de Mesa are singled out as examples of this model (88–96).

24. See Bernard Lonergan, *Method in Theology* (New York: Herder and Herder, 1972) 235–44. For a detailed study of Lonergan's notion of conversion, see Michael L. Rende, *Lonergan on Conversion: The Development of a Notion* (Lanham, MD: University Press of America, 1991).

25. See Bernard Lonergan, *Insight: A Study of Human Understanding* (New York: Philosophical Library, 1958) and *Method in Theology*, especially 6–20.

26. See *Models of Contextual Theology* , 97–102. Two examples of this model are given: Sallie McFague and Justo L. González (103–112).

27. Bevans discusses the merits of each model in his book. With regard to his choice of examples, it is of interest to our theme in that all of them, except John Paul II, are theologians currently working in the United States representing different denominations.

28. Théoneste Nkeramihigo has strongly criticized those who reject western culture and the "Eurocentric" character of Christianity for being dangerously abstract. He argues for maintaining the specificity of historical Christianity: "If Christianity does not concretize a universal, but rather universalizes the concreteness of the man Jesus and of the incarnation of God in him, the separation between Christianity and Western civilization, heir of Jerusalem and Athens, must be seen as false and abstract. It was therefore unavoidable that Christianity was offered in its Western specificity." See "Inculturation and the Specificity of Christian Faith," in Arij A. R. Crollius (ed.), *Inculturation*, vol. 5 (Rome: Editrice Pontificia Università Gregoriana, 1984) 25. Nkeramihigo suggests that inculturation does not start with the rejection of western culture or the western forms of Christianity; rather, it consists in reconciling the conflicts between the already active presence of western culture in the local culture before the arrival of Christianity and the local culture itself by means of the message of the gospel of Jesus.

29. Connected with this is the thorny issue of the hierarchy of truths. Does this hierarchy of truths, however established and identified, remain unchanged from culture to culture? If it is true, as Karl Rahner has argued, that the subjective appropriation of this hierarchy of truths

varies with individuals, can it be argued that the same is true with a particular culture? For instance, in a culture that places an immense religious and ethical significance on the veneration of ancestors, such as the Confucian and African cultures, the Christian practice of veneration of saints, which, objectively speaking, cannot be said to occupy a central place in the hierarchy of truths, will be seen as crucially important. For Rahner's reflections on the hierarchy of truths, see *Foundations of Christian Faith*, trans. William Dych (New York: The Seabury Press, 1978) 382–84.

30. For a discussion of these tools of cultural analysis, see Robert Schreiter, *Constructing Local Theologies* , 42–74; Louis J. Luzbetak, *The Church and Cultures*, 139–56. Obviously, each of the five models of contextual theology privileges one or more of these tools, depending on its interests. Both Schreiter and Luzbetak regard the semiotic method as the most useful for inculturation, though they are aware that it is abstract and difficult.

31. For instance, it is well known that feminists reject the way men define culture. But even among feminists, some black, Asian and Hispanic women reject the way white, middle-class feminists universalize their particular experiences as "woman's experience" and use the term "womanist" to differentiate their own view from the "feminist" one.

32. Stephen Bevans, *Models of Contextual Theology* , 11. It is well known that some feminist theologians have found "usable tradition" in "heretical" Christian traditions, pagan (e.g., goddess-tradition) resources, and modern post-Christian resources. See Rosemary Radford Ruether, *Sexism and God-Talk: Toward a Feminist Theology* (Boston: Beacon Press, 1983) 20–46.

33. Robert Schreiter proposes five criteria: Does the local theology cohere with mainline Christian symbols? Does it facilitate prayer and worship? Does it lead to Christian praxis? Is it open to the judgment of other churches? Does it present prophetic challenges to other churches and to the world? See his "Local Theologies in the Local Churches," *Proceedings of the Thirty-Sixth Annual Convention* of the Catholic Theological Society of America, ed. Luke Salm (1981) 109–111; and *Constructing Local Theologies* , 117–21. See also Stephen Bevans, *Models of Contextual Theology* , 17–20.

34. Cultural anthropologists often distinguish three levels of culture. (1) At the surface level are the individual building-blocks of culture, the meaningless forms, the signs and symbols minus their meaning of who,

what, when, where, how, and what kind. (2) At the intermediate level the society relates such forms to one another through function to create a system of meanings (the immediate whys). (3) On the third and deepest level, these meanings are integrated together into a cultural system resulting in a worldview or mentality. This worldview, which is cognitive, emotional, and motivational in nature, is expressed in a people's religion, mythology, and ritual. For a detailed description of these three levels of culture and their application to missiology, see Louis Luzbetak, *The Church and Cultures* , 223–91.

35. One can think of recent reversals of doctrines such as religious freedom and separation of church and state and the non-reception of encyclicals such as *Humanae vitae*. It is quite possible to regard inculturation as a channel for dogmatic development. See William Reiser, "Inculturation and Doctrinal Development," *The Heythrop Journal* 22:2 (1980) 135–48.

36. See Robert Schreiter, *Constructing Local Theologies* , 16–20.

37. See, for instance, Rodger Van Allen, "Catholicism in the United States: Some Elements of Creative Inculturation," in Arij Crollius, *Inculturation*, vol. 8 (Rome: Editrice Pontificia Università Gregoriana, 1986) 57–76; David O'Brien, "The Historical Context of North American Theology: The U.S. Story," in *Proceedings of the Forty-First Annual Convention* of the Catholic Theological Society of America, ed. George Kilcourse (1986) 1–15; idem, "The Church and American Culture During Our Nation's Lifetime, 1787–1987," in Cassian Yuhaus (ed.), *The Catholic Church and American Culture: Reciprocity and Challenge* (New York: Paulist Press, 1990) 1–23; Joseph A. Tetlow, "The Inculturation of Catholicism in the United States," in Arij Crollius (ed.), *Inculturation*, vol. 2 (Rome: Editrice Pontificia Università Gregoriana, 1983) 15–45; William L. Portier, "Catholic Evangelization in the United States from the Republic to Vatican II," Kenneth Boyack (ed.), *The New Catholic Evangelization* (New York: Paulist Press, 1992) 27–41; John A. Coleman, *An American Strategic Theology* (New York: Paulist Press, 1982) 155–83.

38. See his "The Church and American Culture During Our Nation's Lifetime, 1787–1987" cited above, 10–23. O'Brien suggests that in the future public Catholicism will not be contained exclusively in any one of the three styles but in a combination of all three of them. The social history of the Catholics of the third and fourth phases has been documented by Andrew Greeley's *The American Catholic: A Social Portrait* (New York: Basic Books, 1977). Greeley terms them "the communal Catholic."

39. The proceedings of these conventions have been published by the society, the first edited by Luke Salm, the second and third by George Kilcourse.

40. Some of the papers will appear in a book edited by Peter C. Phan under the title "Ethnicity, Nationality and Religious Experience" to be published by University Press of America.

41. These theologians form a group called "John Courtney Murray Writers' Group." They include Jesuits Donald Gelpi, J.J. Mueller, Frank Oppenheim, William Spohn, and John Stacer. They draw on the classical thinkers of the American tradition: Charles Sanders Peirce, William James, Josiah Royce, John Dewey, William Hocking, and Alfred North Whitehead in religious philosophy, and Jonathan Edwards, H. Richard Niebuhr, and Bernard Meland in philosophical theology. Their writings have been published in Frank M. Oppenheim (ed.), *The Reasoning Heart: Toward a North American Theology* (Washington, D.C.: Georgetown University Press, 1986).

Besides this group, there are others who attempt to construct a North American theology from the perspective of liberation theology. Three deserve mention: the American Catholic John Coleman, *An American Strategic Theology* (New York: Paulist Press, 1982); the American Presbyterian Mark Kline Taylor, *Remembering Esperanza: A Cultural-Political Theology for North American Praxis* (Maryknoll, NY: Orbis Books, 1990); and the Canadian Protestant Douglas John Hall with his projected three-volume work, the first volume of which is *Thinking the Faith: Christian Theology in a North American Context* (Minneapolis: Augsburg, 1989).

42. For a brief discussion of Catholic demographic data, see Peter C. Phan, "Preparation for Multicultural Ministry," *Seminary News*, vol. 30, no.1 (September 1991) 15–19. For data on Hispanics in particular, see Allan Figueroa Deck, *The Second Wave: Hispanic Ministry and the Evangelization of Cultures* (New York: Paulist Press, 1989) 9–25.

43. For a documentary history of black theology, see the two massive volumes edited by Gayraud S. Wilmore and James H. Cone, *Black Theology: A Documentary History, 1966-1979* (Maryknoll, NY: Orbis Books, 1979). This volume has now been revised with new essays, introductions and bibliography and is due in 1993 as the first of a two-volume work. Volume II is *Black Theology: A Documentary History, 1980-1992*. I am using the old edition in this essay. The history of the term black theology is discussed briefly by Gayraud Wilmore in the first volume, 67.

44. "Theology as Intellectually Vital Inquiry: A Black Theological Interrogation," *Proceedings of the Forty-Sixth Annual Convention* of the Catholic Theological Society of America, ed. by Paul Crowley (1991) 49.

45. James Cone associates the beginning of black theology with three contexts: the civil rights movement, Joseph Washington's book *Black Religion*, and the black power movement. See his "Black Theology" in *The Westminster Dictionary of Christian Theology*, ed. Alan Richardson and John Bowden (London: SCM Press Ltd., 1983) 72–74.

46. For the dialogue between black theology on the one hand and African, Latin American, and feminist theologies on the other, see the analysis by James Cones in *Black Theology: A Documentary History, 1966–1979* , 363–67, 445–62.

47. M. Shawn Copeland, "Theology as Intellectually Vital Inquiry: A Black Theological Interrogation," 50. See also her entry "Black Theology," in Joseph Komonchak, et al. (eds.) *The New Dictionary of Theology* (Wilmington, DE: Michael Glazier, 1987) 138–40).

48. See his *Black Religion: The Negro and Christianity in the United States* (Boston: Beacon Press, 1964). However, in his later books, *The Politics of God* (Boston: Beacon Press, 1967) and *Black Sects and Cults* (Garden City, NY: Doubleday, 1972), Washington sees the necessity of joining political struggle with religion in the black church for survival and proposes a new program for black theology.

49. James Cone's principal works include, besides the already mentioned *Black Theology and Black Power*, *A Black Theology of Liberation* (Philadelphia: Lippincott Co., 1970), reissued with new introduction and critiques as twentieth anniversary edition by Orbis Books in 1986; *The Spirituals and the Blues* (New York: Seabury Press, 1972); *God of the Oppressed* (New York: Seabury Press, 1975); *For My People: Black Theology and the Black Church* (Maryknoll, NY: Orbis Books, 1984); *My Soul Looks Back* (Maryknoll, NY: Orbis Books, 1986); *Speaking the Truth: Ecumenism, Liberation, and Black Theology* (Grand Rapids, MI: Eerdmans, 1986); *Martin & Malcolm & America: A Dream or a Nightmare* (Maryknoll, NY: Orbis Books, 1991).

50. See Deotis Roberts, *Liberation and Reconciliation: A Black Theology* (Philadelphia: Westminster Press, 1971); *A Black Political Theology* (Philadelphia: Westminster Press, 1974); *Black Theology in Dialogue* (Philadelphia: Westminster Press, 1987). For Major Jones, see his *Black Awareness: A Theology of Hope* (Nashville: Abingdon Press, 1971) and *Christian Ethics for Black Theology* (Nashville: Abingdon Press, 1974).

51. See his "Structural Similarities and Dissimilarities in Black and African Theologies," *Journal of Religious Thought*, vol. 33 (Fall–Winter 1975) 9–24; and "Perspectives for a Study of Afro-American Religion in the U.S.," *History of Religions*, vol. 2 (August 1971) 54–66 in which he suggests a method for studying black religion other than the social science approach.

52. See his *The Identity Crisis in Black Theology* (Nashville: AMEC, 1975).

53. See his *Black Religion and Black Radicalism* (Garden City, NY: Anchor Press/Doubleday, 1973).

54. See his *Is God a White Racist?* (Garden City, NY: Anchor Press/Doubleday, 1973). For James Cone's discussion of the critiques of his fellow black theologians, see "Epilogue: An Interpretation of the Debate Among Black Theologians," in *Black Theology: A Documentary History, 1966–1979*, 609–623.

55. See "Toward a Black Catholic Theology," *Freeing the Spirit*, vol. 5, no. 2 (1977) 3–6.

56. See Frances Beale, "Double Jeopardy: To Be Black and Female," in Toni Cade (ed.) *The Black Woman* (New York: Signet, 1970); Theressa Hoover, "Black Women and the Churches: Triple Jeopardy," in Alice Hageman (ed.), *Sexist Religion and Women in the Church* (New York: Association Press, 1974) 63–76. Says Hoover, "To be a woman, black, and active in religious institutions in the American scene is to labor under triple jeopardy" (63); Pauli Murray, "Black Theology and Feminist Theology: A Comparative View," *Anglican Theological Review*, vol. 60, no. 1 (January 1978) 3–24.

Contemporary black feminist theologians include, besides the three mentioned above, Katie G. Cannon *Black Womanist Ethics* (Atlanta, GA: Scholars Press, 1988); Jacquelyn Grant *White Women's Christ, Black Women's Jesus: Feminist Christology and Womanist Response* (Atlanta, GA: Scholars Press, 1989); Delores S. Williams *Sisters in the Wilderness: The Challenge of Womanist God-Talk* (Maryknoll, NY: Orbis Books, 1992); and Jamie Phelps, Shawn Copeland, and Diana Hayes.

57. See Kwesi A. Dickson and Paul Ellingworth (eds.), *Biblical Revelation and African Beliefs* (London: Lutterworth Press, 1969) and Cain Hope Felder, *Troubling Biblical Waters: Race, Class, and Family* (Maryknoll, NY: Orbis Books, 1989).

58. For the use of social analysis, see Theodore Walker, Jr., *Empower the People: Social Ethics for the African-American Church* (Maryknoll, NY: Orbis

Books, 1991); for the use of Marxist categories, see the works of Cornell West, especially his *Prophesy Deliverance! An Afro-American Revolutionary Christianity* (Philadelphia: Westminster Press, 1982) and *Prophetic Fragments* (Grand Rapids: Eerdmans/Trenton, 1988).

59. One author whose works are often invoked by black theologians is Martin Bernal. See his *Black Athena: The Afro-Asiatic Roots of Classical Civilization of Ancient Greece 1785–1985*. Vol. I: *The Fabrication of Ancient Greece 1785–1985* (New Brunswick, NJ: Rutgers University Press, 1987) and Vol. II: *The Archaeological and Documentary Evidence* (New Brunswick, NJ: Rutgers University Press, 1991).

60. Besides the work of James Cone, see Dwight N. Hopkins, *Shoes That Fit: Sources for a Constructive Black Theology* (Maryknoll, NY: Orbis Books, 1993).

61. For an account of the dialogue between black theology and other liberation theologies (African, Latin American, and Asian), see James Cone, "Black Theology and Third World Theologies: Introduction," in *Black Theology: A Documentary History*, 1866–1979, 445–62. See also George Cummings, *A Common Journey: Black Theology and Latin American Liberation Theology* (Maryknoll, NY: Orbis Books, 1992).

62. For a latest attempt at elaborating a systematic theology from the African-American perspective, see James H. Evans, Jr., *We Have Been Believers: An African-American Systematic Theology* (Minneapolis: Fortress Press, 1992).

63. The word *Hispanic* is used here to cover a variety of Spanish-speaking national groups. Other names are: Hispanic American, U.S. Hispanic, Latino, Latin, and Latin American. Currently the Hispanic population in the U.S. is estimated at twenty million, of which the largest group is of Mexican origin, the second largest group Puerto Rican, and the third largest group Cuban. About 88 percent of the Hispanic population live in urban areas. From a low of 75 percent to a high of 95 percent of the Hispanic population are estimated to be baptized Catholics. For a history of the Hispanic church in the U.S., see Moises Santoval, *On the Move: A History of the Hispanic Church in the United States* (Maryknoll, NY: Orbis Books, 1990).

64. Both of these documents are published by the USCC, Washington, D.C.

65. For a brief account of the history and the goals of the academy, see Allan Figueroa Deck, *Frontiers of Hispanic Theology in the United States*

(Maryknoll, NY: Orbis Books, 1992) xxi–xxiv. The academy publishes a newsletter available at 1050 N. Clark, El Paso, Texas 79905. For a bibliography of Hispanic theology, see Arturo Bañuelas, "U.S. Hispanic Roman Catholic Theology: A Bibliography," *Apuntes* (Winter 1991).

Although Protestant theologians have also a well-developed Hispanic theology, this essay will concern mainly the Catholic version. For Protestant Hispanic theology, see in particular Justo L. Gonzalez, *Mañana: Christian Theology from a Hispanic Perspective* (Nashville: Abingdon Press, 1990).

66. ACHTUS began its own quarterly, *Journal of Hispanic/Latino Theology*, in October 1993.

67. His books include: *Christianity and Culture: An Introduction to Pastoral Theology and Ministry for the Bicultural Community* (Huntington, IN: Our Sunday Visitor, Inc., 1975); *La Morenita: Evangelizer of the Americas* (San Antonio: Mexican-American Cultural Center, 1980); *The Galilean Journey: The Mexican-American Promise* (Maryknoll, NY: Orbis Books, 1983); and *The Future Is Mestizo: Life Where Cultures Meet* (New York: Meyer-Stone, 1988). For a brief discussion of Elizondo's theology, see Allan Deck (ed.), *Frontiers of Hispanic Theology in the United States* , xii–xiv.

68. See in particular his *The Galilean Journey* and *"Mestizaje* as a Locus of Theological Reflection," in: Allan Deck (ed.), *Frontiers of Hispanic Theology in the United States* , 104–123.

69. See Allan Figueroa Deck, *The Second Wave: Hispanic Ministry and the Evangelization of Cultures* (New York: Paulist Press, 1989) 21–25. For an extensive cultural and social analysis of Hispanic population in the U.S., see ibid., 9–91 and idem, "At the Crossroads: North American and Hispanic," in Roberto S. Goizueta, *We Are A People! Initiatives in Hispanic American Theology* (Minneapolis: Fortress Press, 1992) 1–20.

70. For the *pastoral de conjunto*, see *National Pastoral Plan for Hispanic Ministry*, Section VI, A.

71. See his "Theology as Intellectually Vital Inquiry: The Challenge of/to U.S. Hispanic Theologians," *Proceedings of the Forty-Sixth Annual Convention* of the Catholic Theological Society of America, ed. Paul Crowley (1991) 58–69; "Rediscovering Praxis: The Significance of U.S. Hispanic Experience for Theological Method," in Robert Goizueta (ed.) *We Are a People!* , 51–77; "United States Hispanic Theology and the Challenge of Pluralism," in Allan Deck (ed.) *Frontiers of Hispanic Theology in the United States* , 1–22.

72. They include María de la Cruz Aymes, Marina Herrera, Ada María Isasi-Díaz, Gloria Loya, Rosa María Icaza, and María Pilar Aquino, and others.

73. See, for instance, Ada María Isasi-Díaz and Yolanda Tarango, *Hispanic Women: Prophetic Voice in the Church* (San Francisco: Harper & Row, 1988); Ada María Isasi-Díaz, *"Mujeristas*: A Name of Our Own," in Marc Ellis and Otto Maduro (eds.), *The Future of Liberation Theology: Essays in Honor of Gustavo Gutiérrez* (Maryknoll, NY: Orbis Books, 1989) 410–19; María Pilar Aquino, "Doing Theology from the Perspective of Latin American Women," in Roberto Goizueta (ed.) *We Are A People!* 79–105; idem, "Perspectives on a Latina's Feminist Liberation Theology," in Allan Deck (ed.), *Frontiers of Hispanic Theology in the United States* , 23–40; The Hispanic Woman: *Pasionaria* and *Pastora* of the Hispanic Community," ibid., 124–33.

74. See the excellent essay of Fernando F. Segovia, "Hispanic American Theology and the Bible: Effective Weapon and Faithful Ally," in Roberto Goizueta, *We Are A People!* , 21–49 which evaluates the hermeneutical theories of Ada María Isazi-Días, Harold J. Recinos, Virgil Elizondo, and Justo González; C. Gilbert Romero, "Tradition and Symbol as Biblical Keys for a United States Hispanic Theology," in Allan Deck (ed.), *Frontiers of Hispanic Theology in the United States* , 41–61.

75. See Elizondo's reflections on the Virgin of Guadalupe in *La Morenita*; Orlando Espín and Sixto García, "Hispanic-American Theology," *Proceedings of the Forty-Second Annual Convention* of The American Theological Society of America, ed. George Kilcourse (1987) 114–19; Orlando Espín, "Tradition and Popular Religion: An Understanding of the *Sensus Fidelium*," in Allan Deck (ed.) *Frontiers of Hispanic Theology in the United States*, 62–87; C. Gilbert Romero, *Hispanic Devotional Piety: Tracing the Biblical Roots* (Maryknoll, NY: Orbis Books, 1991).

76. See Sixto García, "United States Hispanic and Mainstream Trinitarian Theologies," in Allan Deck (ed.) *Frontiers of Hispanic Theology in the United States*, 88–103; idem, "A Hispanic Approach to Trinitarian Theology: The Dynamics of Celebrations, Reflection, and Praxis," in Roberto Goizueta (ed.) *We Are A People!* 107–132.

77. See Orlando Espín, "Grace and Humanness: A Hispanic Perspective," in Roberto Goizueta (ed.), *We Are A People!* , 133–64.

78. See Virgil Elizondo, "The Hispanic Church in the USA: A Local Ecclesiology," in *Proceedings of the Thirty-Sixth Annual Convention* of the Catholic Theological Society of America, ed. Luke Salm (1981) 155–70.

79. See Allan Figueroa Deck, *The Second Wave: Hispanic Ministry and the Evangelization of Culture.*

80. See María de la Cruz Aymes and Francis J. Buckley, "Case-Study: Catechesis of Hispanics in the United States," in Arij A. R. Crollius, *Inculturation*, vol. 9 (Rome: Editrice Pontificia Università Gregoriana, 1987) 3–28.

81. See Rosa María Icaza, "Prayer, Worship, and Liturgy in a United States Hispanic Key," in Allan Deck (ed.), *Frontiers of Hispanic Theology in the United States*, 134–64.

82. One can think of various attempts at inculturating the Christian faith undertaken in India, the Philippines, Sri Lanka, Indonesia, Korea (*Minjung* theology), and Hong Kong for instance. One organization which is largely responsible for the current theological inculturation is the Asian Theological Conference, a branch of the Ecumenical Association of Third World Theologians (EATWOT). Notable Asian theologians of inculturation include Tissa Balasuriya, Aloysius Pieris, Chung Huyn Kyung, Virginia Fabella, Michael Amaladoss, Stanley Samartha, Samuel Rayan, Carlos Abesamis, Jose M. de Mesa, Leonardo Mercado, and others.

For a discussion of attempts at contextualizing Christian theology in Asia from a liberationist perspective, see Peter C. Phan, "Experience and Theology: An Asian Liberation Perspective," *Zeitschrift für Missionswissenschaft und Religionswissenschaft*, 77 (1993, 2) 99–121.

83. See *Models of Contextual Theology* , 88–92.

84. Song's major works include: *Christian Mission in Reconstruction: An Asian Analysis* (Madras: The Christian Literature Society, 1975; Maryknoll, NY: Orbis Books, 1977); *Third-Eye Theology: Theology in Formation in Asian Settings* (Maryknoll, NY: Orbis Books, 1982; rev. ed. 1990); *The Tears of Lady Meng: A Parable of People's Political Theology* (World Council of Churches, Geneva: Risk Book Series, 1981; Maryknoll, NY: Orbis Books, 1982); *The Compassionate God* (Maryknoll, NY: Orbis Books, 1982); *Tell Us Our Names: Story Theology from an Asian Perspective* (Maryknoll, NY: Orbis Books, 1984); *Theology from the Womb of Asia* (Maryknoll, NY: Orbis Books, 1986); *Jesus, The Crucified People* (New York: Crossroad, 1990). This last book is the first volume of a trilogy under the general title *The Cross in the Lotus World*; the second titled *Jesus and the Reign of God* (Minneapolis, Fortress Press, 1993) and the third yet to appear *Jesus in the Power of the Spirit.*

85. *Theology from the Womb of Asia* , 3.

86. *Christian Mission in Reconstruction*, 197.

87. *Third-Eye Theology*, 95.

88. For examples of these, see *Theology from the Womb of Asia*.

89. See *The Tears of Lady Meng*.

90. See *Jesus, The Crucified People*.

91. This section on Choan-Seng Song is taken with slight modifications from my essay "Experience and Theology: An Asian Liberation Perspective," quoted in note 81.

92. See his *An Asian Theology of Liberation* (Maryknoll, NY: Orbis Books, 1988) 80.

93. In this context questions regarding the intended role of the recently published universal catechism can be raised.

94. See his "Ethnicity and Nationality as Contexts for Religious Experience," in Peter C. Phan (ed.), *Ethnicity, Nationality, and Religious Experience*, to be published by University Press of America.

95. See, for instance, Leonard Swidler (ed.), *Toward a Universal Theology of Religion* (Maryknoll, NY: Orbis Books, 1987).

Response to Peter C. Phan

1. It is, however, interesting to note that, since his exile from Argentina, Dussel's scholarship has been increasingly focused on the theological import of Marx's thought. See, e.g., his *Filosofía de la producción* (Bogotá: Editorial Nueva América, 1984) and *La producción teórica de Marx: Un comentario a los Grundrisse* (México, DF: Siglo Veintiuno Editores, 1985). In so doing he has gone against the general trend in Latin American liberation theology, which has increasingly relativized socioeconomic analysis. In his Introduction to the 15th anniversary edition of *A Theology of Liberation*, for example, Gustavo Gutiérrez writes: "The socioeconomic dimension is very important but we must go beyond it....Diverse factors are making us aware of the different kinds of opposition and social conflict that exist in the modern world....Attention to cultural factors will help us to enter into mentalities and basic attitudes that explain important aspects of the reality with which we are faced. The economic dimension itself will take on a new character once we see things from the cultural point of view; the converse will also certainly be true." Gutiérrez, *A Theology of Liberation: History, Politics, and Salvation,*

revised edition with a new introduction (Maryknoll, NY: Orbis Books, 1988) xxiv–xxv.

2. Allan Figueroa Deck, S.J. (ed.) Introduction, *Frontiers of Hispanic Theology in the United States* (Maryknoll, NY: Orbis Books, 1992) xiv–xv, xx.

3. Ibid.

4. Ibid., xix.

5. Ibid.

6. John Brenkman, *Culture and Domination* (Ithaca, NY: Cornell University Press, 1987) 69.

7. See Enrique Dussel, *Philosophy of Liberation* (Maryknoll, NY: Orbis Books, 1985) 137–52.

8. Brenkman, *Culture and Domination*, 71.

9. Ibid., ix, 77.

10. Antonio Gramsci, *Selections from the Prison Notebooks of Antonio Gramsci*, Quintin Hoare and Geoffrey Nowell-Smith, eds. and trans. (London: Lawrence and Wishart, 1971) 5; Thomas Nemeth, *Gramsci's Philosophy: A Critical Study* (Sussex: The Harvester Press, 1980) 87.

11. Brenkman, *Culture and Domination* , 107.

12. Ibid., 46–47.

13. Anthony Giddens, "'Habermas' Social and Political Theory," *American Journal of Sociology* 83 (1977) 198–212; Robert Wuthnow et al., *Cultural Analysis: The Work of Peter L. Berger, Mary Douglas, Michel Foucault, and Jürgen Habermas* (Boston: Routledge and Kegan Paul, 1984) 232–39.

14. Helmut Peukert, *Science, Action, and Fundamental Theology: Toward a Theology of Communicative Action* (Cambridge, MA: The MIT Press, 1984) 123.

15. Daniel Lazare, "The Cult of Multiculturalism," *The Village Voice* (May 7, 1991) 29.

16. Justo González, *Mañana: Christian Theology from a Hispanic Perspective* (Nashville: Abingdon, 1990) 56.

17. Enrique Dussel, *Philosophy of Liberation* (Maryknoll, NY: Orbis, 1985) 63.

18. Brenkman, *Culture and Domination* , 69ff.

19. The productive character of culture is reflected in the fact that the words "culture" and "cultivate" have a common etymological root.

20. See Roberto S. Goizueta, *Liberation, Method, and Dialogue* (Atlanta: Scholars Press, 1988) 98.

21. Robert Wuthnow et al., *Cultural Analysis* , 236.

22. Deck, Introduction, Allan Figueroa Deck, ed., *Frontiers of Hispanic Theology in the United States*, xx.

23. Mario Barrera, Carlos Muñoz, and Charles Ornelas, "The Barrio as an Internal Colony," in F. Chris García, ed., *La Cusa Política: A Chicano Politics Reader* (Notre Dame, IN: University of Notre Dame Press, 1974); see also Rodolfo Acuña, *Occupied America: The Chicano's Struggle Toward Liberation* (San Francisco: Canfield Press, 1972).

24. Barrera, Muñoz, and Ornelas, "The Barrio as an Internal Colony," 282.

25. Ibid., 283–98.

26. See Orlando Fals Borda, "Investigating Reality in Order to Transform it," *Dialectical Anthropology*, 4 (1) 33–56; Muhammad Anisur Rahman, "The Theory and Practice of Participatory Action Research," in Orlando Fals Borda, ed., *The Challenge of Social Change* (London: SAGE, 1985).

27. Fals Borda, "Investigating Reality," 49.

28. Rahman, "The Theory and Practice of Participatory Action Research," 125.

29. Ibid., 120.

30. Ibid.; cf. Clodovis Boff's discussion of the theologian's social commitment and three models of social engagement, in *Theology and Praxis: Epistemological Foundations* (Maryknoll, NY: Orbis, 1987) 159–74.

The Pastor and the Theologian

1. See Lambert, W.G., *Babylonian Wisdom Literature* (Oxford: Clarendon Press, 1960) 150–212.

2. Gen. 4:1–6. See Testa, P.E., O.F.M., *Genesi. Introduzione-Stona Primitiva* (Rome: Marietti, 1969) 105–108; also Pritchard, J.B., ed., *Ancient Near Eastern Texts* (Princeton: Princeton University Press, 3rd. ed. 1960) 41f.

3. See Ruidor, Ignacio, S.J., Vizmanos, Francisco De B., S.J., *Teologia Fundamental para Seglares* (Madrid: Biblioteca De Autores Cristianos, 1963) 860f.

4. The Greek word *hairetikos* (found in the New Testament only in Ti. 3,10) comes from *haireo*, to choose.

5. See Congar, Y., O.P., *I believe in the Holy Spirit* (New York: Seabury Press, 1983) 5–64.

6. I Jn. 4, 2f.

7. Sacramentality belongs to the principle of Incarnation, because in Christ, through him and from him the sacraments receive their efficacy. See *Sacrosantum Concilium* , n. 5–11.

8. Lk 9:23.

9. Gal 2:19.

10. Ibid., 5:24.

11. Rom 6:3f.

12. 1 Cor 1:18–23.

13. Ibid., 15:17.

14. Gal 6:14.

15. Lk 24:25f.

16. Phil 3:18.

17. 1 Cor 15:14.

18. See *Codex Juris Canonici* (1983), c. 1752. For the sources see *Codex Juris Canonici Fontium Annotatione et Indice Analytico Auctus*, s.l.

19. Lk 17:2.

20. Rom 14:13.

21. Ibid., 16:17.

22. 1 Cor 8:13.

23. Rom 14:19.

24. Ibid., 15:1f.

25. 1 Cor 8:1.

26. See Rom 12:4–5; 1 Cor 12:12–30; Eph 4:4–6; Col 3:11. See also Léon-Dufour, X., S.J., ed., *Vocabulaire de Théologie Biblique: Corps du Christ* (Paris: Editions du Cerf, 1979–1980); Orr, W.F. and Walther, J.A., *I Corinthians, The Anchor Bible,* v. 32 (New York: Doubleday & Co., 1976) 283–289.

27. See 1 Cor 14:1–40.

28. Ibid., 12:1–11.

29. See Rahner, Karl, S.J., ed., *Sacramentum Mundi* (New York: Herder & Herder, 1970) v. 6, 232f. Also see Söhngen, Gottlieb, "Die Weisheit der Theologie durch den Wegder Wissenschaft," *Mysterium Salutis* (Zurich: Benzinger Verlag, 1965) V.I, 905–977; Spanish translation, *Mysterium Salutis, Manual de Teologie Como Historia de la Salvación* (Madrid: Ediciónes Cristiandad, n.d.) V.I, 997–1052. Reference to the Spanish translation follows.

30. See *Dei Verbum,* n. 2–6; see also Söhngen, 977–1011.

31. See Rahner, l.c., 232f.

32. The question of the correct theological method is of great importance, but I cannot discuss it here. I would assume, perhaps too optimistically, that the correct method is always followed. See Söhngen, l.c., 1034–1036, 1045–1049.

33. See Rom 1:5, 16:26. See *Dei Verbum,* n. 5. The Greek text calls it *hypakoē pisteōs.*

34. *Dei Verbum,* ibid.

35. See Söhngen, l.c., 992–996; also Rahner, l.c., 233f.

36. *Lumen Gentium*, n. 9; see also *Evangelii Nuntiandi n.* 13.

37. See Söhngen, 1026–1029.

38. See the Ignatian *Spiritual Exercises*, n. 352–370.

39. Mt 11:25.

40. 1 Cor 1:19.

41. See Söhngen, ibid.

42. See Thomas Aquinas, *Summa Theologiae*, 1 pars, 1 ques., 4 art.; see also Rahner, l.c. 233f.

43. On the kerymatic character of theology, see Rahner, ibid; also Söhngen, 1021–1036.

44. See Smith, G. A., *The Historical Geography of the Holy Land* (New York: Harper Torchbook, 1966) 210f.

45. See Is 40:11; Jer 23:1–6; Ez 34:1–31; Zec 11:4–17; Ps 23:1–4.

46. See Mt 18:12–14; Mk 6:34; Lk 15:4–7; Jn 10:1–18.

47. See Jn 21:15–17.

48. *Lumen Gentium*, n. 20.

49. *Christus Dominus*, n. 1.

50. *Lumen Gentium*, ibid.

51. *Presbyterorum Ordinis*, n. 2.

52. Rahner, ibid.

53. I Tm 2:4.

54. *Dei Verbum*, n. 11.

55. See *Evangelii Nuntiandi n.* 23.

56. *Dei Verbum*, n. 10.

57. Ibid., n. 12.

58. See *Evangelii Nuntiandi*, n. 60.

59. Acts 20:28.

60. *Gaudium et Spes*, n. 58.

61. *Evangelii Nuntiandi*, n. 20 et passim.

62. *Redemptoris Missio*, no. 52–54.

63. *Evangelii Nuntiandi*, n. 63.

64. Ibid., n. 20 & n. 55.

65. Ibid.

Response to Bishop Enrique San Pedro, S.J.

1. Joseph Donders, *Non Bourgeois Theology* (Maryknoll, NY: Orbis Books, 1985).

2. Avery Dulles, *The Reshaping of Catholicism* (San Francisco: Harper and Row, 1988).

3. Andrew Greeley and Mary Durkin Greeley, *How to Save the Catholic Church* (New York: Elizabeth Sifton Books, 1984).

4. See Lawrence Cunningham, *The Catholic Experience* (New York: Crossroads, 1986).

5. Cain H. Felder, *Troubling Biblical Waters* (Maryknoll: NY, Orbis Books, 1991) 176.

NOTES ON CONTRIBUTORS

EDWARD BRANCH, D.MIN., is campus minister and director of the Catholic Center, Atlanta University Complex, Atlanta, Georgia. He also lectures on catechesis and evangelization in the Pastoral Ministry Institute, Spalding College, Louisville, Kentucky. A graduate of Howard University and former chaplain at The Catholic University of America, he speaks frequently on issues of black ministry.

WILLIAM CENKNER, O.P., PH.D., is Professor of History of Religions and former Dean of the School of Religious Studies, The Catholic University of America. He is the author of *The Hindu Personality in Education: Gandhi, Tagore, Aurobindo* (Columbia, MO: South Asia Books, 1976); editor and co-author of *Religious Quest* (College Park, MD: University of Maryland, 1983); and *A Tradition of Teachers: Śankara and the Jagadgurus Today* (Delhi: Motilal Banarsidass & Columbia, MO: South Asia Books, 1983).

MARY COLLINS, O.S.B., PH.D., is Associate Professor and former Chair of the Department of Religion and Religious Education, The Catholic University of America, where she teaches in the areas of liturgical studies, spirituality, and women and religion. She is co-editor of *The New Dictionary of Theology* (Wilmington, DE: Michael Glazier, 1987). Recent writing includes; *Contemplative Participation: Sacrosanctum Concilium Twenty-Five Years Later* (Collegeville, MN: Liturgical Press, 1990); and numerous articles, one most recent is "Eucharist and Christology Revisited: Body of Christ," *Theology Digest,* 1993.

M. SHAWN COPELAND, PH.D., is an Associate Professor at Marquette University in systematic theology and African-American religious experience and culture. Her dissertation from Boston College was a genetic study of the idea of the human good in the thought of Bernard Lonergan. She has taught at Yale University Divinity School, Institute for Black Catholic Studies at Xavier University of Louisiana, St.

Norbert College, and Harvard Divinity School. She is a contributor to *A Troubling in My Soul: Womanist Reflections on Evil and Suffering* (ed. Emilie Townes, Orbis Books, 1993), *The New Dictionary of Catholic Social Thought* (ed. Judith Dwyer, Liturgical Press, 1994), and co-editor of a recent *Concilium* volume, *Violence Against Women* (SCM Press and Orbis Books, 1/1994).

ORLANDO O. ESPÍN, TH.D., is Associate Professor of Theology, University of San Diego. He is the founding editor of the new *Journal of Hispanic/Latino Theology*. He was the 1993 president of the Academy of Catholic Hispanic Theologians of the United States. His recent articles include: "Grace and Humanness," R.S. Goizueta, ed., *We Are a People! Initiatives in Hispanic American Theology* (Minneapolis: Fortress Press, 1992); "Tradition and Popular Religion: An Understanding of the Sensus Fidelium," in A.F. Deck, ed., *Frontiers of U.S. Hispanic Theology* (Maryknoll: Orbis Books, 1992).

ROBERTO S. GOIZUETA, PH.D., is Associate Professor of Theology, Loyola University of Chicago. He is the former co-director of the Aquinas Center at Emory University, Atlanta, and past president of the Academy of Catholic Hispanic Theologians of the United States. He is associate editor of the *Journal of Hispanic/Latino Theology*. His publications include: *Liberation, Method, and Dialogue* (Atlanta: Scholars Press, 1988); editor of *We Are A People! Initiatives in Hispanic-American Theology* (Minneapolis: Fortress Press, 1992). His articles include "Liberating Creation Spirituality," *Listening* 24 (1989) 85–115.

DIANA L. HAYES, S.T.D., PH.D., is Assistant Professor of Theology, Georgetown University. Her publications include: "Church and Culture: A Black Catholic Womanist Perspective," in William J. O'Brien, *The Labor of God: An Ignatian View of Church and Culture*, (Washington: Georgetown University, 1991) 67–87; "Emerging Voices, Emerging Challenges," in David G. Schultenover, ed., *Theology Toward the Third Millenium* (Lewiston, NY: Edward Mellen, 1991), 41–59; "Black Catholic Revivalism: The Emergence of a New Form of Worship," *Journal of the Interdenominational Theological Center*, 14 (Fall 1986–Spring 1987) 87–107.

MARINA A. HERRERA, PH.D., is a writer and consultant on multicultural issues. She is former lecturer and consultant on multi-cultural ministry for the Washington Theological Union; she also established, in 1977, the Office of Multicultural Catechesis, United States Catholic Conference, Washington, D.C. One of the early and more prolific writers among U.S. Hispanic theologians, her recent publications are: *Laser: Creating Unity in Diversity* (Washington, D.C.: National Catholic Conference on Interracial Justice, 1985); *The Cross: Our Heritage and Our Hope* (Washington, D.C.: National Conference of Catholic Bishops, 1991); "Third World Theology for the Third Millenium," in David G. Schultenover, ed., *Theology Toward the Third Millennium* (Lewiston, NY: Edward Mellon, 1991).

JOSEPH A. KOMONCHAK, PH.D., is Professor of Theology in the Department of Religion and Religious Education, The Catholic University of America. He was chief editor of *The New Dictionary of Theology* (Wilmington, DE: Michael Glazier, 1987). His recent publications include: "Modernity and the Construction of Roman Catholicism," in George Gilmore, Hans Rollma, and Gary Lease, ed., *Modernism as a Social Construct* (Mobile, AL: Spring Hill College, 1991) 11–41; "The Local Church and the Church Catholic: The Contemporary Theological Problematic," *The Jurist* 52 (1992) 416–47; "The Catholic University in the Church," in J.P. Langan, ed., *Catholic Universities in Church and Society* (Washington: Georgetown University Press, 1993) 35–55.

PETER C. PHAN, S.T.D., PH.D., born in Vietnam and a 1975 refugee to the U.S., is Professor of Theology and former Chair of the Department of Theology, The Catholic University of America. His books include: *Eschatology and Culture, The Iconographical Vision of Paul Evdokimov* (New York: Peter Lang, 1985); *Eternity in Time: A Study of Karl Rahner's Eschatology* (Cranbury, NJ: Associated University Press, 1989); ed., *Grace in the Human Condition* (Wilmington, DE: Michael Glazier, 1988); ed., *Christianity and the Wider Ecumenism* (New York: Paragon House, 1990).

DAVID N. POWER, O.M.I., S.T.D., is the Shakespeare Caldwell-Duval Professor of Theology in the Department of Theology, The Catholic University of America. His editing for *Concilium* and extensive writings over three decades include: *Unsearchable Riches: The Symbolic Nature of Liturgy* (New York: Pueblo Publishing Co., 1984); *The Sacrifice We Offer: The Tridentine Dogma Reinterpreted* (Edinburgh and New York: T. & T. Clark and Crossroad, 1987); *The Eucharistic Mystery: Revitalizing the Tradition* (New York and Dublin: Crossroad and Gill & Macmillan, 1992. Reprint, 1993); "Calling up the Dead," ed. with K. Lumbala, *The Spectre of Mass Death, Concilium* (New York: Orbis, 1993) 111–120.

BISHOP ENRIQUE SAN PEDRO, S.J., S.T.D., S.S.L., was bishop of Brownsville, Texas. He died in July, 1994. Prior to his appointment in 1986 as Auxillary Bishop of Galveston-Houston, he was a seminary professor of scripture and theology. He became Bishop of Brownsville in 1991; he also chaired the Committee on Hispanic Affairs of the National Conference of Catholic Bishops.

GERARD S. SLOYAN, PH.D., is Professor Emeritus of New Testament and Roman Catholic Studies at Temple University and recently Visiting Professor at The Catholic University of America and Visiting Professor at Iowa State University. His extensive writings in New Testament, liturgy, religious education, and theology span five decades. Recent writing includes: *John. Interpretation Series: A Bible Commentary for Teaching and Preaching* (Atlanta: John Knox Press, 1987); *Bursting the Bonds? A Jewish-Christian Dialogue on Jesus and Paul,* with L. Dean, L. Eran, and L. Swidler (Maryknoll, NY: Orbis, 1990); *What Are They Saying about John?* (Mahwah, NJ: Paulist Press, 1991).

GENERAL THEOLOGICAL SEMINARY
NEW YORK